£6·95

PAPAL PROVISIONS

PAPAL PROVISIONS

ASPECTS OF CHURCH HISTORY CONSTITUTIONAL, LEGAL AND ADMINISTRATIVE IN THE LATER MIDDLE AGES

By GEOFFREY BARRACLOUGH

Fellow of Merton College, Oxford; sometime Scholar of
Oriel and Merton Colleges, Bryce Student in the University
of Oxford, and Scholar of the British School at Rome

GREENWOOD PRESS, PUBLISHERS
WESTPORT, CONNECTICUT

Originally published in 1935
by Basil Blackwell, Oxford

First Greenwood Reprinting 1971

Library of Congress Catalogue Card Number 74-109707

SBN 8371-4198-2

Printed in the United States of America

Romae scimus veritatem obscurari posse, nunquam tamen, si fuerit agnita, reprobari. Thronus ille justitia est, equitatem sedes illa judicat.

GILBERTUS FOLIOT.

PREFACE

THE FOLLOWING pages are concerned predominantly
with the intervention of the papacy in the disposal of
benefices in the mediaeval Church: in more technical
terms with the question of 'Papal Provision' during
the thirteenth and fourteenth centuries. This prosaic
definition I make immediately—in order to dispose of
it immediately. If the subject were in fact as technical
and specialized and arid as these words make it sound,
it could have no claims on the reader who was not a
highly specialized historical student. Antiquities of
Church government are of no interest—except to anti-
quarians; but there is still, I believe, a general public
which is interested in the great historical movements
of the past, such as the decline of the mediæval papacy
and the impulse which produced the Reformation.
Both papacy and Reformation are historical facts
which belong as much to the present as to the past:
they have actuality to-day, arouse thought to-day,
command present loyalties, direct present personalities. And they cannot be understood apart from their
history. In matters of Church, past and present are
inextricably intertwined. The interpretation of the past
is of immediate, present significance: it cannot be
ignored by anyone to whom Church, faith, religion,
ideals are words which still conserve a meaning. And
the present essay is—in intent and, I hope, in effect—
not a historical thesis on a technical subject, but an
attempt to re-interpret the crucial years with which the
Middle Ages ended.

It may seem, at first sight, a long cry from papacy
and reform to the question of the distribution of
benefices in the thirteenth-, fourteenth- and fifteenth-
century Church. But we have to bear in mind that the
character of the Church itself, and its potentialities for

vii

good, in the final analysis depended necessarily and irrevocably on the character of its ministers. And we have to remember also that mediæval criticism—which was in itself in every way as radical and as challenging as historical criticism to-day—was in no two minds about the significance of the distribution of benefices as a prime factor in all the major problems of Church and State. Papal provisions and papal finance were at the heart of the opposition which culminated in Protestantism: they were not technicalities, but central points of strategy and objects of heated contest for reformers in the fifteenth and sixteenth centuries.[1] Nor is it difficult to see why this should have been the case. During a few weeks in the year 1342 the Papal Curia at Avignon disposed of no less than *one hundred thousand* benefices.[2] This is a central fact which deserves to be singled out and stressed as it has never been stressed before. Circumstances in 1342 may have been unusual, numbers such as these may not have been repeated: but the fact remains that the figures for that year provide us with the only adequate standard by which the significance of papal control over the Church's benefices can be measured. There was nothing exceptional, there was nothing trivial about the practice of provision. In every country in Europe benefices were affected, and in every year benefices were affected in thousands and perhaps even in tens of thousands. This is the explanation of the insistence of mediæval critics in regard to what seems at first sight a side issue. If the question of papal provision were merely a technical matter of ecclesiastical administration, it would have no historical significance to-day: in actual fact, the very vastness of the system made it the

---

[1]Cf. *infra*, pp. 16-18: for all who desire more detailed treatment, Prof. Haller's brilliant *Papsttum und Kirchenreform* is still unsurpassed.—From the point of view of taxation and finance, I take the opportunity to refer to Prof. W. E. Lunt's important volumes entitled *Papal Revenues in the Middle Ages*, which appeared too recently to be used here.

[2]Cf. *infra*, p. 31, n. 2, pp. 105-106.

most practical, obvious, actual, unavoidable issue in
Church politics during the later Middle Ages. Round it
the other issues were grouped: to understand it aright,
we must survey the whole life of the Church in the
fourteenth and fifteenth centuries—survey it, and all
its facets, as it appeared at that date, and survey it in
its historical setting, as it had developed in changing
circumstances from the time of the Barbarian Invasions
onwards.

This is a conviction which has forced itself on me in
writing the pages which follow. And it is a conviction
with a corollary. That corollary I state for what it is
worth: the further conviction that, in concentrating on
one particular historical problem and in attempting to
explain it in all its complexity, it is possible to throw
new light on the whole subject involved—in this case,
the mediæval Church—to open up new perspectives
and illuminate well-worn facts. Histories of the Church
in the later Middle Ages exist in abundance; and
assuredly they will not be displaced, nor their useful-
ness decreased, by the essay which follows. But I
believe—and I hope not presumptuously—that the
following pages contribute something new towards
understanding the spirit of the mediæval Church, and
that the reader who passes from this volume to more
general and more wide-ranging histories will find that
the events and facts there narrated take on a new
significance, when viewed from the standpoint here
adopted. Readers of the following pages will find that,
apart from and above the problems arising directly
from the history of papal provisions, one central fact
is emphasized and emphasized again: the significance
of the legal, constitutional and administrative history
of the Church for a proper understanding of mediæval
history as a whole. For this very reason, because this
is my profound personal conviction, I have not shirked
legal and formal technicalities, where some discussion
and knowledge of them has seemed essential to the

right interpretation of cardinal facts. But under no other circumstances have technicalities found a place. It is precisely the facility with which a superficial view can be formed, that impedes the progress of our knowledge of the mediæval Church: and I therefore believe that no reader will grudge a few pages of technical discussion of administrative and legal problems, if, as a result, a more profound and a more satisfactory, a more vivid and a more illuminating conception of the mediæval Church and its problems can be formed.

What follows is an essay, not a treatise; but it is the result of a fairly long period of work in Germany and Italy as well as in England, and the conclusions it contains are drawn, in part at least, from more detailed and technical studies, of which only a few have as yet appeared in print. It should be unnecessary to add that my only object in writing has been to contribute to the best of my ability to historical knowledge; but the assumption is still made, in certain quarters, that no one who writes about canon law or Church politics does so without ulterior motives. Therefore it should not be thought idle if I echo the disclaimer which even so undisputed a scholar as Maitland was forced, a generation ago, to make: I am neither a member of the Catholic nor of any of the Protestant Churches, and in writing what I have written I am not conscious of having been influenced by any belief, except the firm belief that the truth is interesting and valuable in and for itself.

From the time that the manuscript of this essay was first drafted until the volume was through the press, I have received much valuable encouragement and help. Professor F. de Zulueta, Professor F. M. Powicke, Mr. E. S. Cohn and Mr. J. R. H. Weaver each read and criticized the original draft, and to each I owe an equal debt of gratitude. Mr. Cohn further brought to my notice the sentence of Gilbert Foliot, quoted on p. vi, which expresses the core of what I have to say;

Professor de Zulueta suggested and drew up for me the original draft of the table of contents; and Professor Powicke convinced me that the inclusion of a bibliography would not be superfluous. I am indebted also for advice and bibliographical help to Canon E. W. Watson and to the Rev. J. F. Rogers, S.J. Finally I must express gratitude to all who have interested themselves in and furthered my work during the last five years, both at home and abroad; to my father and mother in the first place, to Professor Rudolf von Heckel and Professor Paul Lehmann of the University of Munich, and finally to Mr. H. L. Schollick, under whose supervision publication has taken place.

G. BARRACLOUGH.

Oxford.
18 *December*, 1934.

TABLE OF CONTENTS

CHAPTER I

No PERIOD in the history of the Church has received more attention than the century and a half which runs from the beginning of Alexander III's pontificate (1159–1181) to the death of Boniface VIII (1294–1303). These are the years during which the papacy achieved its greatest victories over the lay power, put forward its farthest-reaching claims, exercised the most obvious influence over the political destinies of Europe. But they are also the years in which other victories, less remarked but no less significant in its spiritual history, took place. Almost silently Alexander III assumed, for the papacy, the practical headship of the Church, centralizing, collecting the threads of government into papal hands, substantiating and transforming into realities the theoretical claims which were as old as the days of Gregory VII and older. Almost insensibly business, and with it importance, was diverted from the local bishoprics to Rome. The pope became the 'universal ordinary', Rome itself the *communis patria omnium*. Under Innocent III the *plenitudo potestatis* was already put to the widest uses; under Gregory IX the legislative power was brought firmly under papal control. Before the end of the thirteenth century Guy of Baysio, the famous 'Archidiaconus', was able to cut short discussion of the papal right to grant indulgences as superfluous, 'quia hoc patet lippis et tonsoribus'.[1] With the growth of centralization and the accumulation of powers the papal chancery, which even under so active a pope as Gregory VII had consisted of the seven notaries alone, soon came to number five score scribes among its staff, and a corresponding number of higher officials carried

[1] *Quaestiones Bononienses*, fo. 114*b*.

I

B

out the more responsible duties. The papacy busied itself with the smallest detail of Church regiment, it took upon itself the immediate care for the welfare of the clergy, and for the spiritual lives of the laity as well. It did not hesitate to enter into touch with the daily existence of ordinary people, or to guide the individual in his spiritual problems. Not only its powers, but also its jurisdiction and its sphere of influence at the end of the period in question, knew no bounds.

This victory of the papacy, a victory—if not a final victory—over localism and particularism, a victory within the Church and within the spiritual realm, has not received the attention granted to the more splendid struggles and victories in the long contest between the papacy and the Empire. We have no large-scale history of the changes in the constitution and organization of the Church, which first become apparent in the days of Alexander III.[1] We have no clear perception even of the legal construction, which was put together as a basis for the new organization. The continuous development, which went on unbroken and in general outline unchanged from pontificate to pontificate, regardless of the personality of popes, has not been traced in detail. Slowly, methodically, surely, one stone was put on another, and the structure carried farther; but except in a few isolated cases, we do not know who did the work or how each stage of construction was debated and carried out.

This is not the place to write such a history. But though the history remains unwritten, the existence of the momentous changes in the constitution of the Church is not to be ignored. They are as much—to some they may appear to be more—a part of the history of the Church as the political events and the international relationships of the popes, which figure

[1]Good, within its limits, is Ehrhard, *Das Mittelalter u. seine kirchl. Entwickelung.*

so largely in the records of the times. From week to week and from day to day, even at those periods in which political questions demanded all their energies, the great popes of the thirteenth century issued a mass of legal decisions, which even to-day astonish us by their objectivity, their invariably high standard, their careful phraseology and fine juristic sense.[1] When we are reading of political exploits and diplomatic skirmishes, we shall do well to keep this perpetual, day to day administrative and judicial activity in mind. It is not the least important part of the work of the papacy at the period. It is that which touches most nearly the lives of ordinary folk; it is that which makes the papacy a potent force in even the smallest village community. Without exaggeration it can be maintained that the world-wide dominion of the papacy resulted to no greater degree from its leadership in the major affairs of Church and State than from the endless number of petty, constantly repeated, daily recurring transactions—in themselves of small historical interest, but precisely because of their separate insignificance all the more impressive as a body—through which the papal power penetrated to the farthest parts of Christendom and made itself felt in even the lowliest ranks of society.[2]

The internal development of the Church followed its own separate course, independent of the personal characteristics of popes, conditioned in the main by practical legal and administrative factors, based on traditional tendencies, characterized above all by the two predominant qualities of impersonality and continuity. If we say that its history is administrative history rather than Church history, we shall to some degree explain its essential independence of external events; for the administration of the Church is like other administrative institutions and has an intrinsic

---

[1] Friedberg, *Das Kanonische u. d. Kirchenrecht*, 9.
[2] v. Heckel, *Misc. Ehrle* II, 293.

continuity and life of its own. But such a distinction would be mistaken for the very reason that in the general history of the Church no factor is of greater importance, as an index of decline or of progress, than the history of government and administration. It is precisely in day to day business, in the care for small matters of government, in regard for administrative forms, in due observance of the law, in impartial repartition of rights and duties, in balanced distribution of executive power, that the character of the Church, like that of any other social structure, is most clearly expressed. To probe to the bottom the great impersonal movements of rise and fall, which are evident enough when we extend our gaze over long centuries of Church history, we must not neglect the objective study of the Church's legal and administrative institutions. Their significance can hardly be overstressed at any period in history; but at no time is their influence on the development of the Church as a whole more evident than in the century and a half which divides Alexander III from Boniface VIII, the century and a half which saw the practical realization of the theory of papal supremacy and the emergence of the centralized Church.

The pages which follow are concerned with one of the most characteristic innovations of this age. Papal intervention in the bestowal of ecclesiastical benefices is a phenomenon which earlier ages had not known.[1] It stands out among the many acts of prerogative and authority, which the popes of the twelfth and thirteenth centuries began to exercise, as that which had least ground in tradition or in theory. In other directions, direct papal action may have appeared as the culmination of age-long traditions and gradually accumulated tendencies. The right to the disposal of all ecclesiastical benefices, on the other hand, which

[1]Hinschius, *Kirchenrecht* III, 114 n. 1, leaves the upholders of the opposite theory no ground to stand on.

Clement IV formulated in his famous decretal of 27 August, 1265,[1] had actually been acquired by the papacy less through theoretical justification or a legal qualification of the rights of others, than through practical exercise during the course of the immediately preceding century. If we ignore the primatial rights of the Holy See, *quae disponente domino super omnes alias ordinariae potestatis obtinet principatum*,[2] we shall regard it as a new right; in any case, it is the new exercise of a right which had previously been no more than inherent. From an historical point of view, papal provisions belong to the age of ecclesiastical centralization, and are one of the most obvious examples of the way in which that centralization worked.

The history of papal provisions had thus a peculiar and individual significance in the history of the Church during the later centuries of the Middle Ages. Just as papal intervention in the collation of benefices was the most characteristic result of the new tendencies in ecclesiastical government and of the new conception of the ecclesiastical constitution, so also it remained for the rest of the Middle Ages an index of the strength and weakness of the papacy and of the conceptions of Church government for which the papacy stood. The history of papal provisions, unlike that of any other single institution of Church government, reveals to us *en petit* the course followed by the internal history of the Church through the thirteenth, fourteenth and fifteenth centuries to the Reformation. It reveals the influence, policy and administrative methods of the papacy; it throws light on the moral and intellectual level of the clergy at large; it explains the inrush of disorders, the growing decline; it is inextricably connected with the burning question of finance and, together with finance, was the root problem which the movement of practical reform set out to solve; from

[1] c. 2 in VI° 3, 4 (*Licet ecclesiarum*).
[2] c. 23 X 5, 33.

an internal point of view, it can only be interpreted in the light of abstruse but uncontroversial principles of canon law and of the practice of the papal chancery and ecclesiastical courts; from an external point of view—a standpoint which hardly concerns us here—it constituted a highly controversial problem in the political relationships of the papacy with the secular governments of Europe. It is thus one of the permanently important questions in the history of the mediæval Church, and as such demands careful, detailed and objective treatment.

To trace the history of papal provisions through the Middle Ages is not directly the object of the following pages. What follows is rather an attempt at criticism, an attempt to clear the ground of encumbering preconceptions and misconceptions, an attempt to sum up the work, scattered and often not easily accessible, which has already been done, to set the views asserted and the facts alleged by one historian over against the facts and theories of another, to balance them out, and in the final result to point the route which earlier investigations have indicated to be the direct way to a final and objective estimation of the system of papal provision and of its influence on the life of the mediæval Church. At times it involves detailed and technical but ultimately important criticism of the contemporary authorities, documentary, legal and literary; at others, it necessitates a more general consideration of wider aspects of mediæval Church history. At no time, however, is it necessary to stray far from the main lines of Church history. The permanently important fact in the history of provisions is the light it throws on the double problem of the influence of the papacy, for good or for bad, and on the growth of the reformatory movement—a movement directed, from the fourteenth century onwards, against the papacy, a *reformatio in capite* rather than a *reformatio in membris*—within the mediæval Church. It is with these broader, permanently interesting questions in view that, in the following pages, the history and the modern historiography of papal provisions have been approached.

CHAPTER II

THE BROAD historical outlines in the development of the practice of papal provision are already well known, and can be found in any handbook of canon law or ecclesiastical history.[1] Under the influence of current conceptions of papal authority—conceptions identified to-day with the names of Innocent III and Innocent IV and with the doctrine of *plenitudo potestatis*—the practice exercised by twelfth-century popes of recommending clerks for benefices was transformed by the beginning of the thirteenth century into a papal right to confer benefices directly, or to order conferment by others on apostolic authority, without the concurrence and even against the wishes and intentions of the ordinary collator. This right—the right of papal provision—was enforced from the end of the twelfth century by legal sanctions and exercised under judicial forms by means of rescripts, whose resemblance to contemporary English writs of the *Praecipe* class is worth stressing.[2] Its exercise as a legally enforceable right implied the abrogation of the canonical right of the ordinary collator—bishop, chapter or patron, singly or in co-operation—to dispose of his benefices, and this abrogation was justified on the theory that *omnes ecclesie et res ecclesiarum*

[1]Hinschius, *System d. kath. Kirchenrechts* III, 113–164, and Fierens, *Ons Prebendenwezen onder de Pausen van Avignon* are the best surveys; cf. further Baier, *Päpstl. Provisionen* and Mollat, *La collation des bénéfices*. From a wider point of view Haller, *Papsttum u. Kirchenreform*, is also important.—Provisions to major benefices (bishoprics, abbeys and 'consistorial' benefices generally) form a separate subject, and no attempt is made to discuss them here; cf. however, for the earlier period (until the Reservations) Barraclough, *The Making of a Bishop*, for the general Reservations and the later history, Eubel, *Zum päpstl. Reservations- u. Provisionswesen.*

[2]Cf. *infra*, pp. 91 sqq. If I mention this analogy immediately, it is because it is essential to bear in mind throughout the legal nature of what are usually but somewhat loosely regarded as 'papal bulls' or 'letters' rather than *rescripta apostolica*.

sunt in potestate pape.[1] The ordinary right of the ordinary collator and the extraordinary right of the pope existed side by side: pope and ordinary concurred in the power of collation, the one could 'prevent' the other. But in his famous decretal *Licet ecclesiarum* of 27 August, 1265—after setting forth for the first time in theory the right to dispose of all ecclesiastical benefices which the papacy had been exercising and consolidating in practice for well nigh a century— Clement IV claimed an exclusive authority over one particular class, namely those benefices vacated in the Roman curia. These the pope alone could legitimately bestow: they were 'reserved' to the disposition of the Holy See.

Thus to the theory of provision there was added the theory of reservation—a theory capable of almost unlimited expansion. Under Clement IV's successors expansion followed rapidly.[2] Boniface VIII, Clement V, and John XXII in his famous constitutions *Ex debito*[3] and *Execrabilis*,[4] added new classes to the *beneficia reservata*, and the whole system of reservations was codified by Benedict XII, at the beginning of his pontificate, in the constitution *Ad regimen*.[5] Even then development did not stop: new categories were added from time to time, and the most far-reaching reservations made at any period were those promulgated by the popes of the Schism in their Chancery Regulations.[6]

Even before the first general reservation of 1265, however, the part played by the papacy in the distribution of benefices throughout mediæval Europe was very considerable. It has been said that until the

[1]*Cod. lat. Monacen.* 8011 (*Questio Egidii de Fuscarariis*) fo. 86′a.

[2] Cf. Mollat, P. I, cap. 1.

[3] c. 4 *in Extrav. commun.* 1, 3.

[4] c. un. *in Extrav. Iohann.* XXII, 3; cf. Deeley, *Papal Provision and Royal Rights of Patronage.*

[5] c. 13 *in Extrav. commun.* 3, 2.

[6]Cf. Ottenthal, *Die päpstl. Kanzleiregeln*; Haller, *Papstt. u. Kirchenreform,* 125– 28.

days of Innocent III the pope intervened in the bestowal of benefices as far as the ordinaries permitted; from that time forward, on the other hand, the ordinary collators were only able to use their rights in so far as they were not hindered by papal reservations and provisions.[1] This may be an exaggeration; but it is certain that the system was complete in all essentials, juridically and administratively, before the the beginning of the fourteenth century,[2] and there is good reason to think that it was already securely established and maturely developed before the end of the pontificate of Innocent IV (1243–1254).[3] The fact that Alexander IV was compelled to revoke large numbers of mandates of provision in his constitution *Execrabilis* of 5 April, 1255, is unquestionable proof that papal provisions had even then been granted in such large numbers as not only to render the rights of the ordinary collators illusory but even to defeat their own ends. In some cases, Alexander wrote, ten, in others twenty and more 'expectants' were awaiting provision; in some churches the number of expectants exceeded the total number of prebends in existence. The whole system of papal bestowal, in short, had grown to vast and unwieldy proportions.[4]

In these circumstances it is not to be wondered at, that the pontificate of Innocent IV saw a sporadic outburst of radical criticism and a fairly general expression of dissatisfaction with the exercise of the newly acquired right of collation by the papacy and with the growing concentration and centralization of the machinery for the bestowal of benefices in the Roman curia. A first outbreak of popular discontent, directed above all at the practice of beneficing foreign ecclesiastics in England and at the consequent impoverishment of the realm, had already occurred in

[1]Haller, p. 32.   [2]Fierens, pp. 823, 846.
[3]Barraclough, *Formulare f. päpstl. Suppliken.*
[4]Cf. Barraclough, *The Constitution 'Execrabilis'.*

England during the pontificate of Gregory IX.[1]
The chronicle of Matthew Paris, with its estimate of
the annual value of English benefices held by foreign
clerics at 60,000 marks[2] and its later calculation that
the foreign providees of Innocent IV alone
were in receipt of some 70,000 marks per annum,[3]
dwells persistently on the same theme.[4] It is the burden
of the English complaints recited to the pope in 1245
at the First Council of Lyons,[5] and finds even more
radical expression in the *Gravamina Ecclesie Gallicane*
of 1247.[6]

This document[7]—often called the 'protestation of
St. Louis'—is well worth singling out as a characteristic expression of the views of the laity at the turning
point in the history of provisions. It is more radical,
more far reaching and more illuminating than the
parallel English criticism. Starting from the proposition that not only king and magnates but the whole
realm generally were moved and perturbed,[8] the
French agents who expounded the grievances to the
pope, gave a reasoned, logical survey of the situation.
The basic cause of discontent, they said, was *quod
nova facitis, nova et inaudita*, first in regard to taxation
and then in regard to provisions and pensions,
'etiam in illis ecclesiis que sunt speciales ecclesie
domini regis.' They attacked these innovations both

[1] Cf. Mackenzie, *The Anti-Foreign Movement in England*; Marti, *Popular
Protest and Revolt*; Ellis, *Anti-Papal Legislation*, 57–62.
[2] *Chron. majora* IV, 419.   [3] *Op. cit.*, V, 355.
[4] Baier (pp. 112–120) has tried, by statistical methods, to prove Matthew
Paris' contention; but his argument is not convincing. To take but one
point, he assumes (p. 118) that the average period for which a benefice was
held, was 30 years; but Schäfer, *Röm. Quartalschr.* XX, 139 (though referring
to the fourteenth century) estimates it at no more than five years.—All other
recent authorities have assumed that the totals mentioned by Paris are
highly exaggerated; cf. among others, Haller, p. 32 n. 3, A. L. Smith, *Church
and State*, 129.
[5] *Chron. majora* IV, 443.
[6] *Op. cit.* VI (*Additamenta*), 99–112.—The document is referred by Paris to
1245; but cf. Haller, p. 27 n. 3, and Smith, p. 149.
[7] On its authenticity, cf. Berger, *Registres d'Innocent IV* II, cxci sqq.
[8] 'Nec solum moventur super hiis dominus rex et magnates, sed etiam
generaliter omne regnum motum est et turbatum. . . .'

on historical and on legal grounds: 'nec littera nec
historia docet, quod talia facta fuerunt usque modo,
nec in sacris canonibus tale quid invenitur.' Then they
came to their own propositions:[1] namely the king's
right to *temporalia*, which, in spite of the prohibition
of lay interference in the Church, they deduced by
historical argument from Charlemagne's electing of
popes and ordaining of the Holy See, and from the
fact that 'non est multum temporis quod reges Francie
conferebant omnes episcopatus in camera sua.' The
Kings of France, they admitted, had renounced many
things *propter Deum*; but many others they had not
renounced, and had, it was implied, no intention of
renouncing.

It has not always, I think, been realized how searching and radical the French *gravamina* of 1247 really
were.[2] The plenitude of power—or more correctly
and perhaps not insignificantly, *quaedam plenitudo
potestatis*—was as yet accepted: on the other hand, it
was pointed out that there was no canonical authority
for the activities the pope was engaged on under
guise of the *plenitudo potestatis*, and time after time his
actions were characterized in general as innovations.
Thus there is evident, if only tentatively, that recourse
to the ancient law of the Church which was to become
characteristic, in a later century, of Gallicanism. And
on the other hand there is its counterpart, the theoretical construction of a royal right to intervene and to
play a legitimate part in Church affairs, which mani-
fests the true elements of the 'caesaro-papism' of the
outgoing fourteenth and fifteenth centuries. But if we

---

[1] *Chron. majora* VI, 110: 'Nunc itaque veniamus ad propositum nostrum. . . .'
[2] Cf. Smith, pp. 147–8: 'Here we have four times repeated the acknowledge-
ment that knocks the bottom out of all resistance, however justifiable,
however eloquent. It is acknowledged that the pope is above law, that he has
the *plenitudo potestatis*; that his See holds the primacy, that he can act as he
chooses. Then there can be no talk of real resistance in the end; it can only at
highest be expostulation, or no more than humble entreaty. . . . The mighty
theory of God upon earth once accepted, all its consequences must be
accepted too. . . . The only way out of the circle is to break in upon the
theory itself, and this no one was yet ready to do.' Similarly, Haller p. 21.

wish to appraise these elements correctly, it is essential to recognize that the basic motive of the protest, revealed again and again in the course of the argument, was the anger of the king and magnates at the loss of revenues which they regarded as their right. The cardinal thought at the back of the whole argument was: *in depauperatione ecclesiarum depauperatur regnum*,[1] and it is likely enough that if the pockets of the laity had not been touched, there would have been no protestation.[2]

This was the main charge against the practical operation of provisions, but not the only charge. At the same period Bishop Grosseteste of Lincoln was complaining of the incompetence and unsuitability of the papal providees, English as well as foreign, sent for promotion in his diocese.[3] Other complaints of the day concerned the grant of non-vacant benefices, pluralism and non-residence, and there was a general disposition to attack the venality of the curia. *Ecclesia Romana non supplicantium sed dantium preces exaudit*:[4] it was a question, according to the chroniclers of the thirteenth and fourteenth centuries, not of the grant but of the 'sale' of provisions and other 'graces.'

[1] *Chron. majora* VI, 111.

[2] The following passage (pp. 105–6) may fairly be regarded as typical: 'Certe iam ad hoc devenit res, quod episcopi non possunt providere clericis suis litteratis et honestis personis diocesum suarum. Et in hoc etiam preiudicatur domino regi et omnibus nobilibus regni, quorum filii et amici promoveri solebant in ecclesiis. . . . Nunc autem, quia contra omne ius preferuntur extranei indigenis et notis preferuntur ignoti, perit servitium Dei in ecclesiis, pereunt ecclesiarum iura. Isti enim non resident in ecclesiis, immo de multis eorum ignoratur, utrum unquam nati fuerunt; sed hoc vestri faciunt, quod nomine eorum bona ecclesiarum asportantur de regno et in dampnum ecclesiarum et regni, et contra voluntatem eorum, qui fundaverunt ecclesias et dederunt eis bona, que habent ea intentione, ut de ipsis alerentur ministri, qui ibi Domino Deo servirent, et si quid residuum esset, in usus pauperum converteretur et in defensionem regis, si necesse esset'.

[3] That unsuitability and incompetence, not foreign birth, was his ground for opposition, is amply demonstrated by Smith, pp. 111–113.

[4] The quotation is from Boncompagno of Florence, but the same complaint is found in practically every writer on the subject from John of Salisbury onwards. For literature dealing with the question of curial corruption, cf. the references in my *Making of a Bishop*, 302 sqq.

Throughout the later Middle Ages the propensity of the curia to turn its administration of provisions into a money-making apparatus, the conferment of benefices on foreigners, the unsuitability of providees, and the attendant evils of pluralism, non-residence and the burdening of churches with expectancies to non-vacant benefices, continued to be the main practical charges in the indictment which was gradually formulated against the centralized, papal administration of the Beneficial System of the Church. From a constitutional point of view, the opponents of the papal system of provision challenged the legitimacy and the expediency of destroying, as the papacy was alleged to have done, the canonical rights of the ordinary collators, and asserted on the positive side, that the spiritual needs and welfare of the Church were better served by the ordinary methods of appointment to benefices than by the system of papal provisions.

The formation of a constitutional rather than a merely practical opposition, however, hardly began before the fourteenth century and was not transformed into a programme of practical politics till the French withdrawal of obedience from Benedict XIII in 1398. In this place it is out of the question to devote even a few lines to the long and complicated history of the reform movement during this period. But it must be remarked that it was far from being purely religious or ecclesiastical in character. There is perhaps no more difficult question in the history of the Church in the fourteenth century than to determine what share political, what share ecclesiastical motives played in the practical development of the reform programme; but it is no exaggeration to say that political interests provided the practical motive power which directed the movement into the course it eventually took. In regard to provisions themselves, the English Statutes of Provisors are a sufficient indication that it is impos-

sible to separate the religious and the political—the
innerkirchliche and the *kirchenpolitische*—factors. It is
impossible to separate them because already in the
thirteenth century men had begun to doubt whether
they really were separable. Without as yet challenging
the theory of a universal, catholic Church, men whose
thoughts and interests were more closely bound up
with questions of State than of Church, were beginning
both to act and to think on the assumption that nothing
which happened within its bounds was foreign to the
State's interests. Not in abstract political theory but in
practical, concrete measures of government, the conviction slowly and tentatively grew that the political
sovereignty of the State must be complete. This
movement of thought was perhaps above all else a
reaction against the growing encroachment of the
Church into the province of the State, the inevitable
result of its too decisive victory in the struggle with
the Empire, a practical reply to the starker doctrine
of the superiority of the spiritual over the temporal
sword. From the age-long struggle with the Empire
the thirteenth-century papacy emerged victorious;
but almost immediately, in the age of Philip le Bel and
Edward I, it came face to face with the feudal states of
Europe and with the vigorous, if still undeveloped,
principle of national sovereignty.[1] It was this political
conception—the conception which transformed
western Christendom into the independent states of
Europe—that made the question of reform within the
Church a question of politics, and in the final analysis
it was this political conception which determined the
course that the movement for reform was eventually
to take.

Politics may not, in the fourteenth and fifteenth
centuries, have been a religion, but religion was a

[1]Clearly the same factors had operated from time to time at an earlier date;
cf. for example, the interesting remarks in *Epp. Cantuar.*, pp. 80, 300. But
few historians would criticize the view that the reigns of Philip and Edward
mark in this respect an epoch.

part of politics. The distinction between the sphere of
the Church and the sphere of the State—the reality of
which the disputes over the limits of the two in the
days of Gregory VII had only served to accentuate—
became increasingly blurred and increasingly insigni-
ficant. The State was prepared to intervene where it
thought its interests affected, and it is often hard to
distinguish the motive for intervention, particularly
as the real motive was often concealed. Reformatory
intentions, a desire to curb abuse which the papacy
did nothing to hold in check, there may have been;
but political motives were never far distant. This fact
makes it difficult to judge the objective value of attacks
on the papacy and complaints of disorders in the
Church, in so far as they were inspired by the State
or by secular interests. It is certain that there were few
reformatory actions in which political motives played
no part; but it is probable also that there were few
political movements against the papacy in which
reformatory motives remained without influence,
even if the point of view of the reformers was more
that of local ecclesiastical provinces than of the
Church as a whole. In the history of the Church in the
fourteenth and fifteenth centuries, in sum, it is
impossible to separate the ecclesiastical and the
political factors: questions of internal government and
policy had become an integral part of the activities and
transactions which depended on, and fell under the
heading of, the relations of Church and State.

Both from the political and from the purely
ecclesiastical point of view, no sphere of papal administration was more radically challenged in the
fourteenth and fifteenth centuries than the combined
system of provisions and reservations. Even the
lively criticism of finance was directed above all at
Annates, the levying of which, from the days of
Clement V (1305–1314) onwards, had bound inextricably
together the financial and the beneficial policy of the

papacy.[1] Provisions and finance were regarded as the twin pillars of curialism: it was on these, as HALLER has shewn in his brilliant *Papsttum und Kirchenreform*, that for some two and a half centuries the attacks of reformers were concentrated. And this attitude has persisted, substantially unchanged, until to-day. After generations of unmitigated condemnation from the standpoint of morality, religion, politics and government, opinion is slowly swinging round in favour of the fourteenth-century papacy. Virtues— such as the immense administrative vigour of a pope like John XXII—are being brought to light; supposed vices and weaknesses—such as political subservience— are being questioned and former judgements reconsidered. But the work of rehabilitation has stopped short at provisions. Much may be palliated, much explained: they remain as an unquestioned evil amidst much which was fundamentally sound. They are the morbid sore on the body of the mediæval Church, which led to its final decay. 'We can admit that the popes of Avignon deserve no reproach in regard to their attitude towards the princes of Europe,' wrote FIERENS, the Belgian historian of provisions and one of the most balanced critics of the fourteenth-century Church, 'that they supported dogma and devoted their energies to the conversion of the heathen: the main fact still remains that, through their beneficial policy, and through the fiscal policy which is bound up with it, they brought the moral and religious integrity of Europe to a state of calamity. And this evil is so great that no services rendered in any other domain are sufficient to efface it.'[2]

A judgement such as this is in itself a striking testimony to the importance—if only to the tragic and ill-famed importance—of papal provisions. Precisely because of their central position in the whole question

---

[1]Cf. Göller, *Repert. Germ.* I, 55.*
[2]*Ons Prebendenwezen*, 848.

of Church reform, their history—above all in the crucial years of the fourteenth century—demands the closest critical attention. The evidence needs careful weighing and balancing. The separate classes of evidence, literary and documentary, local and central, legal and financial, demand independent criticism and comparative evaluation. These are the essential preliminaries to a final, objective, historical treatment of the subject. How far have they been attained? On what reading of the abundant evidence have the judgements of historians been founded? What questions remain to be solved? From what standpoint, with what attitude to the various classes of evidence, must a historian set out to-day, who wishes to treat objectively the history of provisions in the thirteenth and fourteenth centuries? To some of these questions a historiography of papal provisions can provide an answer, to others an indication of where and how an answer is to be sought. In tracing the attitude of successive schools and generations of historians to the problem, we are enabled to see how one generation has corrected another, how one school has preferred one, another a different class of evidence. In this way the problems to be solved, the results achieved, emerge with a new clarity; and the historian who can look back over decades of research and criticism is enabled to escape from his individual, personal standpoint and innate preconceptions, and take his stand on an objective criticism of the work of past generations.

CHAPTER III

It is, in a more than paradoxical sense, with the Protestation of St. Louis, with the anti-curial commentary of the English chronicler, Matthew Paris, and the misunderstood correspondence of Bishop Grosseteste of Lincoln, that the modern historiography of papal provisions begins. The views there set out are substantially the views which the earlier historians of modern times put forward: they provide the evidence on which the narratives of eighteenth- and nineteenth-century writers are based. From Thomassin[1] and Febronius[2] onwards, to Lamprecht[3] in Germany and Stubbs[4] and Creighton[5] in England, the earlier modern writers derived their opinions almost exclusively from the opponents of Innocent IV, and for the later period, from the anti-papal pamphleteers, publicists and chroniclers of the fourteenth and fifteenth centuries. For this reason, in the main, it has been of interest to see briefly how the views of mediæval critics were formed, what elements contributed to the anti-papal opposition of the Middle Ages.[6] The statements which have come down to us in mediæval chronicles and letter-books were accepted in the first place as trustworthy historical evidence; and in dealing shortly with the first phase of the modern historiography of papal provisions, the essential question which confronts us, is to decide how far evidence of this class is really admissible at face value.

[1] *Vetus et nova ecclesiae disciplina*, P. II, l. i, caps. 43 sqq.
[2] *De statu ecclesiae*, c. 7. §. 4.
[3] Cf. Finke, *Die kirchenpolitischen u. kirchl. Verhältnisse zu Ende d. Mittelalters nach d. Darstellung K. Lamprechts*.
[4] Cf. Maitland, *Roman Canon Law*; Davis, *The Canon Law in England*.
[5] Cf. Haller, *Papstt. u. Kirchenreform*, 7 n. 1.
[6] *Supra*, pp. 10 sqq.

Thus certain questions immediately force themselves on our consideration. Do the criticisms which the earlier modern historians of provisions accepted and, with greater or lesser degree of discrimination, made their own, represent level-headed, objective judgements, or are they merely *ex parte* statements? Are the grievances therein expressed real grievances of the Church, or are they merely the recriminations of interested partisans? Were the reformatory intentions expressed in acts of parliament[1] and diplomatic representations[2] little more than a mask for political ambitions, and the complaints directed against the papacy a pretext for the furtherance of secular interests? For the very reason that the attack on provisions was only a part—if perhaps the most effective part—of a general attack on the papacy and its administration of the Church, we may well turn for an example to the parallel contemporary criticism of papal finance. Historians of the nineteenth century took this vehement criticism at its face value; but when the actual documentary evidence was analysed, the small totals which the papacy raised by its taxation aroused general surprise.[3] Were the cries of financial oppression and shameless pressure, which persisted for two centuries and more, pure exaggeration?[4] FINKE declared:[5] 'all the *gravamina* of the fifteenth century cannot convince me that those who cried for help were in actual fact so greatly in need of help', and KIRSCH, a recognized authority on papal finance in the fourteenth century, pointed out that the real cause of the German opposi-

---

[1] Cf. for example, the admirable summary in Mackinnon, *Const. History of Scotland*, 320, 327–330.

[2] Cf. Haller, p. 6 n. 4.   [3] Finke, pp. 109–111.

[4] The same question arises in regard to the 'sale' of provisions (and other writs)—a favourite topic of the fourteenth-century chroniclers. Tihon, who has examined the only Register of the examiners of providees *in forma pauperum* known to be in existence (*a.* 1407), has shown that, in spite of the reduced tariffs granted to petitioners of this class, only thirty of the fifty-one rescripts which this register contains, were taxed at all—twenty-one were 'gratis pro Deo'; *Bulletin de l'Institut hist. belge* VI, 73.

[5] *Loc. supra cit.*

tion was not so much papal exorbitance as a rooted hostility to all forms of taxation on the part of the nobility and higher clergy—a hostility which found expression also in an exactly similar attitude towards imperial levies.[1] In the same way in regard to provisions, is not the key note of the French gravamina of 1247, which have been briefly analysed above,[2] the somewhat naïve statement: 'in hoc preiudicatur domino regi et omnibus nobilibus regni, quorum filii et amici promoveri solebant in ecclesiis?'[3]

The grievances so expressed are, of course, real grievances, and demand as such every consideration; but they represent the point of view of one party alone, and therefore need careful checking. Moreover, they are the grievances of a party whose aspirations in regard to the Church could in the long run only be satisfied by an Erastianism which was the very contradiction of the ideals of the mediæval Church.[4] We may well judge that the small regard which the papacy of the thirteenth and fourteenth centuries paid to provincial feeling in its disposal of benefices was ill-considered, that its catholicity, its internationalism, was too sweeping; but, unless we are prepared to go farther and maintain that the whole ideal of Christendom was mistaken, there is, as A. L. Smith has forcibly argued,[5] no necessity for wholesale capitulation to the views of the nationalist opposition. Moreover, even

---

[1] *Die päpstl. Kollektorien*, lxxi. Cf. also Knöpfler, *Lehrbuch d. Kirchengesch.* (1895), 428; Sägmüller, *Tätigkeit u. Stellung d. Cardinäle*, 96 n. 5.
[2] *Supra*, pp. 11–13.
[3] Matth. Paris. *Chron. majora* VI, 105.
[4] It can be summed up in the proverbial (if unhistorical) phrase: *Dux Cliviae est papa in terris suis*. Parallels, such as Rudolf of Austria's declaration: 'I myself will be pope, archbishop, bishop, archdeacon and dean in my lands', or a similar statement on the part of the duke of Bavaria in 1367, were already frequent in the fourteenth century; cf. Hashagen, *Staat u. Kirche*, 550–557, Werminghoff, *Neuere Arbeiten*, 167, and *Verfassungsgesch.*, 89. Within the Church we find similar statements put forward by members of the Paris university party at the time of the withdrawal of obedience from Benedict XIII; cf. Valois, *La France et le grand schisme* II, 429–430, Barraclough, *Un document inédit*, 113 n. 3.
[5] *Church and State*, 135–6.

in the Middle Ages the opposite point of view had its upholders.[1] At the time of the Council of Constance the growing 'caesaro-papism' of the age was put forward in itself as a basic argument for the maintenance of annates and provisions. If the rights of the papacy were not maintained, it was said, its position in the Church was doomed. 'Reges et principes . . . de presenti . . . intromittunt se de factis ecclesiarum usque ad ultimum de potentia; ideo ecclesie fere in toto mundo male stant.'[2]

Thus the one side blamed the papacy, the other the secular power, for the decline of the Church which all admitted. It is the former conception which has taken the stronger hold to-day; that the centralized administrative practices of the papacy were at fault. But if we ask why this view is preferred, we shall see that the reason is, in the main, the assumption that the international church was doomed to failure; that with the Reformation Christendom was destined to break up into the nations of Europe, the universal Church to split into a number of national Churches.[3] Yet even if Erastianism eventually won the day—within the Church hardly less than outside it—that is, in itself, no valid reason why the criticism of an opposition which was political and nationalist more than anything else in character, should be accepted at its face value as far as the situation in the thirteenth and fourteenth centuries was concerned.

Thus the first forward step in the modern historiography of provisions—as in the historiography of the reform of Church and papacy as a whole in the later Middle Ages—was the criticism of the literary authorities on which the judgements of the earlier modern historians were based. In this way PASTOR, among the earliest critics, put forward as an incon-

[1]Thus, notably, Nicholas de Clemanges; cf. Barraclough, *Un document inédit*, 111.
[2]Finke, *Die kirchenpol. u. kirchl. Verhältnisse*, 7.
[3]Smith, *loc. cit.*

testable fact the uselessness of seeking from the
majority of Italian chroniclers an equitable judgement
on the popes of Avignon.[1] Subsequently MOLLAT,
accepting PASTOR'S view, and noting that no less a
person than Benedict XII, had remarked the vehe-
mence with which adversaries had sought to blacken
his predecessor's memory,[2] set himself the task of
judging John XXII's character, 'en rapprochant des
sources littéraires les documents d'archives'.[3] This
was the method which the opening of the Vatican
Archives by LEO XIII rendered possible, indeed
imperative. FINKE put his finger on the weak point in
earlier research when he wrote: 'a sound judgement has
not been reached because accurate appraisal of the
historical authorities has been omitted. . . . The most
subjective are used with predilection—the acrid
phrases of preachers, for example, or the boundless
accusations of *Gravamina* literature'.[4] HALLER who,
in his *Papsttum und Kirchenreform*, made the most
brilliant, critical use of the subjective, literary authorities, dwelt on the same point;[5] but at the same time
he went a step further. 'No one,' he wrote, 'has
hesitated to base his judgement almost exclusively on
admittedly reformatory or polemical writings. Of the
documents in which the activities of the curia as a
governmental machine have been set down, historical
works have long taken no notice.' Yet 'these documents
exist, and exist moreover in an abundance which no
other government, even that of England, can boast'.
Thus 'with the help of this unparalleled material we

[1] *Geschichte d. Päpste* I, 60.
[2] 'Memoriam eiusdem predecessoris denigrare ac dilacerare sub murmura-
tionibus temerariis'.
[3] *Jean XXII fut-il un avare?* 525.
[4] *Op. cit.*, 8–9.
[5] *Papstt. u. Kirchenreform*, 6–7: 'Aus den mehr oder weniger absichtlichen
Deklamationen der Zeitgenossen ist wenig zu gewinnen. Man sollte deshalb
aufhören, Schilderungen der kirchlichen Zustände am Ausgange des Mittelalters aus Bruchstücken von Dietrich Vrye und Nikolaus von Clemanges
zusammenzusetzen. Nur insofern sind diese Schriften von grossem Werte,
als sie uns ein Bild der herrschenden Stimmung geben'.

are able to set over against the subjective picture which contemporaries drew of the papacy as it seemed to them, the objective description of the papacy as it really was'.[1]

This was the method of historical research which the opening of the Vatican Archives in 1881 made possible.[2] With particular regard to provisions, HALLER again pointed the way. 'Before Innocent III,' he wrote,[3]

the pope exerted an influence over the disposal of benefices by means of requests and recommendations, in so far as the ordinaries permitted: later the ordinaries retained the disposal of the benefices in their spheres of jurisdiction, in so far as papal expectancies and provisions constituted no hindrance. How often this was the case, to what degree the papacy put into effect its theoretically unlimited rights, is a question which forces itself upon our consideration, to which however we must probably be content to receive no satisfactory answer. Complaints of exorbitant burdening with provisions, such for example as the chronicle of Matthew Paris is fond of repeating from about 1240 onwards, prove nothing. The suspicion of exaggeration is too obvious. How is it that the chronicler, who is attempting to create the impression of a veritable flood of papal provisions, nevertheless dwells so persistently and so illuminatingly on isolated cases? There is no documentary support for his notices, even in cases where, in spite of the heaviest losses of material, at least some traces might be expected to be recorded among the acts.[4] Very different is the position when in 1248 documentary evidence proves that in the cathedral chapter at Constance, out of twenty existing prebends, seventeen had been filled by pope or legate, and that even then fourteen expectancies remained. . . . And again no one will refuse to believe the bishop of Angers, who announced at the Council of Vienne, that in thirty-five

[1]*Op. cit.*, vi-viii.
[2]'De opening van het Archivum Vaticanum doet thans sinds veertig jaar den geleerden het middel aan de hand om het oordeel der kronijkschrijvers aan de oorspronkelijke bronnen te toetsen'; Fierens, p. 812.
[3]Pp. 32-33.
[4]E.g. when he notes (*Chron. majora* IV, 31 sq.) an order in 1240 for the provision of 300 Romans.—Cf. similarly Baier, p. 187.

or more vacancies in his own church during the last twenty years, he had only twice been able to make use of his right of collation. But that does not prove that it was necessarily so, always and everywhere. In order to proceed with certainty, the only method is to make use of the Papal Registers: they ought, one would suppose, to yield clear statistics.

Thus the way was pointed to a statistical use of the Papal Registers as a method of checking the assertions of chroniclers, letter-writers, poets, reformers and pamphleteers. The first essential was the publication in one form or another of the documents in the Registers themselves; but in many cases, if not in all, publication of the documentary material and analysis and criticism of the contents of the volumes published, were in practice combined. The *Analecta Vaticano-Belgica*, published by BERLIÈRE and other members of the Belgian School at Rome, SAUERLAND's collections for the history of Lothringen and of the Rhineland, RIEDER's *Römische Quellen zur Konstanzer Bistumsgeschichte*, LANG's *Acta Salzburgo-Aquilejensia* and the *Repertorium Germanicum* compiled for the pontificate of Clement VII by GÖLLER,[1] all contain valuable studies of the operation of provisions in the fourteenth century, based predominantly on the material there brought to light.[2] Finally BAIER and MOLLAT, the one for the thirteenth, the other for the fourteenth century, have produced independent studies, the main characteristic of which is careful analytical use of the long series of Calendars of the Papal Registers published by the *École française de Rome;* and a penetrating analysis of the Belgian

---

[1] Cf. also the 2nd volume, for the pontificates of Urban VI, Boniface IX, Innocent VII, and Gregory XII, *ed.* G. Tellenbach; the volume for Martin V is being prepared by K. A. Fink.

[2] In addition, there are large numbers of smaller works, valuable mainly for local history, which cannot be discussed here; cf. Wehrmann, *Deutsche Geschichtsblätter* VIII, 93 sqq., Schmitz, *Röm. Quartalschrift* VII (1893), 209 sqq. and in criticism, Haller, *Theol. Literaturzeitung* (1905), 404–406.

fourteenth-century material has been furnished by FIERENS.

What have been the results of this phase in the historiography of papal provisions? Has the publication of a huge mass of documentary evidence provided an accurate check on the subjective literary authorities? Has a clear, objective, incontrovertible—we may well say, an authentic—picture of the operation of provisions and of their effects on the mediæval Church resulted? Without doubt, the study of the documentary authorities has given a new degree of ballast and objectivity to the views which have been expressed. But the fact remains that it has proved scarcely less difficult to appraise at its just value the documentary evidence than it is to determine the objective worth of the literary and propagandist authorities.

In the first place, it has become abundantly evident that the problem is not one which can be reduced to terms of statistics and thus solved by more or less mechanical means. The number of documents entered up in the Papal Registers of the thirteenth century, considerable though it is, is not too large to be surveyed at one time; and BAIER has conscientiously worked through the material. But his result, as he himself was first to admit, is negative.[1] We do not know what class or what proportion of letters were registered; we do not even know that the proportion registered remained fixed—indeed the mass of provisions appearing in the Register for the third year of Urban IV's pontificate,[2] is evidence that it did not. In these circumstances, as JORDAN has

---

[1] *Päpstl. Provisionen*, 47–48: 'um es am Schlusse dieser Ausführungen nochmals auszudrücken, ist meine Überzeugung die: Der grösste Teil der Provisions-mandate während des ganzen 13. Jahrhunderts ist verloren infolge der Unvollständigkeit der Register. Der Wirklichkeit entspricht nur das Bild, das wir über das dritte Jahr Urbans IV. gewinnen'.

[2] *Op. cit.*, 44.

noted,[1] mere figures can tell us nothing of importance. Even the broadest contrasts cannot be made with certainty. LAMPRECHT, for example, pointed out that the correspondence for the whole nine years of Boniface VIII's pontificate was contained in one volume,[2] that for the first year of Clement VII, on the other hand, filled twenty-one—a contrast that, in the words of FINKE, 'wäre vorzüglich für den Sozialstatistiker zu verwerten', if only we knew the rules of registration.[3] Actually the rules of registration seem to have varied from pontificate to pontificate;[4] and even though there is reason to think that greater uniformity was introduced in the fourteenth century,[5] we still know nothing of the principles in use, and have no means of bringing statistical calculations into relation with real numbers.[6] One of the fundamental questions to which an answer is needed is the relative numerical proportion between the different classes of provision-mandate; yet TIHON has shown that the *forma pauperum*— the simple mandate which was sued out in such numbers that its issue was limited to special occasions, such as the beginning of a new pontificate[7]—was not

---

[1]*Revue historique* CX (1912), 93: ' . . . Quelle en était l'étendue, quelles en ont été les phases d'aggravation ou d'atténuation et sur qui en retombait la charge? M. Baier a demandé une réponse à la statistique. . . . On peut se demander pourtant si M. Baier a été bien payé de sa peine. . . . Nous ne pouvons nous flatter de connaître qu'une faible partie des mandats de provision réellement expédiés. Dans ces conditions, les chiffres absolus n'ont pas grand intérêt; les chiffres relatifs peuvent en avoir, si les différences sont assez grandes pour ne pas s'expliquer par le hasard. Mais tel n'est pas le cas le plus ordinaire. . . . M. Baier aurait été mieux inspiré en faisant porter son principal effort sur d'autres aspects de son sujet, sur les côtés juridique, politique, économique'.

[2]This statement seems to be incorrect: to-day there are four volumes of letters of Boniface VIII, formerly there were six; cf. *Sussidi per la consultazione dell'Archivio Vaticano* I, 58. The broad contrast is, however, not affected thereby.—For Clement VII, cf. Göller, *Rep. Germ.* I, 15*sqq.

[3]*Die kirchenpol. u. kirchl. Verhältnisse*, 111–112.

[4]The right to register a rescript was undoubtedly originally, and perhaps for the major part of the thirteenth century, granted to private parties as a special privilege; cf. v. Heckel, *Untersuchungen zu den Registern*, and more generally, *Das päpstl. u. sicilische Registerwesen*.

[5]Cf. Barraclough, *Public Notaries*, 123–4.

[6]Cf. Guiraud, *Revue historique* LIX (1895), 189–190.

[7]Cf. Tihon, *Les expectatives*, 63–64, 91; *infra*, pp. 105–106.

registered throughout the whole period.[1] Thus the
very type of mandate which represents the ordinary
routine of administration, the ordinary man's writ
which demands the particular attention of those
interested not in abnormalities and special cases, but
in day-to-day practice, is lost sight of; and the Registers, studied alone, overstress the importance of the
special concessions to cardinals and *curiales*, who had
unusual facilities for obtaining particular advantages
and privileges.

This is the main but not the only factor which
renders it as difficult to obtain the whole truth from
the documents in the Papal Registers as from the
statements and personal opinions of contemporary
critics and chroniclers. In conjunction with it must
also be considered the unwieldiness of the huge mass
of material.[2] The immeasurable numbers of documents preserved defeat, of themselves, the objects of
the historian. It is beyond human capacity to survey
the thousands of provisions and related documents,
which the various series of fourteenth-century Papal
Registers contain. For this reason no one has really
attempted to analyse the fourteenth-century material
as BAIER analysed that of the thirteenth century.
MOLLAT relies in the main on single documents of
particular note: other more specialized workers such
as SAUERLAND, use the material they have collected as
illustration for the general impression they have
formed of the contents of the Registers. As far as the
fourteenth century is concerned, the statistical method
has proved impossible to apply.

The publication and historical use of a long series
of documents from the Vatican Archives has therefore
resulted in little more than a confirmation of what few
would be found to deny; namely, the growing corrup-

---

[1]With the exception of graces *in forma pauperum* accorded to graduates;
Tihon, 57-59.

[2]The situation is very fairly described, though in a different connexion,
by Kehr, in his Introduction to the *Repertorium Germanicum*, vol. I.

tion of the Church during the Avignonese period.[1] BERLIÈRE, the best judge of the fourteenthc-entury Vatican material, sums up the results of his researches with the sentence: 'c'est à Avignon qu'on peut aller chercher les origines de la Réforme protestante',[2] and LUX, following MUNCH,[3] adds that blame for this result is fundamentally to be ascribed to the operation of provisions.[4] But we have every right to look for more profound results than these. As HALLER has said, the object of the historian is to show 'how it came about'.[5]

Broad ethical judgements present no view of the actual facts and their formation. Immediately we seek a living presentation of the facts, other questions arise. Was every part of papal administration in the fourteenth and fifteenth centuries so radically bad? What were the specific faults? Was the curia really corrupt throughout? Are not the criticisms of the controversialists in themselves likely to be exaggerated? Are there not at least certain distinctions from period to period? And above all, was the effect on the Church as a whole of the corrupt state of the curia really so great that the papacy must be accounted the principal cause of the decline of Church institutions?

It is when questions such as these are approached, when an attempt is made to explain and to estimate the actual effect of papal provisions on the life and character of the fourteenth-century Church, that the conclusions of those who have sought to make use of the documentary evidence have met as radical criticism as the *ex parte* statements of contemporaries. SAUERLAND'S verdict on nine volumes of Vatican documents is summed up in the words: 'a more and

---

[1] Mollat's *Les papes d'Avignon* is the only apologetic work of importance.
[2] *Suppliques d'Innocent VI*, xxii.
[3] *Archivalische Zeitschrift* IV, 104.
[4] 'Es gibt wenige Umst nde, welche das Ansehen der Kurie so untergruben und die Gemüter zum Abfall für die Reformation derartig vorbereiteten, als gerade jenes ungemein verhasste Provisionssystem', *Die Besetzung d. Benefizien in d. Breslauer Diözese*, 4–5.
[5] *Papstt. u. Kirchenreform*, vii.

more unbridled chase for benefices, more and more lavish distribution on the part of the curia, ever growing demands by the *camera apostolica* on the financial resources of the clergy, ever increasing accumulation of cures of souls in the Rhineland by members of the papal curia at Avignon, uncanonical accumulation of incompatible benefices by younger sons of the nobility, and the unashamed support of noble bastards with fat livings'.[1] Even if we ignore SAUERLAND's more exaggerated statements,[2] such an indictment needs careful checking. In what way, we must therefore ask, has SAUERLAND approached his evidence? He admits[3] that a distinction must be made between curial and non-curial impetrants; but nowhere, in actual fact, does he make such a distinction. Though it is generally admitted that the Papal Registers contain, in an overwhelming majority, provisions *in forma speciali*,[4] though TIHON has even suggested that registration occurred mainly when a cumulation of benefices was in question,[5] SAUERLAND has made no attempt to estimate the relative proportions of the provisions in the Registers to the whole number issued. Frequent though they were, special graces and dispensations to hold a number of benefices were nevertheless abnormal if we consider the beneficial system of Europe as a whole.[6] SAUERLAND, on the other hand, with his eye on the too frequent 'professional' pluralists, the worldly clerks who made the collection of benefices their life-work,[7] and on the

---

[1]*Urk. z. Gesch. d. Rheinlande* I, xvii; cf. III, lv-lvi, lix, lxiii; IV, viii-ix, xlv; V, xix, xxix.

[2]E.g. *op. cit.*, V, xii, regarding the moral corruption of *curia* and *curiales*. —Such remarks as: 'Die an der Kurie weilenden oder zur Kurie eilenden Pfründenbettler aber waren wie die Bettler aller Orte und aller Zeiten gewesen sind. Nur äusserst wenige von diesen suchen Arbeit und Geld; bei weitem die meisten, ja fast alle verlangen Geld ohne Arbeit' (IV, ix) are—apart from anything else—out of place in a serious historical work.

[3]V, xxv. [4]Cf. Fierens, p. 820.

[5]*Les expectatives*, 58. [6]Fierens, p. 845.

[7]For examples of notorious *Pfründenjäger*, cf. Sauerland, *op. cit.*, III, lvii n. 1; IV, xii sqq.; V, xlii sqq.; *Vat. Urk. z. Gesch. Lothringens* II, ii-iii.

Massenexpektanzen, as he names them, by which cardinals were entitled to hold benefices to a total value of a thousand marks and more,[1] treats the exceptional as the rule. The *pauperes clerici*, who used the system in tens and even hundreds of thousands,[2] their examination and the local proof required of their moral and personal capacities, the *rotuli* of the universities and the importance attached to university-degrees in the curia,[3] are given little prominence in his survey.[4] For him the provisions system in Avignonese times was nothing but organized nepotism and favouritism.[5]

Apart from these broader issues, however, his estimate of the effects of papal provisions on the distribution of benefices in the Church as a whole, has met with radical criticism. Using SAUERLAND's own material, SCHÄFER has estimated the number of

---

[1] E.g. Sauerland, *Urk. z. Gesch. d. Rheinlande* III, 71 (5 Oct. 1342) to *Guido, tit. s. Cecilie presb. card.* On the question of the cardinals, cf. *infra*, p. 74 sq.

[2] Peter of Hérenthals (who apparently had trustworthy official information) estimated the number of impetrants between 19 May and 25 June, 1342 at 100,000 (Baluze-Mollat, *Vitae paparum Avenionensium* I, 298); Bucglant, the proctor of the city of Hamburg, writing on 11 June, gives his information as 80,000 (Schwalm, *Das Formelbuch d. Heinrich Bucglant*, xlii; 'et ad ecclesiam nostram Hamburgensem de nostris civibus et aliis clericis ultra quadraginta suas porrexerunt supplicaciones'). Cf. also Haller, *Papstt. u. Kirchenreform*, 124 n. 1, where however no definite figure is mentioned.—That these figures are not exaggerated is shown by the fact that some 6,000 candidates from the dioceses of Mainz and Köln alone were examined in the curia; cf. Berlière, *Suppliques de Clément VI*, 579.

[3] Cf. Fierens, p. 836.

[4] His remarks on examination in *scientia* and *vita* (III, lvii-lix) are not only inadequate but unjust; cf. Tihon, pp. 71-83.

[5] Fierens (pp. 832 sqq.) expresses an equally strongly worded judgement: 'bij de begeving der beneficiën door den Heiligen Stoel niet gelet werd, eerst en vooral, op den eisch der plaatselijke behoeften en noodwendig-heden, maar wel op geheel daarbuitenliggende motieven: het was een vriendjespolitiek die gevoerd werd ten voordeele van al wie goed stond met het pauselijk hof, veel meer dan een bedacht zijn op de geestelijke vereischten der Christenheid. . . . Onder die hoogwaardigheidsbekleeders nemen van zelf sprekend de Kardinalen de eerste plaats in . . . er zijn kerkambten die feitelijk van de eene kardinaalshand tot de andere overgingen, zoo bijna alsof ze een private of althans een voorbehouden eigendom van het heilig College uitmaakten'.—But, in marked contrast to Sauerland, his verdict on this side of the system, is balanced by a careful appreciation of the other factors.

provisions in the Rhineland at the height of the
Avignonese centralization, not, in SAUERLAND'S
phrase, as 'immeasurable', but as affecting about
9 per cent. of the total number of benefices; the cases
in which papal providees and the candidates of the
ordinaries were forced into litigation as involving at
the highest ⅛ per cent. of the livings in the district.[1]
A higher percentage of benefices, he concludes, was
disposed of by the French crown in virtue of the *ius
regale* than by the papacy by means of provisions.[2]

Without attempting for the moment to determine
how far either SAUERLAND or SCHÄFER succeeded in
establishing a final judgement, we can safely draw one
conclusion from the controversy: the use of the Papal
Registers, without a thorough preliminary investigation of their construction—the mere citation of isolated
documents, and even statistics drawn from larger
groups—falls hardly less under the influence of the
particular point of view of the individual writer than
the use of literary authorities. From among the
thousands of documents in the Registers, hundreds
can be cited in support of practically any contention,
particularly when all classes of material are used
indiscriminately with the sole object of extracting
isolated facts from single documents. Thus RIEDER
has rightly insisted on the necessity of an investigation
of the numbers and inter-relation of the different
classes of documentary evidence.[3] It has been declared
that, from the point of view of provisions, the
Registers of petitions are more instructive than the
papal letters.[4] But, as RIEDER has shown, it is above
all the Registers of petitions which have to be used

---

[1] *Zur Kritik mittelalterl. kirchl. Zustände*, 139–140; Sauerland's reply (IV, ix)
seems to me to be beside the point; but it would be superfluous to criticize it
in detail.
[2] *Op. cit.*, 140; cf. Imbart de la Tour, *Origines* I, 103, where the king of
France is said to have been compared by his lawyers with the pope on account
of his influence over the disposal of benefices.
[3] *Röm. Quellen*, xxix-xxxix.
[4] Fierens, p. 814.

with care. For, notwithstanding the fact that only petitions which the pope had sanctioned, were registered—and there can be no doubt that a really considerable proportion was rejected[1]—for practically half the petitions collected by him for the period 1305–1378 there is no corresponding bull in evidence.[2] Only the most superficial student of the papal archives, however, would dare to ascribe this result to the incompleteness of the material. The documents themselves point in no doubtful manner to certain quite definite reasons, among which may be named the presentation of two or three petitions by one person,[3] only one of which could ordinarily be admitted, an erroneous statement in the petition itself by which its value was destroyed, failure to pass the prescribed examination,[4] and finally omission on the

[1]Cf. Rieder, p. xxxviii: 'Da in die Supplikenregister nur die signierten, nicht aber die überhaupt eingelaufenen Bittschriften registriert wurden, wird es uns bei dem derzeitigen Stand unserer Kenntnisse völlig unmöglich sein, ein Urteil darüber zu fällen, wieviel von den eingelaufenen Bittschriften und nach welchem Gesichtspunkt sie signiert wurden. . . . Auf der anderen Seite belehren uns gerade die Supplikenregister, dass ein grösserer Prozentsatz der Suppliken nicht signiert wurde. Aus Versehen nämlich registrierten oft die Supplikenregistratoren die eine oder andere nicht signierte Supplik, die dann nachträglich mit einem Tilgungsvermerk versehen wurde. Diese Stücke allein—und wer die Supplikenregister kennt, weiss, dass es deren viele sind—bilden uns heute einen Anhalt für die Feststellung nicht signierter Suppliken . . . Schon diese Beispiele zeigen zur Genüge, dass nicht jeder, der nach Avignon kam, um eine Gnade zu erbitten, dieselbe auch gewährt erhielt'. 'Das ist hier um so mehr zu betonen, als man vielfach der Meinung begegnet, die Kurie habe unterschiedslos ohne vorhergehende Prüfung sämtliche Suppliken kurzerhand signiert'.

[2]*Op. cit.*, xxxi.

[3]The object was obviously to make sure that one at least of the supplications would be acceded to. In the same way, if a petition was refused, the same request was repeated at a later date, and if necessary two or three times, 'um trotz erstmaliger Abweisung am Ende doch noch zum erwünschten Ziele zu gelangen . . . Daraus folgt aber, dass nicht die Gewinnsucht der Kurie oder das Bestreben der päpstl. Kanzlei, durch möglichst viele neue Klauseln die Einnahmen der Kammer zu vermehren, in erster Linie an der Weiterentwicklung des Suppliken- und überhaupt des Formelwesens Schuld war, sondern die Petenten selber oder deren Prokuratoren, die um jeden Preis in den Besitz der erwünschten Gnade kommen wollten' (*op. cit.*, xxxix).

[4]Thus a certain sign on a petition signified 'quod illi adhuc restant examinandi et quod nondum sunt conficiende littere super petitionibus illis, quamvis per dominum nostrum sint signate, donec examinati existant et reperti fuerint habere illas sufficientes qualitates, quas dominus noster eos vult habere'. Teige, *Beiträge*, 429, no. 42.

D

part of the impetrant to have his bull drafted, due often to the realization that another was in legal possession of the benefice in question, or that the probability of his gaining possession himself was so remote that he was not prepared to undertake the attendant expense.

Every petition, therefore, does not imply a provision, and every fact alleged by a petitioner is not to be understood as an objective description of local conditions. And all the arguments which lie against taking the evidence of the Registers of Supplications at face value, apply to the Registers of Papal Letters. It is the particular merit of what we may call the Belgian school of criticism to have taken this point into serious consideration.[1] Just as RIEDER has shown that the petitions need checking by reference to the papal letters, so BERLIÈRE has shown that the letters in their turn must be checked by reference to the accounts of the papal collectors, whose detailed statements of annates paid or owed offer final proof whether a providee eventually obtained real possession of his benefice or not.[2] Although others have given the question incidental attention,[3] it is, however, to the acute and penetrating work of TIHON and BAIX that we must turn for an independent treatment of the question of the *real*—the final and effective—value of papal mandates of provision.

'Du "droit" au "fait" il y avait loin':[4] that is the starting-point of their argument. Even the rights conveyed by a papal rescript, TIHON showed,[5] were subject to narrow limitations which are rarely understood by modern historians—a point which can be left out of consideration here, but with which we shall have to deal briefly later.[6] Even more restricted, however,

[1] Kurth stands apart; but he has been severely criticized by Baix, p. 66.
[2] *Les collectories*, xli.
[3] E.g. Hanquet, *Documents relatifs au Grand Schisme* I, xxxiv.
[4] Baix, *De la valeur hist. des actes pontificaux de collation*, 59.
[5] *Les expectatives*, cap. III.   [6] *Infra*, capp. VII and IX.

than the legal value of a rescript was its practical worth. Individual cases of papal providees who were unable to obtain satisfaction from their letters, can be counted in hundreds. Jan Boesman of Montenaeken,[1] a poor clerk of the diocese of Liège, went to Avignon at the beginning of Clement VI's pontificate, to take part with 80–100,000 others of his class in the general issue of graces which marked the occasion.[2] He waited ten years for his provision to take effect, and then the death of the pope rendered his letters null. On the election of Innocent VI he again set off for Avignon, but fell ill on the way, and did not arrive till the issue of *gratie communes* had been discontinued. As compensation, the pope granted him an expectancy in special form; but even this availed him nothing, and twelve years later he was still without a benefice. Jan Reyners[3] received provisions successively from Clement VI, Innocent VI and Urban V, but none of them won him a benefice. Simon de Maneslies[4] engaged in litigation for eighteen years to get possession of a benefice to which he had been provided at Saint-Omer; and when he found that even judgement on his behalf did not bring him success, he renounced his rights in order to prosecute a provision to a canonry in the cathedral at Paris. Robert Fabri[5] complained in 1362 that he had been waiting *sub expectatione* for more than thirty years; and even officials of the curia found themselves in the same unfortunate situation.[6]

Such isolated cases, of considerable interest in themselves, are typical of hundreds; but for the very

[1]Cf. Tihon, p. 94.   [2]Cf. *supra*, p. 31 n. 2.   [3]Tihon, *loc. cit.*
[4]Fierens, p. 828.   [5]Fierens, p. 829.
[6]Cf. the following petition of 26 Jan. 1359, printed by Sauerland, *Urk. z. Gesch. d. Rheinlande* III, lviii: 'Pater sanctissime! Pro isto infelice et infortunato servitore vestro, qui camere apostolice et bo. me. domino Francisco notario vestro XI annis vel circiter fideliter et laboriose servivit, die noctuque continue scribendo, expensis suis propriis absque gratiis vel premio seu remuneratione quacumque, signastis hactenus successive quatuor supplicationes super diversis beneficiis, que nullum sortite sunt nec sortiri possunt effectum, ymmo sunt sibi non solum inutiles sed dampnose. Quare supplicat sibi gratiam fieri intuitu premissorum. . . .'

reason that they are individual examples, they must be discounted. More significant evidence is furnished by the frequent *Rotuli pauperum clericorum, qui fuerant inutiliter assignati,*[1] and by general declarations of the worthlessness of provisions, such as those attested by the clergy of Liège in 1350.[2] But the most impressive evidence, as BAIX insists, is that furnished by statistics drawn from the accounts of collectors. 'In a total of 196 benefices conferred by letters of Clement VII from 31 October, 1387, to 30 October, 1392, in those parts of the dioceses of Cambrai, Tournai and Thérouanne within his obedience, the collector recognized that ninety-seven provisions were of no effect; eighty-eight had acquired a real value, and eleven cases seemed doubtful. Thus even at the final stage in the development of provisions a 50 per cent. wastage occurred, from the point of view of actual effectiveness'.[3] Moreover, even after the collector had verified the papal letters and collected annates, the impetrant did not always get possession: cases occur where, failure to get possession being alleged, the collector notes that the taxes paid have been returned,[4] and the percentage of cases in which the issue of letters actually resulted in the conferment of a benefice is therefore reduced still further.

The broad result of the critical studies of RIEDER, BAIX and TIHON is thus to prove beyond all question that we can no more take the documents in the Papal Registers at their face value than we can accept without qualification the hostile statements, for example, of Petrarch or St. Catherine of Siena. The factors which limited and in many cases completely destroyed the value of letters of provision have been enumerated by BAIX under the following headings:[5] revocation of graces; delusiveness of expectancies;

---

[1]Cf. Lux, *Die Besetzung d. Benefizien,* 24 sq.; Schwalm, *Das Formelbuch d. Heinrich Bucglant,* 159 sq.; Rieder, *Römische Quellen,* nos. 98, 99.

[2]Schoolmeesters, *Recueil de lettres,* 28–34; cf. Fierens, p. 830, Tihon, p. 93, Haller, p. 151.

[3]Baix, p. 59.   [4]*Op. cit.,* 60.   [5]*Op. cit.,* 66.

disproportion between supplications, letters and the actual acquisition of benefices; benefices granted by the pope but not accepted, or disputed; fictitious or surreptitious resignations and permutations; concessions replaced by others; dispensations and indulgences by which papal grants were neutralized,[1] errors in the documents themselves. If the statistics which have been drawn up are accurate, it would appear that, through the operation of factors such as these, only about half of the supplications acceded to led to the issue of letters, and only about half of the letters issued resulted in the actual conferment of a benefice.

Important as it is to establish a proportionate relationship of this sort, significant as it is as a check on the calculations of those who have seen in every provision issued by the Papal Chancery, or even in every petition presented to the pope, the unconditional destruction of a positive canonical right of the ordinary collator, there are few historians who will not agree that it is almost as dangerous to proceed on the basis of a broad, general estimate of this sort as on the uncritical lists of provisions abstracted from the various series of Registers by SAUERLAND, for example, or by KURTH. In the first enthusiasm after the opening of the Vatican archives, it was imagined that the lists of Church dignitaries, compiled from local evidence, would need to be drawn up again as a body with the help of the Vatican material:[2] now it is more truly seen that the Vatican documents demand the most thorough collation with the local evidence, can in no event be accepted where they disagree with the local evidence, and ought, if no collateral support is

---

[1]It is too often supposed (e.g. Stubbs, *Const. History* III, 321, Baier, *Päpstl. Provisionen*, cap. VI, *passim*) that indulgences *ne ad provisionem inviti cogantur* were rendered useless by *non obstante* clauses. Yet such a privilege was granted for example, to the cathedral-chapter of Gnesen by Innocent IV in 1247, and there is no evidence of a papal provision in this church till the middle of the fourteenth century; cf. Binder, p. 21.—On *non obstantia* in general, cf. *infra*, pp. 86 n. 2, 95 n. 6, 113 sqq.

[2]Cf. Kurth, *Liège et la cour de Rome*, 19, 21.

forthcoming, only to be accepted as final after the most intensive research and criticism.[1] A final judgement on the provisions system, it is becoming clear, is to be sought not in Rome but in the provinces.

This fact was already observed, with fine insight, by FINKE, at the end of the last century, not in regard to provisions alone, but in regard to the whole state of religion in the fourteenth and fifteenth centuries. A final judgement, he wrote, is possible, if historians begin not, according to the usual scheme of studies, at the top, allowing themselves to be satisfied with a superficial criticism of the Roman curia, but attempt by means of the most thorough-going exploration of local history to penetrate into the heart of the people.[2] Already the facts have borne out this judgement. RIEDER's independent analysis of the situation in Constance[3] provided a first indication of the decisive results which could be obtained by a careful comparison of the Roman and the local documentary evidence. But not until the scores of monographs produced by members of the historical schools of STUTZ and SCHULTE—and particularly of the latter—could be considered as a body, was the fundamental importance of a penetrating study of local history for those spheres of ecclesiastical administration which had previously been considered the prerogative of the worker in the Vatican Archives, placed beyond all doubt. STUTZ' theory of the *Eigenkirchenwesen*[4] and SCHULTE's conception of the part played by aristocratic influence and class-conceptions in the mediæval Church[5] were ideas which only a detailed study of the history of small localities, of individual chapters and churches and of the religious life of single towns, could prove or

[1] Baix, p. 66; Berlière, *Les collectories*, xli.
[2] *Die kirchenpol. u. kirchl. Verhältnisse*, 11.
[3] *Röm. Quellen*, lxix-xc; also K. A. Fink, *Die Stellung d. Konstanzer Bistums z. päpstl. Stuhl.*
[4] *Gesch. d. kirchl. Benefizialwesens; Die Eigenkirche als Element d. mittelalt.-germanischen Kirchenrechts*, etc.
[5] *Der Adel u. d. deutsche Kirche*, etc.

disprove. But the historians who set out to test the
validity of these theories for thirteenth-, fourteenth- and
fifteenth-century history had necessarily to consider
other factors, among which none was more important
than the Roman curia. If the influence of the centralized, curial administration of the popes of Avignon
was so great, what was the significance of the
Eigenkirchentum and of the ascendancy of the nobility
within the Church? If the aristocracy and the *Eigenkirchenwesen* played a dominant part in Church history,
to what degree were the efforts of the papacy to control
the Church effective? In answering questions such as
these, the followers of STUTZ and SCHULTE were
immediately brought face to face with the question of
papal provisions.[1]

We cannot do better, in a limited space, than to see
in what words the more outstanding of these local
historians have summed up the results of their researches on the question of provisions. From the very
beginning their conclusions were surprising and
provocative. KISKY, for example, in studying the
situation in Cologne, Mainz and Trier, arrived at the
conclusion that 'the popes had mostly little success
in the provision of *curiales*, who naturally did not meet
the requirements of the chapters in regard to matters
of class or rank. On the other hand, it was often the
case that the papal providee belonged to the same
class as the other canons: in that case little or no
difficulty was made, and the providee was normally
admitted. In sum, papal intervention was not of such
a type as to frustrate a particular tendency within the
chapter. Our lists show how the chapters were able

---

[1] Stutz and Schulte themselves, who were more directly concerned with the
proof of their own theories, gave no more than casual attention to provisions.
—The following remarks do not claim to cover all the monographs on the
two subjects in question, many of which have not been available to me in
England, at the time of writing. I have merely singled out those which have
made a marked contribution to the history of provisions as notable examples
of a large and growing class of historical literature. In general, cf. Werminghoff, *Ständische Probleme*.

almost without exception to carry out a policy of complete caste exclusiveness. Thus a relatively small number of families managed throughout to maintain their position in a chapter, and we see the same names occurring again and again with inexhaustible frequency'.[1] In the cathedral at Cologne, 'the popes only attained their object when the chapter had no objection to the providee—that is, no objection to his parentage—which rarely happened, since the popes practically only put forward members of the curia without consideration of their rank'.[2] It must, however, be admitted that in Cologne, where it was customary to admit only the highest ranks of the nobility to the chapter, opposition to papal provisions and providees was unusually intense.[3] KISKY remarks that 'papal providees such as Bindus of Siena and Anselm of Wasselnheim, who stand isolated in the long list of canons at Cologne, are not uncommon in Mainz and Trier'.[4] But when in 1325 the pope tried to grant a canonry to a commoner at Mainz (where simple nobility alone was demanded) the remonstrances of the archbishop and chapter quickly induced him to revoke his act.[5] The other side of the picture is seen when in 1374, for example, Gregory XI deferred the provision of John de Trlag to a canonry at Gnesen until assurance had been given that he was of noble birth.[6]

From this point of view, no conclusions are more striking than those which KOTHE has drawn from his analysis of the Strassburg evidence. 'The increasing conferment of canonries by papal provision altered the existing situation but little; for the curia throughout showed understanding for the wishes of the

[1] *Das freiherrliche Stift St. Gereon*, 45.
[2] *Die Domkapitel d. geistl. Kurfürsten*, 16.
[3] *Op. cit.*, 11–12.   [4] *Op. cit.*, 16.
[5] Op. cit., 12, 'together with a similar example from Trier. For further instances, cf. Rauch, *Stiftsmässigkeit u. Stiftsfähigkeit*, 741.
[6] Binder, *Das Domkapitel zu Gnesen*, 11.

chapter; and it could not do otherwise, since the canons preferred to suffer suspension and excommunication rather than give way on the question of class. Among the numerous provisions to cathedral prebends in the fourteenth century we find the names of but two providees of lower than baronial rank—a Ritter von Fourpach and a Herr von Baionna—and neither seems to have contrived to get possession of his benefice. No further mention of them occurs. Otherwise it was old acquaintances like the von Geroldseck, Lichtenberg, Rapoltstein and other families of high baronial rank, who made use, on account of the excessive competition for benefices, of the shorter and safer process of papal provision on the recommendation of a relative'.[1] Thus although in the three most important churches of Strassburg the years 1324–1330 saw no less than thirty-nine papal provisions, there is every reason to ask whether the intervention of the papacy substantially altered the position within the chapters. 'The curia adapted itself, as far as the class of its providees was concerned, practically without exception to the prevailing custom —an indication of shrewd respect for facts, which no doubt rendered its unpopular administrative measures more palatable to the canons whose rights of election were affected'.[2]

The same fact is emphasized by RIEDER at the conclusion of his detailed investigation of the position at Constance. 'The names of the providees', he writes, 'seem to me to indicate that at any rate a large number of candidates would never have approached the pope without the preliminary approbation of the chapter: the families of Pfefferhard, Last, Güttinger, Nellenburger, Sätteli, v. Steinegg, v. Toggenburg, v. Montfort and their relatives are, as we might say, 'native' in the cathedral chapter. If all these facts are taken into

[1] *Kirchl. Zustände Strassburgs*, 12.
[2] *Op. cit.*, 31–32.

consideration, the effective influence of the papacy on the distribution of benefices in the cathedral at Constance must be set very low'.[1]

But even if provisions were used in churches of this type by families whose influence had always predominated in the chapter, the proportion of petitioners who eventually achieved their objective, remained remarkably small. During the period 1316–1378 we know of ninety-eight aspirants to papal provision at Constance. Of these ten were unsuccessful in obtaining papal letters, and eight of the remaining eighty-eight had to renew their petitions. Eventually thirty-seven (or perhaps thirty-three) got possession of a prebend, of whom eleven (or seven) were immediately promoted to vacant places.[2] In Augsburg the effect of provisions was to all appearance even smaller. According to LEUZE's statistics, only seventeen in a total of 125 admissions to canonries were due to papal intervention.[3] Where, on the other hand, papal influence seems to have been considerable, it can usually be explained by special circumstances: thus, for example, in regard to the cathedral chapter of Ermland,[4] in the colonized lands of the German Order. Here there was no aristocratic influence to counterbalance the influence of the papacy,[5] no statutory limitation of the right of admission to the chapter to any particular class,[6] and papal provisions (which incidentally exercised a salutary check on the attempts of the German Order to incorporate the bishopric, as it had incorporated those of Kulm, Pomesanien and Samland)[7] were consequently

---

[1]*Röm. Quellen*, lxxxviii.
[2]*Op. cit.*, lxxxvi; for more detailed statistics, cf. pp. lxxiii sqq.
[3]*Das Augsburger Domkapitel*, 33.
[4]Cf. Pottel, *Das Domkapitel v. Ermland*.
[5]*Op. cit.*, 26; cf. Brunner, *Grundzüge*, 154.
[6]Pottel, p. 7.
[7]*Op. cit.*, 92.

numerous.[1] In Ermland the papacy contrived to bring considerable influence to bear on the chapter, and its provisions were unusually effective; but the abnormal circumstances are an adequate explanation of the constitutional situation and show that Ermland, if it was an exception, was the sort of exception which proves the rule.

'Canonries were the staple commodity of the papal market.'[2] Modern historians have undoubtedly good reason to begin with the detailed study of the situation in the larger cathedral and collegiate churches; for it was here that papal provisions had most effect. But their use was in no wise confined within these limits. It is true, and must be emphasized, that the pope did not normally interfere with livings in lay patronage: although, in canonical theory, they fell within his plenitude of power,[3] he did not in this connexion put his prerogative powers into exercise.[4] For a time, indeed, perhaps until the pontificate of Innocent IV, there seems to have been some ambiguity in practice;[5] but it was not long before it became established, as a fixed rule, that lay patronage should not be regarded as affected, unless the papal rescript contained a specific clause: *non obstante si predicta ecclesia ad presentationem laici pertineret*. Such clauses are in fact very uncommon.[6] The principles of equity, which nowhere received

---

[1]*Op. cit.*, 25, 27, 95. He counts sixty provisions in the period 1344–1400; but it is not clear whether he is referring to papal letters or effective investitures. By the time of Bishop John Stryprock (1355–1373) the chapter contained only 'päpstlich gesinnte Kleriker' (p. 102).

[2]Maitland, *Canon Law*, 67.

[3]See c. 2 in VI° 3, 4 *gl. ad v.* 'Collatio'; but cf. c. 34 X 3, 5 *gl. ad v.* 'Regis' (*et ad v.* 'Frivolam').

[4]Bonaguida, *Consuetudines*, 16: 'quod per litteras generales domini pape, ut provideatur alicui de aliquo beneficio cum cura vel sine cura, non possit ei providere aliquo modo in ecclesia, in qua sunt patroni laici, et si fiat provisio, quod sit nulla. Sic curia tenet et servat'.

[5]Cf. Hinschius III, 120 n. 4; Haller, p. 31 n. 2; but see further Roffredus, *Opus libellorum*, tit. *De preb.*, §. *Quomodo concipiatur libellus* (fo. 89′a).

[6]But cf. for example, *Reg. Vat.* 29 (*Urbani IV, a.* 3), fo. 277, n. 1447 (Guiraud, n. 2398); *Reg. Vat.* 44 (*Nich. IV, a.* 1), fo. 27, n. 110 (Langlois, n. 211).

such lasting recognition as in the law of the Church, made special consideration of the rights of lay patrons not only a political expedient but also a moral obligation;[1] and there is overwhelming evidence that the papacy did not countenance real interference with these rights in any country of mediæval Europe.[2]

At the same time, there were other benefices, besides canonries and prebends, in the patronage of the clergy, and from a social and religious point of view, they were of considerable importance. Natural though it is to concentrate critical attention on the situation in the collegiate churches, those who see in papal provisions a corrupting, degrading influence on the moral and religious life of the whole Church, and through the Church on the people at large, must necessarily demand a similar attempt by local historians to gauge the effect of provisions in outlying districts and throughout whole dioceses. Such a study, as a supplement to the work of RIEDER, has been carried out for the diocese of Constance by K. A. FINK.[3] Under the popes of Avignon, he finds, there occurred 106 provisions to benefices with cure of souls, a figure which is not excessive for a period of seventy years; and of these providees only two were foreigners. From a somewhat different point of view HILLING has arrived at similar results in regard to the diocese of Hildesheim at the end of the Middle Ages. His analysis of the material in the archives of the Rota

[1]Cf. Bern. Parm. *ad* c. 28 X 3, 28 *v*. 'Presentare': 'sed istud maiori nititur equitate, ut patronus ratione patrimonii, quo dotavit ecclesia, non privetur iure suo, nec fiat ei hec iniuria, et propter hoc subtraherentur et ipse et alii a fundatione ecclesiarum; et hoc est verum'.

[2]Schulte, *Kirchenrecht* II, 327 n. 3, claims that in Germany alone was lay patronage exempt from papal intervention. But cf. for France, Haller, *Papstt. u. Kirchenreform*, 36 n. 2; for England, Maitland, *Canon Law*, 67, and Deeley, *Engl. Hist. Review* XLIII, 497 sqq.; and in general Hinschius, *Kirchenrecht* III, 144 n. 3.—The cases cited p. 43 n. 6 are exceptional; and in the second, moreover, (which appears to be an important test case), the party supported by the patrons, not the providee, was successful. Cf. further *Reg. Vat.* 44 (*Nich. IV, a.* 2), fo. 263', n. 679 (Langlois, n. 1813), with the stipulation: 'si nulli alii debeantur, nec in ipsis ius patronatus ad laicum spectet'.

[3]*Die Stellung d. Konstanzer Bistums z. päpstl. Stuhl*, cap. III.

Romana—the central law-court of the Church—shows on the one hand that litigation affected canonries and prebends in collegiate churches to a far greater degree than parishes and cures of souls,[1] and secondly that only rarely are foreigners found engaged in litigation for possession of Hildesheimer benefices.[2] In Brandenburg, as PRIEBATSCH has shown, the position at the end of the Middle Ages was fundamentally the same. 'There is absolutely no reason for perpetual repetition of the complaints raised in contemporary German invective concerning the numerous Italians who got possession of German benefices by means of papal provision. The number of Italians in possession of German—and above all of North German—benefices can be counted with ease: they were certainly far and away less numerous than the Germans who made their fortune in Italy at the papal curia, but who were then, of course, classed as 'courtiers' and identified with the foreigners. The curia gave the question of nationality much deeper consideration than is usually supposed, and tried to select as far as possible acceptable candidates for provision'.[3]

These independent results, and above all their general agreement on the question of the provision of foreigners, are not without interest. But a great deal more remains to be done before even an indication of the position in the remoter country districts can be said to have been obtained. Above all, as HILLING has said, 'to guard against an exaggeration of the significance of the abuses which no doubt were actually present in the central administration and judicature, no judgement of the number of provisions and of litigation over provisions should be regarded as final, except in relation to the total number of benefices in existence. Through such a comparison alone is it possible to arrive at a dependable percentual ratio,

---

[1] *Die Römische Rota u. d. Bistum Hildesheim*, 38 sqq., 160.
[2] *Op cit.*, 44.   [3] *Staat u. Kirche in d. Mark Brandenburg*, 428.

on the knowledge of which an objective judgement of the good and evil consequences of any particular practice necessarily depends'.[1]

In this regard, however, our knowledge is very limited. KALLEN has produced valuable statistics of the benefices in Upper Swabia for the period 1275–1508, and LEINEWEBER has published a similar work for the *beneficia curata* in the Duchy of Westphalia. Similarly HILLING has estimated that in the three chief towns of the Hildesheimer diocese no less than 500-600 benefices were in existence at the end of the Middle Ages.[2] These enormous figures, as he rightly remarks, provide us with the background in which the large numbers of papal provisions and equally frequent litigation *in beneficialibus* must necessarily be placed. But the statistics for many more towns and districts must be compiled before we are in a position to generalize on the proportion of provisions to benefices. For this purpose the thirteenth-century surveys, such as in England the Valuation of Norwich or the Taxation of Nicholas IV, are of little use, in the first place because they were not complete lists of all benefices in existence,[3] more particularly because the fourteenth century, which saw the widest extension of papal provisions, saw also a sudden and unparalleled outburst of pious bequests, as a result of which very large numbers of new foundations, particularly of chantries, came into existence.[4] Thus the only statistics which could answer our purpose would be carefully drawn up historical statistics, in which the different periods from the thirteenth to the end of the fifteenth century were distinguished, and the contemporary material critically reviewed.

Such statistics, as has been said, are still rare and the same is true of all classes of monographs dealing with

[1]Hilling, *op. cit.*, 64.   [2]*op. cit.*, 66.
[3]Graham, *The Taxation of Pope Nicholas IV*, 453–4.
[4]Cf. Kothe, pp. 33 sqq., 114 sqq., Kallen, p. 270.—For England, cf. Wood-Legh, *Some Aspects of the History of the Chantries.*

the local history of ecclesiastical benefices and their distribution. In Germany alone have the ideas of the *Eigenkirchenwesen* and of aristocratic influence in the Church been studied in any degree of thoroughness, and even there the detailed monographs are still too few to permit of definitive generalization, as far as the question of provisions is concerned. The situation during the fourteenth and fifteenth centuries in other parts of Europe, on the other hand, remains to all intents and purposes unknown.[1] Every reader of the Papal Registers of the period must be impressed by the frequency of provisions in the dioceses, for example, of Cambrai, Lincoln or Liège—a frequency for which further research would probably show that there were quite definite economic reasons.[2] But what proportion of these provisions took effect? To what class did the providees belong? Was there the same standard of class-exclusiveness in the chapters in question as in German chapters at the same period? Do certain family connexions maintain a position of dominance, notwithstanding papal intervention? What proportion of foreigners are found in possession of *beneficia*

---

[1]Cf. however, for England, Böhmer, *Das Eigenkirchenwesen in England*, Stutz, *Das Eigenkirchenwesen in England*; for Spain, Bidagor, *La iglesia propia en España*, *Id.*, 'La iglesia propia medieval española', *Razon y Fe* XC (1930), 481–499, M. Torres, 'La doctrina de las "Iglesias propias" en los autores españoles', *Anuario de historia del derecho español* II (1925), 402–461, *Id.*, 'El origen del sistema de "iglesias propias" ', *Anuario* V (1928), 83–217; for France, R. Génestal, 'Les origines du droit ecclésiastique franc', *Nouvelle revue hist. de droit* XXXVIII (1914), 524–551, Imbart de la Tour, 'Les paroisses rurales dans l'ancienne France', p. III, *Revue historique* LXVII (1898), 1–35, LXVIII (1898), 1–54, P. Fournier, 'La propriété des églises dans les premiers siècles du moyen-âge', *Nouvelle revue hist. de droit* XXI (1897), 486–506.— But in all these works attention is concentrated on the earlier Middle Ages: the situation during the period with which we are dealing, and the effects of the *Eigenkirchenwesen* on the system of provisions and on the efficacy of provisions, still remain very obscure. This is partly because Stutz', rather than Schulte's, views have attracted the widest attention; yet in the later Middle Ages, face to face with the Romanistic conceptions maintained by the papacy, the influences emphasized by Schulte remained more powerful than the *Eigenkirchenrecht*, which had been radically challenged by the popes from the days of Gregory VII onwards.

[2]Cf. for the moment, Fierens, p. 838 sq., in comparison with Sauerland's remarks (IV, xlviii) on the relative poverty of German benefices.

curata? How far, moreover, are cures of souls affected by the intervention of the papacy? Before these and other parallel questions can be answered a long series of detailed, independent studies of individual churches and smaller ecclesiastical districts in England, France and those ancient dioceses which fall within the modern boundaries of Belgium and the Netherlands will be necessary, and if a balanced judgement is eventually to be obtained, these also will need supplementing by parallel studies of the ecclesiastical situation in those southern lands where Germanic influence never made itself felt, or was counterbalanced by the survival of much that was Roman or otherwise non-Germanic in origin.

'The mediæval German Church', wrote SCHULTE, at the end of his epoch-making work, 'was more singularly German than has been supposed';[1] in no other land but Germany, in other words, was the aristocracy so strongly privileged and so firmly entrenched within the Church.[2] It remains to be seen how true this conclusion is.[3] Already BÖHMER, in a brilliant essay, has shown that the peculiar constitutional features of mediæval Church government which SCHULTE and STUTZ have laid bare, are to be regarded less as German (*deutsch*) than as Germanic (*germanisch*); that they are as native to the Anglo-Saxon or the Frankish kingdom, for example, as to the lands between the Rhine and the Oder.[4] It is worth suggesting, on the other hand, that their character may be less Germanic or racial than feudal, and that if at the height of the Middle Ages—as perhaps few would doubt—the German Church was more deeply penetrated by these constitutional features than any other, the reason lay precisely in the particular development which feudalism took in Germany, as contrasted for example with

[1] *Der Adel u. d. deutsche Kirche*, 301. [2] *Ibid.*, 92.
[3] For certain important qualifications regarding Germany itself, cf. Werminghoff, *Ständische Probleme*, 58 sqq.
[4] *Theol. Studien u. Kritiken* LXXXVI, 165–280.

France or England. It is difficult to estimate *a priori* how far the English Church, which was certainly under the overpowering influence of the *Eigenkirchenwesen* and other Germanic conceptions at about the time of the Norman conquest, remained under such influence in the thirteenth, fourteenth and even in the fifteenth centuries; and it would be hazardous to offer an opinion now, whether Germanistic conceptions were still strong enough to check and in practice to overpower the Romanistic conceptions of Church government which were inherent in the Canon Law, and perhaps even more strongly marked in the administrative practice of the highly centralized papacy of the fourteenth century. But such broad issues must be faced before any final judgement on the influence of provisions over the Church at large can be attempted. The trenchant, suggestive results achieved in the work already performed on the history, in particular, of single churches and chapters make any other course of future investigations in this sphere of Church history unthinkable. For one district after another old firmly-rooted conceptions and preconceptions have been destroyed: the fundamental question which now remains to be decided is the geographical extension of 'Germanic Christianity'. Future research may prove that its limits were hardly less wide than the limits of mediæval western Christendom: on the other hand, they may show that the Church in many parts of Europe was, by the thirteenth and fourteenth centuries at any rate, comparatively free from local influence and Germanic forms, and under the sway of the centralized papacy. Only after long years of detailed work will a final decision of this question be possible.

CHAPTER IV

EVEN TO-DAY, it is not without interest to survey shortly the indications which recent research into the detail of local Church history has necessarily forced into consideration, if only to provide a working contrast with those conceptions of Church history in the later Middle Ages which have so long held sway. The main fact has already been stressed by BÖHMER in his brilliant essay, *Das germanische Christentum*. 'Most of the much censured abuses in the conferment of ecclesiastical benefices,' he writes,[1] 'which Luther, for example, considered without any qualification whatsoever as the invention of Roman greed—pluralism, incorporation or appropriation, and all the remarkable legal usages springing therefrom—are logical consequences of the novel, material conception of the spiritual office which sprang up on Germanic soil, and as such can be proved to have been in existence in the early Middle Ages.' Pluralism is seen to result from the cessation of new benefactions to the older foundations, together with the decline in the value of the individual benefice and the consequently increasing claims of the occupants of benefices to an income which would enable them to live according to their rank—claims which could only be satisfied by the accumulation of a number of benefices in the hands of one person.[2] Examples of pluralism which are no less striking than those SAUERLAND has collected for the fourteenth century,[3] meet us already in the middle of the twelfth century;[4] and at Augsburg the first complaint of non-residence—the immediate consequence

[1]P. 257.
[2]Werminghoff, *Ständische Probleme*, 48; cf. Schulte, 287.
[3]*Supra*, p. 30 n. 7.
[4]Werminghoff, *op. cit.*, 48 n. 6.

of pluralism—was raised by Gerhoh of Reichersperg in 1120.[1]

The origin of the system of vicarages, as SCHÄFER has shown in criticism of SAUERLAND, is to be traced to the same causes. As far as the fourteenth century is concenred, it is easy to blame the papacy for the grant of dispensations which made the institution of vicars a necessity; but 'in order to understand this undeniable evil, the less obvious causes of the system and the older ecclesiastical arrangements for regulating the same must be taken into account. That the official occupant of a cure of souls handed over his duties to a vicar is attested—quite apart from the abuses of the germanic *Eigenkirchenwesen*—long before the fourteenth century, in England and in the Frankish kingdom. Numerous examples can be produced from the twelfth century, and in the thirteenth century the substitution of a vicar for the actual holder of the benefice appears in many parts as an ancient custom'.[2] If we turn to the fourteenth century we find that, although in the period 1294-1352 about 100 parishes in the Rhinelands were (mostly for a short period of one or two years) in the hands of clerks without priest's orders or of non-resident priests, less than twenty of these were conferred by the curia. 'The larger proportion was in the hands of young clerks of noble family, whose fathers or relatives had the right of patronage,[3] or in the possession of canons, whose canonries were frequently united with a parish church.'[4]

The incorporation or appropriation of parish churches by collegiate bodies, secular and regular, was, however, in itself perhaps the most weighty and, as far as the later centuries of the Middle Ages were concerned, the most lasting consequence of the

---

[1]Leuze, p. 6 n. 1.
[2]Schäfer, *Z. Kritik mittelalt. kirchl. Zustände*, 131–132.
[3]Cf. similarly Schulte, p. 284.
[4]Schäfer, p. 130.

germanic *Eigenkirchenwesen*.[1] By the beginning of the fourteenth century the process of unification was everywhere practically complete. 'The good old days in which every parish had its parish-priest were long ago past . . . the majority of independent town parsons (*rectores ecclesiae*) had already made way for the *perpetui vicarii* set up by the chapters.'[2] The results of this change can be well illustrated by the facts expounded by one Thomas Seccheton in a case brought by him against the Premonstratensian abbey of Cockersand in the court of Rome in the years 1369–1370.[3] The parish of Mitton in Lancashire (the object of the litigation), he writes, is large: it contains nine *villae*, is ten miles long and six miles broad, so that 'per unum presbiterum absque alio adiutorio commode et honeste gubernari non potest'. Thus the late rector, William of Tatham (like his predecessors), had employed 'duos vel tres commensales presbiteros et alios quatuor vel quinque familiares clericos et laycos in dicta ecclesia deservientes in subsidium suum et ad supportandum curam animarum parrochianorum dicte parrochialis ecclesie et ad serviendum dicte ecclesie et eius parrochianis laudabiliter in divinis', and it is claimed that 'temporibus rectorum huiusmodi dicte ecclesie et eius parrochianis in divinis officiis et aliis ad curam huiusmodi pertinentibus fuit et erat laudabiliter deservitum'. On William's death, however, the monks of Cockersand claimed to have legitimately appropriated the church; but they were opposed by Thomas, who contended that their appropriation was illegal, and that in the eyes of the law they had merely detained

---

[1] 'Zweite Tochter des Eigenkirchenrechtes und . . . jüngere Schwester des Patronates'—such is Stutz' description of incorporation; *Gratian u. d. Eigenkirchen*, 12.

[2] Kothe, p. 33.

[3] *Arch. Vat. Collect.* 417 A.—The Rev. J. McNulty has kindly consented to transcribe and edit the documents for publication in the Journal of the Yorkshire Archæological Society, and extracts from them are included also in a volume which I hope shortly to publish under the title: *Anecdota et diplomata, quae praesertim in beneficialibus processum ecclesiasticum spectant*.

the church (as they were still detaining it) 'indebite occupatam'. Various legal arguments were put forward by him, both in support of his own claim and as a rejoinder to that of the abbey; and one of these is of particular interest here. From the time of the appropriation onwards, Thomas declared,

solum et dumtaxat fuit ibi unus presbiter deputatus, qui curam animarum parrochianorum dicte ecclesie exerceret, et quod solum unus presbiter a temporibus predictis absque alio adiutorio huiusmodi curam, licet minus sufficienter et indebite, exercuit et exercet, et quod propter insufficientiam et paucitatem ministrorum ecclesie . . . plures infantes absque baptismo et plures mulieres in puerperio cubantes et plures alii infirmi parrochiani dicte parrochialis ecclesie absque viatico et sacramentis ecclesiasticis consuetis talibus ministrari (licet ea ipsi et eorum parentes instantissime peterent et postularent eis dari) obierunt; quod vix in diebus dominicis et festivis, nisi quando oblaciones fieri debent, misse et alia divina officia a dictis temporibus et citra dicta fuerunt aut erant celebrata . . . ac quod propterea grave scandalum est subortum. Et sic se habet communis opinio, reputatio, credulitas communis et vulgaris assertio, communeque ac verum, publicum et notorium fuit et est palam publice et notorie.[1]

In these words we see Thomas Seccheton attributing to the baneful influence of the English *Eigenkirchen-wesen* many of those disastrous moral and social aspects of Church government in the later Middle Ages, responsibility for which, almost without break from the sixteenth century onwards, has been laid to the charge of papal provisions. What he did not attribute to the *Eigenkirchenwesen* we can with good reason attribute to the dominance which the feudal aristocracy was able to exercise over the Church in the

---

[1] *Cod. cit.*, ff. 51'–52.—Evidence such as this makes it difficult to agree with K. L. Wood-Legh (*The Appropriation of Parish Churches*, 22) 'that, in many cases, the evils resulting from appropriations may have been less apparent to contemporaries than they are to us'. Cf. Kallen, p. 271, and in general Hartridge, *History of Vicarages*, where the appropriation of Mitton is mentioned (p. 171) on authority of papal letters of 1396.

maintenance of its own interests. That these interests were rarely the interests of the Church is a fact which hardly calls for proof.[1] In sum, they amounted to little more than the interest of a dominant class in the accumulation of property; and it was, as Böhmer has shown, the influence exerted from the very earliest times by the essentially material interests of the aristocratic classes which rapidly made it normal to regard the religious vocation from the standpoint not of *officium*, but of *beneficium*.[2] This point of view was hardly less habitual in the eleventh and twelfth centuries—at any rate within the ranks of the secular clergy—than in the fourteenth and fifteenth. At Augsburg, for instance, a century before papal provisions had begun to take effect, the cathedral chapter contained more subdeacons than deacons, more deacons than priests: already in the twelfth century canons without priest's orders were in a definite majority.[3] No other result was possible at a time when religious houses, secular and regular, were regarded mainly as institutions for supporting the younger sons and daughters of noble families, without any regard to their vocational qualifications, and when such clerics were determined to leave the way open for a return to secular life and marriage, if family policy and family profit turned on the establishment of a marriage connexion.[4]

For the maintenance of aristocratic and family influence in the chapters, however, no question was

---

[1]Cf. however, from a somewhat different angle, the contemporary criticism of the parvenu Bishop Lamprecht of Strassburg (1371–1374): 'weil er kein Graf oder Freiherr war, so war er gehasst von allen Edlen, so dass er wehrlos war und sein Land nicht beschirmen konnte' (Kothe, p. 23), and the exactly parallel remarks of Aeneas Sylvius, quoted by Werminghoff, *Ständ. Probleme*, 63 n. 2.

[2]*Das germ. Christentum*, 256.

[3]Leuze, p. 7.

[4]Cf. Schulte, *Der Adel u. d. deutsche Kirche*, 282; Werminghoff, *Ständ. Probleme*, 48; Böhmer, *D. germ. Christentum*, 253–255. For details of the large number of modern princely families descended from renegade clerks, cf. Schulte, pp. 264–273, 295–296, Böhmer, 254 n. 1, Werminghoff, 50.

more important than the control of admission. Thus we find that during the thirteenth century, if not before, not only was the bishop forced step by step to surrender his rights in regard to the creation of canons— a constitutional issue of some magnitude which seems to have been fought out in all countries of Europe[1]— but also the old system of canonical election was supplanted in most collegiate churches by a procedure of simple nomination, in accordance with which each canon in turn was able to name a new member of the chapter. 'The results of such a procedure are self-evident. A family which had once obtained a firm foothold in the chapter was able to maintain its position for centuries, since the canons naturally gave first consideration to the claims of their relatives in the nomination of new members.'[2] Thus there grew up a practice of family connexions and nepotism (*Vetternwirtschaft*), the extension and ramifications of which only become obvious when the detailed history of individual chapters is subjected to independent treatment. Next to family, however, rank was the chief consideration with the electors. The rapid decline in the number and size of aristocratic families in the later Middle Ages,[3] combined with the ever more stringent regulation and ever increasing exclusiveness of the qualifications demanded from candidates for places in collegiate churches, sooner or later made it impossible for the aristocratic families resident within a diocese to provide enough members to fill the local chapters. In these circumstances, rather than allow families of inferior standing to fill the vacant places, the canons

[1]Cf. Kothe, pp. 14–20; Gnann, p. 60; Rieder, p. lxxxix; Kisky, *Domkapitel*, 14; Bradshaw I, 316–317; Amiet, pp. 21–27; and in general Schneider, *Die bischöfl. Domkapitel*, Hergenröther-Kirsch, *Kirchengeschichte* II, 643 and Sägmüller, *Kirchenrecht*, §§. 74, 96.—The efforts of the chapters were not, of course, uniformly successful: in England, for example, the bishop seems normally to have managed to maintain his rights. An independent treatment of the problem, on a broad European basis, would be of great value.

[2]Kisky, *Die Domkapitel d. geistl. Kurfürsten*, 14; Kothe, *Kirchl. Zustände*, 11.

[3]Schulte, caps. XXI and XXII.

recruited their ranks from distant dioceses.[1] The 352 canons of Cologne during the fourteenth and fifteenth centuries sprang from in all thirty dioceses; not a third belonged to the diocese, only about two-fifths to the province of Cologne; the rest were recruited from such distant parts as Utrecht, Bremen, Ratzeburg, Meissen, Freising, Constance, Geneva and Arras.[2]

Thus whatever we think of the papal policy of transferring clerks from one diocese to another by means of provisions—a policy the effects of which have certainly been exaggerated[3]—it is clear that the popes were doing little that the canons themselves had not done, or were not at any moment prepared to do. From time to time, and in some countries more than others, there may have been real objection to providees on account of their nationality; but it is obvious that local considerations did not weigh heavily on the nominators to canonries; they showed no desire to confine membership of the chapter to those with a knowledge of and an interest in local affairs, and where they raised objections to papal providees questions of class were more likely to be at issue, except in times of high political tension, than the question of nationality.[4] Thus, even if provisions were often used to further family interests and connexions,[5] it is generally admitted that papal intervention, in counteracting the growing spirit of exclusiveness and

---

[1]Schulte, p. 53; Kisky, p. 23; Werminghoff, pp. 49–52.

[2]Werminghoff, p. 51; Kisky, p. 23. For similar figures regarding Mainz, cf. Werminghoff, p. 52.

[3]Cf. *supra*, pp. 39–45.—In this connexion, some interest attaches to a case (Rieder, no. 350) from the year 1363, in which Johann Molhart, a priest of the diocese of *Constance*, supplicated for a canonry 'sub expectatione prebende' in the cathedral of *Augsburg*: the pope, however, replied: *habeat . . . in ecclesia Constantiensi*. The object of the alteration was evidently to keep the providee in his own diocese, and it would be interesting to know if such modifications in the terms of a petition were of common occurrence.

[4]It might, on the other hand, be objected that the real evil of the promotion of foreigners was not their provision to canonries, but to parishes and other *beneficia curata*; on this point, in addition to *supra*, pp. 44–45, cf. *infra*, pp. 117–118.

[5]*Supra*, pp. 40 sqq.

nepotism and introducing new elements into the chapters, exercised a salutary influence in cathedral and collegiate churches.[1] Even the Italians and other foreigners appointed by the papacy, for the very reason that they usually won admittance only because they were able to lay claim to a higher class of education and university training than that possessed by the scions of noble families who formed the majority in most chapters,[2] cannot be condemned as an unjustifiable burden. 'Anyone who works through the list of providees will not be disposed to deny the fact that altogether outstanding people appear among them. Candidates who have not reached the statutory age or are marked out by illegitimate birth, are unable to obtain admission, even when persons of high rank lend them their support. From the time of Benedict XII onwards it can be shown that the majority of providees had studied at the famous universities of Bologna, Padua, Paris or Prague, and had distinguished themselves in their studies. Others again were in the service of cardinals, bishops or temporal magnates, or had been appointed as collectors by the papal Treasury or as ambassadors by secular princes. Considered as a whole, it was certainly not indifferent material which was brought into the cathedral chapter at Constance in virtue of papal provisions.'[3]

Such a judgement as this cuts right across the old-fashioned estimate of provisions as an instrument of papal greed and unscrupulous materialism, used above all in the interests of bastards, minors, courtiers, foreigners and unqualified, uneducated upstarts. It cuts across the theory that they were used above all to the detriment of poor but worthy clerks, who had acquired a suitable education but not the necessary

[1]Cf. Kothe, p. 30; Schulte, p. 66; Werminghoff, p. 61.—Thus, in regard to Strassburg cathedral, Erasmus remarked that 'Christ himself could not have been admitted into this college without dispensation'. (Schulte, p. 248)
[2]Kothe, p. 30; cf. also Schulte, pp. 43, 121.
[3]Rieder, p. lxxxii.

influence for a benefice, and were exercised by constant and shameless pressure at the expense of the episcopal right of collation;[1] for talent and personal merit were more sure of recognition in the *curia Romana* than in the provinces, and the episcopal right of collation was destroyed, not by the papacy, but by the growing pretensions of the chapters of collegiate churches[2] and of lay patrons[3] during the thirteenth and fourteenth centuries. On the other hand, the criticism directed against provisions by Pierre Leroy in the French synod of 1406: 'Aucune fois une personne seroit bonne et convenable en un lieu qui ne seroit pas opportune en un autre lieu: comment porra le pape connoistre les personnes, les habitudes des églises et la manière comment il y faut vivre'?[4]—a criticism at which perhaps no one a generation ago would have carped—takes on a sinister meaning when we consider that 'les habitudes des églises' were formidable customs of class-exclusiveness, the 'manière comment il y faut vivre' conformity with aristocratic standards, and the question of personal suitability rarely more than a question of birth and rank. In sum, we can with BÖHMER[5] reasonably maintain that if we approach the Church history of the fourteenth and fifteenth cen-

---

[1]Cf. Bishop William Lemaire of Angers' criticism in 1311: 'prelati hodie non possunt bonis personis de beneficiis nec beneficiis de bonis personis, obstante numerosa multitudine talium impetrancium, providere' (Haller, p. 56 n. 2; similarly Duranti, *op. cit.*, 62 n. 3); but cf. *op. cit.*, 140 n. 2, and the very different-sounding complaint of bishop Grandison of Exeter (1327–1369): 'per multos annos non potui familiaribus meis aut nepotibus providere' (Bannister, p. 182 n. 2).

[2]Cf. *supra*, p. 55 n. 1.—In view of the statement quoted *supra*, p. 24, an investigation of the relative rights of bishop and chapter in the nomination of canons at Angers would be of interest. That provisions actually were used by bishops to enable them to break through the 'förmliche Ringbildung des Domkapitels, welche sich einerseits gegen das päpstliche Reservationsrecht richtete und auf der anderen Seite jede Einwirkung des Bischofs auf die Besetzung der Stellen ausschloss', has been demonstrated e.g. by Rieder, p. lxxxix.

[3]Cf. Kothe, pp. 83 sqq., 117; Schulte, p. 292.—That the declining influence of the bishops was due to financial weakness, to be ascribed to economic causes, is of course well known; cf. Kothe, p. 18.

[4]Bourgeois du Chastenet, p. 170.

[5]*Loc. cit.*, *supra*, p. 50 n. 1.

turies in a direct line from the tenth, eleventh, and twelfth centuries, instead of considering it as an isolated period—with perhaps an occasional glance at the preliminary development in the thirteenth century of the theory and practice of papal supremacy—the abuses which have ordinarily been ascribed to the centralized administrative practices, and above all to the centralized administration of Church benefices through the papacy, appear as the result of developments which were already inveterate long before the days of the Babylonish exile at Avignon.

Thus, in the most balanced survey of the fourteenth-century history of provisions which the last decade produced—in spite of the fact that the subject is there still considered in isolation from the general course of mediæval Church history—the question of the responsibility of the Avignonese popes through their system of provisions and reservations for the decline of the Church receives an answer which would have been unthinkable even a generation ago. According to FIERENS their responsibility consisted not in misplaced or unprincipled activity, but in inactivity or mere opportunism. 'As far as the popes themselves are concerned', he writes, 'they were distinguished, from Clement V to Urban V, by a deficiency in ability to offer resistance: they went with the stream, instead of rowing against it. Above all they were lacking in strength of judgement and clearness of vision.'[1]

With this opinion few in general would quarrel. But in so far as its place and policy brought the papacy

[1]*Ons Prebendenwezen*, 847–848; cf. further p. 846: 'Verondersteld dat die ontwikkelingsgang juist zij, welke is dan de verantwoordelijkheid van de pausen van Avignon? Op het oogenblik dat Clemens V den stoel van Petrus bestijgt, was het apostolisch begivingsrecht . . . reeds op vaste juridische grondslagen gegrondvest . . . de verschillende begivingsvormen hadden reeds hun gestereotypeerde uitdrukking gevonden en ter pauselijke kanselarij had het raderwerk, dat voor de uitvaardiging der apostolische mandaten vereischt werd, zich reeds nagenoeg volledig ontwikkeld. Plicht ware het geweest voor Clemens V en zijn opvolgers, voorzeker, van het verderfelijke stelsel, dat voor hen en buiten hun toedoen geboren was, niet te laten voor-twoekeren. . . .'

into opposition with the aristocratic element in the Church—and the existence of such an opposition in idea as well as in practice cannot be denied[1]—it would be a mistake to judge the failure of the papacy too harshly. Such constitutions as John XXII's *Execrabilis* mark a definite attempt to hold the evil for which the germanic *Eigenkirchenwesen* was responsible, in check; but they were defeated by the blind factious opposition of the noble classes.[2] The strength of the aristocratic influence in the Church must therefore not be underestimated. At Augsburg, at the middle of the fourteenth century, the chapter devoted earnest discussion to the attitude to be adopted in face of the harassing demands of noble families for benefices,[3] and at Constance a series of statutes from 1326 onwards was directed against the importunity of the same classes.[4] Similar also was the position in the central Rhinelands. 'No complaint by a Rhenish chapter concerning papal provisions is known to me', writes SCHÄFER: 'well known, on the other hand, are their complaints of constraint and coercion on the part of powerful magnates regarding admission to places in the chapter.'[5] These complaints are striking, when we consider that such chapters—for whom the importunity of the nobility was a perpetual embarrassment—had little or no difficulty, as for example at Gnesen, in defeating royal pretensions to fill vacant places:[6] at Cologne, Mainz and Trier, as KISKY has shown, they were even able to force the crown to give up the attempt to enforce its well-established *ius primariarum precum*.[7]

---

[1]Cf. Werminghoff, *Ständische Probleme*, 58 sqq.
[2]Schulte, p. 285.   [3]Leuze, p. 34 (n. 2).   [4]Rieder, p. lxxxviii sq.
[5]*Zur Kritik mittelalt. kirchl. Zustände*, 140, quoting Joerres, *Urkundenbuch von S. Gereon*, 265 (a .1305): 'Ex preteritorum experientia temporum frequenter persensimus, quod vacantibus quantuliscunque modicis beneficiis, nos tam per nobilium et potentium quam maiorum armatas preces et instantias importunas . . . offensas potius et odia incurrimus, adeo etiam ut sepe coacti simus providere indignis'.   [6]Binder, p. 20.
[7]*Die Domkapitel d. geistl. Kurfürsten*, 16 sqq.

These facts help us to understand how powerful were the influences which any attempt on the part of the papacy to root out or even to check such evils as pluralism or non-residence, was bound to drive into opposition. If we give them due consideration, we shall be inclined to wonder, not that the popes were never able wholly to defeat the forces in opposition, but that they did consistently maintain an influence which provided the only effective check on the dominance of strictly material class interests within the Church. In this connexion, it is essential also to bear in mind that, from the middle of the thirteenth century onwards, the papacy looked not to the secular clergy but to the Mendicants as a bulwark of the Church and a mainstay of papal influence.[1] With a clear realization that they could not hope to infuse into the seculars an effective spirit of religious animation,[2] the popes concentrated their efforts less upon the reform of this branch of the hierarchy than upon setting in their place, as the vitally active agents of the *ecclesia Romana*, the Franciscans and Dominicans and other preaching orders. It may not have been for the ultimate good of the Church that the secular clergy was thus reduced to a position of secondary importance; but it is beyond denial that wholehearted support of the friars offered the most immediate promise of success, and this feature of papal policy proved in actual fact to be comparatively successful. At the same time it must be admitted that the papacy did not at all times maintain that opposition to the secularization of the secular clergy and to the dominance of aristocratic lay interests within its ranks, which we have every right to expect from it. WERMINGHOFF has pointed out with acumen that the Renaissance popes of the

---

[1] Cf, among many others, Hergenröther-Kirsch II, 647 sqq., III, 80 sqq.; Dufourcq, pp. 668–674; Kothe, pp. 90–100; Paulus, *Welt- und Ordensklerus beim Ausgange d. 13. Jhs. im Kampfe um d. Pfarr-rechte;* Gratien, *Histoire de la Fondation et de l'Évolution de l'Ordre des Frères Mineurs,* Append. 2.

[2] Cf. Gibbs and Lang, *Bishops and Reform,* p. III, particularly the conclusion.

fifteenth century must, by reason of their very character, have felt considerable sympathy with the preponderating aristocratic influence both in Church and in State.[1] The same is without doubt true of popes such as Clement V and Clement VI, and there can be no doubt that many pontificates in the fourteenth and fifteenth centuries saw a tacit understanding between the aristocracy and the papacy, which was certainly not to the credit of the latter. In this way the aristocratic element within and without the Church secured papal sanction, in some connexions tacitly, in others through explicit privileges and concessions, for the exercise of a *de facto* control of the provincial Churches, which provided the political foundation for the Erastian Church organization of the Reformation period.[2]

The limits of our subject do not allow more than mention of the important question of the late fourteenth and fifteenth century *Summepiskopat* and *Landeskirchentum*.[3] But it is impossible to pass the question by without remarking that, to those who view the history of the mediæval Church as a whole, it must appear far less as a phenomenon of the fifteenth

[1] *Ständ. Probleme*, 63–64:'. . . Auf der anderen Seite wird hervorzuheben sein, dass gerade das Papsttum der Renaissance sich hingezogen fühlen musste zu jener Aristokratie, die im Territorium und Bistum das Übergewicht behauptete. Es sind keine Gegensätze, wenn jenes Papsttum durch seine Privilegien das landesherrliche Kirchenregiment förderte und kräftigte, wenn es gerade um die Wende des 15 und 16 Jahrhunderts in ausführlichen Bullen die gemischtadlige und freiständische Zusammensetzung einer Reihe von Domkapiteln anerkannte'.

[2] Cf. among writers previously cited, Finke, pp. 5 sqq.; Werminghoff, *op. cit.*, 61 sq.

[3] The very considerable and somewhat scattered literature is ably dealt with by Hashagen, *Staat u. Kirche vor d. Reformation*; nevertheless cf. the severe criticism e.g. of Finke, *Hist. Jahrbuch* LI, 218–229, which is certainly justified as regards inaccuracy in detail. Used with care, however, the work still remains an indispensable guide. For more serious criticism—which in any case affects not only Hashagen, but historians of established reputation, such as Werminghoff—cf. *infra* in text.—See also Wunderlich, *Die Beurteilungen d. Vorreformation*; Haller, *Die Ursachen d. Reformation;* v. Below, *Die Ursachen d. Reformation;* Werminghoff, *Nationalkirchl. Bestrebungen*, and *Neuere Arbeiten über d. Verhältnis von Staat u. Kirche*. For the extensive local literature, cf. Hergenröther-Kirsch III, 293 sqq., and Sägmüller I, 67 sqq.

century than as the logical conclusion of the age-long efforts of the privileged classes to dominate the Church in their own interests.[1] The creation of national Churches was the logical means of defeating, if not the aristocratic papacy of the fifteenth century, at any rate the conception of Christendom for which the papacy stood.[2] It is difficult to think that this motive—even if it rarely became conscious—was not infinitely more powerful than the wish for national autonomy as a means of reform. Yet modern historians have practically unanimously regarded the *Landeskirchentum* more than anything else as a feature of, or parallel tendency to, the movement of reform.[3] The idea that it was the preponderating aristocratic influence and above all the conversion of the Church and its property to the uses of the landed nobility that in the final analysis necessitated reform, remains curiously unfashionable.[4] HASHAGEN devotes a whole section to the lay influence in the Church as an effective remedy for ecclesiastical disorders;[5] but a parallel chapter on the disorders as the result of lay influence is totally lacking.[6] Yet

[1]That it became a factor of first-rate importance at this time was, of course, the direct result of the weakness of the papacy after the Schism and the French subtraction of obedience, which led the popes to attempt to regain their old position by means of concessions and compromises; cf. Sägmüller I, 66. See, moreover, Hergenröther-Kirsch III, 303.

[2]Werminghoff, *Ständ. Probleme*, 61–62: 'der Freienadel stand in engster verwandschaftlicher Wechselwirkung zu dem aufstrebenden laikalen Fürstentum der zahlreichen Territorien, der hohe und der niedere Adel waren ihm durch Teilnahme an der landständischen Organisation verbunden und kaum grundsätzlich geneigt, die Ansätze territorialer Landeskirchen zu verhindern, da sie in Einvernehmen mit den Landesherren grössere Sicherheit für ihr Bestehen erwarten durften als in der Unterwerfung unter jene plenitudo potestatis des Papsttums, die jegliche Selbständigkeit und in ihr jegliche Besonderheit schmälerte oder gar aufhob'.

[3]Werminghoff, *op. cit.*, 62: ' . . . Jedenfalls werden in den Ansätzen von Landeskirchen, in den Rufen nach Reform während des Schismas und im Zeitalter der grossen Konzilien zwei einander parallele Richtungen erblickt werden dürfen;' cf. also *Neuere Arbeiten*, 157, 171.

[4]Cf. however, Dittrich, *Beiträge*, 326–7, where this standpoint is ably suggested.

[5]Cap. III ('Der Laieneinfluss in der Kirche als tatsächliche Gegenwirkung gegen kirchliche Missstände').

[6]Cf. notably pp. 308 sqq., where he limits himself to the remark: ' . . . vielmehr kann es diesen erst hervorgerufen haben'.

such is essentially the conclusion indicated by the monographs which the historical schools of STUTZ and SCHULTE have produced in abundance.

No historian will deny that a multitude of causes contributed to produce the decline and corruption of the Church at the end of the Middle Ages. But among these none were more inveterately and consistently powerful than the selfish influence and the material interests of the landed classes. It cannot be denied that at many periods the papacy gave way too readily before the deep-seated, long-established power of the aristocracy: it lacked the resolution and courage to deal with the evil radically, it temporized and compromised. But who can say that, given the utmost determination and steadfastness, it could have eradicated from the western Church evils which had been inherent in the Church and had grown with the Church without break or permanent check since the conversion of the Germanic barbarians? The popes were only men: we must guard against expecting them to act as super-men. The better the history of the fourteenth-century Church is known, the clearer it becomes that throughout that century determined efforts at reform followed one another at close intervals: that the popes alone or even principally were responsible for the failure of these efforts is still not proven, and is rapidly becoming less probable. Nor should we argue *ex post facto* from the Reformation itself; for no one who knows the history, for example, of the English Church from the sixteenth to the nineteenth century, will deny that the real reformers of the Church were, not Henry VIII or Elizabeth, but the Ecclesiastical Commissioners appointed by Peel in 1835.[1] It is for the very reason that aristocratic interests continued to dominate the Lutheran churches as they

[1] I have to thank Prof. E. W. Watson for much valuable information in this connexion.—Cf. as regards other Protestant countries, Böhmer, *Das germ. Christentum*, 259, and in general Sägmüller, *Kirchenrecht* I, 68 (with abundant literature).

had dominated the pre-Reformation church,[1] that, as an instrument of real internal betterment, the Reformation was itself less effective than the Counter-Reformation.[2] From a political point of view, the break with Rome may have been necessary and inevitable: from a cultural and intellectual point of view, it is possible that the setting up of two opposed camps was a salutary and progressive step.[3] But it is a vicious argument that the needs of reform demanded the substitution of local, Erastian Churches for the one united, universal Church. The historian who gives due attention to the question of the lay influence in the mediæval Church cannot logically conclude that the remedy for the abuses thereby engendered was an increasing control of the Church by the laity. As BÖHMER has said,[4] the Germanic nations lost nothing by their christianization; but the Church lost heavily and lost irretrievably by its pervasion with material Germanic conceptions and secular Germanic interests.

[1] I use the word 'aristocratic' (or class) advisedly, leaving aside the question of State as apart from class control. That both influences were in contradiction with the nature of Protestantism is a matter of general agreement; see e.g. Drews, *Entsprach das Staatskirchentum der Ideale Luthers?* For further literature, cf. Sägmüller, *loc. cit.*

[2] So much can be said without fear of contradiction; that parallel tendencies —Gallicanism, Jansenism, Febronianism, Josephinism—were at work in the Catholic Church after the Reformation, is, of course, not to be denied. As far as real internal reform is concerned, the essential difference is perhaps that, whereas Catholicism knew how to use the reformatory spirits, the Protestant combatants for an internal renaissance were for the most part driven into sectarianism, persecuted, and long prevented from exercising either a wide or a lasting influence.

[3] I.e. in relieving thought (as the phrase runs) of its mediæval bondage.

[4] *Op. cit.*, 275.

CHAPTER V

As WE HAVE followed the course of investigations into the real significance of papal provisions in the mediæval Church, we have been led farther and farther away from the isolated investigation of provisions themselves. This very fact is in itself significant. It indicates a growing realization that a subject of such weight for the whole history of the Church cannot be studied apart from the general course of Church history; it indicates the failure of the older conception of historiography—of the system in which different aspects of a large subject were left to specialists and their separate investigations co-ordinated in a masterly synthesis by a master hand. If there is one thing which the historiography of papal provisions teaches, it is that no attempt to deal with them as an independent historical problem can be successful. As the centre of interest has moved from the chroniclers to the papal archives and from the papal archives to the local churches, each new stage in the scheme of investigations has driven home the same conclusion. On the one side, the history of papal provisions cannot be isolated from the history of papal administration and of Church reform: on the other, it must be considered as a factor in the local history of single churches and dioceses. As things were—a living synthesis of forces, ideas and interests —so they must be studied.

In this sense, the results of the historical work of the last generations are negative. Far from achieving a final judgement on the effects of provisions on the Church, the objective value of one class of material after another has been subjected to searching criticism, the illusion of finality and objectivity has been time and again exploded, and it has been established that the historical problem, far from approaching its final solution, has only in the present generation become manifest in all its complexity and with all its ramifications. From another point of view, this is a positive achievement: it can reasonably be maintained that the successive waves of destructive criticism have ultimately cleared the way for an approach to the historical problem which, from a methodological point of view, is beyond criticism. But it is a method of approach which offers no easy or rapid solution of the problem. It is the method of building on the solid foundations of local history, of approaching the central organization by slow stages from the outermost parts. From a practical point of view, it means that historians must turn, not to the accessible collected material in the Vatican, considered *per se* as a self-sufficient unity, but to the scattered inaccessible material in single towns, dioceses and provinces, of which nevertheless the respective Vatican material is an important but a subordinate part. When we have the results of investigations conducted according to this scheme, there is every reason to suppose that they will be final; but in adopting this method of procedure it is necessary to postpone indefinitely the hope of reaching final conclusions. In this regard, the position is the same as in regard to the investigations of the political origins of the Reformation, which received short mention above:[1] as long as the monographs dealing with single regions are incomplete and isolated, all attempts to build up a synthesis from them are bound to be of provisional character.[2] Before the history of provisions and particularly the question of their influence on the general history of the Church can be treated for themselves, careful scientific investigations of the position of the clergy in all representative dioceses and chapters of England, France, Germany,

[1]pp. 62 sq.
[2]Hashagen, *op. cit.*, 1; G. Wolf, *Quellenkunde d. deutschen Reformationsgesch.* I (1915), 290.

Italy, Spain, Belgium, the Netherlands, the Slavonic lands and the northern countries during the thirteenth, fourteenth and fifteenth centuries must be available—investigations in which the methods followed by such pioneers as RIEDER, KISKY, KOTHE, and SCHULTE are put to critical use. In this regard again, the present position of investigations is negative: the work is only at the beginning, and outside of Germany few historians realize which are the important problems, what approach to the evidence is desirable.[1] The bulk of the laborious pioneer work remains to be done; but the way is pointed out, the method of approach demonstrated, and an incentive to rapid, willing work has already been provided by the invigoratingly fresh, original and even iconoclastic results which the few previous workers in the field have achieved.

These results in themselves are again negative, but negative in a higher sense of the word. They deny, in other words, or at any rate query the older theory of the principal responsibility of the papacy and the central administration for the decline of the Church in the fourteenth and fifteenth centuries. There is no need to recapitulate the results themselves, or the arguments on which they are based. But it is essential to repeat that they are only tentative, and that none of the writers concerned has attempted to extend their bearing beyond the geographical limits to which his work was confined. This is the task of future historians: the results of their work, in all parts of Europe, will alone enable us to gauge their radius of application and the degree to which they can be applied in different parts of Christendom. Moreover, there is no question of the ousting of an old theory and the substitution of an-

---

[1] Cf. for example, the otherwise valuable work of Bannister, *The Cathedral Church of Hereford*.—Since this section was written, interesting observations on the personnel of the higher ranks of the clergy in England during the thirteenth century have appeared in Gibbs and Lang, *Bishops and Reform*; but more detailed work than this is necessary, and I hope in the near future to be able to investigate the effects of papal provisions on the composition and personnel of certain English cathedral chapters.

other: the failure of the papacy to perform its duty or at least to make its reformatory measures effective is not denied. The decline of the Church may have been mainly due to factors which already in the earlier centuries of the Middle Ages had obtained an ineradicable influence over the Church's destinies; but it was precisely the function of the papacy to counteract and to provide remedies against such interests, and few would deny that the popes rarely performed this task vigorously or resolutely and at some periods approached it very half-heartedly. The question of responsibility is therefore a relative question: what is to be decided is whether the immediate and obvious cause of decline, namely lax and to some degree admittedly corrupt administration at the centre was actually of such effect that it must be accounted the principle cause of disorders in the Church constitution and ecclesiastical government throughout Europe,[1] or whether these disorders are more truthfully to be ascribed to long-standing abuses in the provincial Churches, which were powerful enough to withstand the efforts of reformers from the centre, which outlived such days of vigorous reform as the Hildebrandine epoch, forced weaker popes than Gregory to capitulate and eventually reduced the universal Church to a state of materialism, decline and ill-repute.

Few would be so hasty, in the present state of knowledge, as to attempt to apportion blame between the immediate and the long-standing, remoter causes of decline. But it is clear enough that the disorders in the fourteenth- and fifteenth-century Church cannot be ascribed to any single group of causes, and any attempt to-day to settle the whole burden of responsibility on the papacy and its administration of benefices and finance is doomed to failure. On the other hand, we must be careful not to go too far in the opposite direction. There is ample evidence that the papal

[1]Cf. *loc. cit.*, *supra*, p. 29 n. 5.

administration of benefices by means of provisions and reservations was felt in the fourteenth, and indeed from the middle of the thirteenth century, to be a grievous and unjustifiable burden. The objective value of the literary evidence is small; but the evidence itself is very considerable in quantity, and the very uniformity of its tone provides a valuable indication of the prevailing sentiments of the day. Thus, although the last thing we should expect from contemporaries is a capacity to distinguish between immediate and remoter causes, between the important and the trivial, or between the ostentatiously obvious and the indirectly powerful, and in spite of the fact that few chroniclers could forgo the effectiveness of *ex parte* statement for the less immediate satisfaction of balanced judgement, the adverse criticism to which the literary authorities have long been subject, does not render them utterly valueless as evidence. As WER-MINGHOFF has said, 'we should certainly be going too far, were we to see in the complaints of the fifteenth century over curial encroachments into the constitution and administration of the Church in German lands, or even the intrusion of foreign *curiales* into offices and benefices, nothing but an outcry of the German landed classes for the maintenance of their predominance within the Church'.[1] The root causes of pluralism, vicarages, non-residence, unwillingness to accept higher orders, and even of nepotism and favouritism may lie farther back; but the central administration during the fourteenth and fifteenth centuries certainly had its faults, and made its own regrettable contribution to the general decline. From the archives of the central government, among the long series of acts of the curial administration, we should even now be able to discover in what directions it was at fault, in what ways it exercised an unhealthy influence over the Church.

[1] *Ständische Probleme*, 63.

CHAPTER VI

THE FUNDAMENTAL charge which can be made against the curia is undoubtedly the one which perhaps no writer on the subject has omitted to make; namely that, like the landed classes which dominated the provincial churches, it placed infinitely more stress on *beneficium* than on *officium*. In this regard, however, we must guard against exaggerated idealism. The attitude of the curia was certainly more suited to the standards of a society in which rewards were graded according to talents and services than to the precepts of the Testament or even of the Decretum;[1] but, as HALLER has remarked, 'to expect pietism from the curia is to demand the squaring of the circle'.[2] The standard of life according to which an auditor of the Rota has a right to expect a higher salary than a parish priest is still an accepted standard; and if the only charge against the papacy were that it did not break with secular standards and enforce the ideals of the Fraticelli or the Lollards, it could be refuted as easily on grounds of doctrine as of practical common sense.[3]

The serious charge against the curia, however, is that instead of providing for the central officials from the revenues of the central administration, it granted them benefices in distant churches, simply as benefices, with little or no regard for the *officium* with a view to

[1] C. XII, q. i.
[2] *Papstt. u. Kirchenreform*, 89.
[3] Here, it seems to me, Fierens' criticism (pp. 839, 845) is too extreme. Thus he writes: 'De kerkambten welke de beschermelingen van den Heiligen Stoel trachten te bekomen zijn niet die welke de meeste geestelijke en zedelijke toewijding vereischen, niet die welke toelaten op godsdienstig gebied het meeste goed te doen; het zijn die welde stoffelijkerwijze gesproken het meest opbrengen'. 'De gunstelingen van den Heiligen Stoel zoeken steeds de rijkste beneficiën.' But it would be curious were it not so: we cannot in reason demand of every cleric, or even of every priest, an overpowering missionary ardour.

which the *beneficium* had been established.[1] To this charge, in the final analysis, no answer can be made. But the papacy had nevertheless good reasons for resorting to this expedient. In the first place, the proposals made as late as the days of Honorius III (1216–1227) for providing a revenue for the central government had been defeated by the implacable hostility of the provincial churches.[2] In the second place, the Avignonese popes were deprived of, or had at any rate great difficulty in obtaining, the regular revenue supplied by the Italian lands of the papacy; and it is thus understandable, if not excusable, that John XXII used the machinery of provisions as a means of escaping financial shipwreck.[3] That the papacy always acted with circumspection in this regard is, however, not the case; and its failure and neglect to insist on the co-ordination of *beneficium* and *officium* was not only the root cause of most of the other ills which arose from the curial administration, but also the reason that the papacy was never in a position to offer a determined opposition to such abuses as pluralism and non-residence, which—though deriving their strength from the local circumstances of provincial churches—were the consequence of the same materialistic conception of the ecclesiastical office as dominated the curia.

To what degree this state of mind in the curia was due simply to an unwillingness to face the implications of the rule: *beneficium datur propter officium*, to what degree it may have resulted from an inability to withstand the pressure of petitioners, in whose minds the object of the religious profession was benefice and not office, is a more difficult question. But RIEDER has shown that the continual complaints of the popes

[1]'Beneficium datur propter officium', c. 15 in VI° 1, 3.
[2]Barraclough, *Making of a Bishop*, 305–6; Haller, *op. cit.*, 164–5; cf. Pfaff, *Kaiser Heinrichs VI. höchstes Angebot an d. röm. Kurie.*
[3]Fierens, p. 847; Mollat, *Jean XXII*, 531.

over the *execrabilis ambitio, cupido, interpretatio maligna* and *perniciosa subtilitas* of petitioners are not to be regarded as mere rhetoric,[1] and there can be no doubt that extreme pressure was put on the papacy not merely to grant benefices but also to sanction pluralism and non-residence. This pressure explains to some degree the way in which the popes disposed of benefices (in the phrase of contemporary critics) as if they were chattels in a market, and was also, as RIEDER has said, the main factor in forcing forward the development of the provisions-system;[2] but the fact remains that the duty of the papacy was to withstand such pressure, and that in allowing the purely material conception of Church benefices to penetrate into the curia, and to obtain a foothold there as firm as that which it held in the provinces, the popes showed failure to appreciate their duty.[3]

By the fourteenth century the tendency to regard a benefice exclusively as a source of income was characteristic, and was everywhere recognized as characteristic, of the curia. HILLING's investigations of the material in the Rota Archives (which unfortunately take us no farther back than the middle of the fifteenth century) show conclusively that the major part of the litigation arising from provisions was promoted by *curiales*.[4] The Registers of the fourteenth century are proof that the share which officials and members of the curia had in provisions was quite out of proportion to their place in the Church.[5] If a ratio could be established

---

[1] *Röm. Quellen*, xxxix; cf. Haller, who relates (p. 160 n. 4) Gascoigne's anecdote of the pope who, harassed by the importunity of a petitioner, finally exclaimed: 'ad diabolum, fiat ut petitur'!

[2] *Loc. cit., supra*, p. 33 n. 3; Barraclough, *Bernard of Compostella*, 493.

[3] This fact is well brought out by Hostiensis (*Summa* ad tit. *De prebendis*, §. *Et qualiter prebenda sit conferenda*) in writing of pluralism: 'Scit enim papa hanc generalem consuetudinem et tollerat; ergo videtur approbare ... maxime hodie, cum in hac compilatione nova non constituerit ius expressum, et bene sciebat hanc dissensionem'.

[4] *Die Röm. Rota u. d. Bistum Hildesheim*, 60–63, 66.

[5] On this subject, cf. v. Hofmann, *Forschungen z. Gesch. d. kurialen Behörden* I, 289–296.

between the different classes of provisions, it would probably shew that a much larger proportion of papal letters than has usually been supposed fell to the share of poor clerks, university graduates and local nominees.[1] But without awaiting the results of such an investigation, we can maintain on the strength of the *gratie speciales* in the Registers of the fourteenth and fifteenth centuries that the officials of the curia profited by the system beyond all measure. Even so, it is reasonable to suppose that the provisions conferred on them—collected together in the Vatican Registers and without the almost immeasurable but no longer existing *gratie communes* to counterbalance them—are more impressive to-day than they were to contemporaries, when divided out over the churches and dioceses of Europe. But one class of provision must always have made a deep impression and an unfavourable impression: I refer to the concessions to cardinals on which SAUERLAND has laid such stress.[2]

No statement throws more light on this question than cardinal Guillaume d'Aigrefeuille's computation of the value of the benefices held by himself and other cardinals in England at the outbreak of the Schism.[3] Personally he was receiving 'peacefully and quietly' from the English benefices in his possession the sum of 3,000 florins a year; Guy de Malsec (*dominus Pictaviensis*) and Pierre de Vergne received about 2,000 florins each, the cardinal-bishop of Albano no less than 5,000 florins, Pierre Flandrin (*dominus s. Eustachii*) a large but unspecified sum of money, and many other French cardinals, he added, were in a similar position of affluence. Such accumulations had their reason. As Pierre Dubois had pointed out at the beginning of the fourteenth century,

[1] *Vide supra*, pp. 27–28.
[2] *Vide supra*, p. 31.
[3] Gayet, *Le grand schisme d'occident d'après les documents contemporains* II, *pièces justificatives*, 71. Important material on this subject appears also in the recently published *Diplomatic Correspondence of Richard II*.

although the cardinals, as important dignitaries of the Church, had *secundum ritum vivendi modernum* high and costly positions to keep up, the income they derived from their titular churches was negligible, *paucos quasi nullos habent redditus suis titulis appropriatos*; and it was therefore a not unnatural result if *tanquam mercenarios oportet eos quasi vivere de rapina*.[1] But such abnormal accumulations on the part of the very body which was entrusted with an important share in the good government of the Church—though in no way a necessary consequence of the practice of papal provision[2]—were an evil of the first order. Without doubt the responsibility of the cardinals for the abuse of provisions was heavy; but it was their own responsibility. In this connexion again, the popes of the fourteenth century showed striking lack of resolution in withstanding the power of a factious interest;[3] but to understand their position aright the long and often bitter constitutional struggle between the papacy and the college of cardinals, which was waged throughout the period, must be taken into consideration. This question cannot be opened up here;[4] but its consequences in relation to provisions were weighty. Only at the risk of a grave constitutional crisis could the popes oppose the interests of the cardinals, and most popes of the fourteenth century preferred to give way on the question of benefices in order to obtain

---

[1] Barraclough, *Making of a Bishop*, 303–4.
[2] Haller, p. 169.   [3] Sauerland IV, xlv.
[4] Cf. Sägmüller, *Tätigkeit u. Stellung d. Cardinäle*; Id., 'Die oligarchischen Tendenzen d. Kardinalkollegs bis Bonifaz VIII', *Theol. Quartalschrift* LXXXIII (1901), 45–93; Lulvès, 'Päpstl. Wahlkapitulationen. Ein Beitrag z. Entwicklungsgesch. d. Kardinalats', *Quellen u. Forsch. a. ital. Arch.* XII (1909), 212 sqq.; Id. 'Die Machtbestrebungen d. Kardinalats b. z. Aufstellung d. ersten päpstl. Wahlkapitulationen', *Quellen u. Forsch.* XIII (1910), 73 sqq; Id. 'Die Machtbestrebungen d. Kardinalkollegiums gegenüber dem Papsttum', *Mitteil. d. Inst. f. österr. Geschichtsforschung* XXXV (1914), 455–483; Souchon, *Die Papstwahlen v. Bonifaz VIII. bis Urban VI. u. die Entstehung d. Schismas* (1888); Id., *Die Papstwahlen in d. Zeit d. grossen Schismas. Entwicklungs- u. Verfassungskämpfe d. Kardinalates v. 1378 b. 1417* (1898); Baumgarten, 'Wahlgeschenke d. Päpste an d. heilige Kollegium', *Röm. Quartalschr.* XXII (1908), 36–47; Schelenz, *Studien z. Gesch. d. Kardinalats im 13. u. 14. Jh.*

their point in regard to the major constitutional
issues.[1] Thus throughout the fourteenth century the
cardinals as a body were able to conduct an independent policy in regard to provisions, both in maintaining their own private interests and in using their
influence on behalf of others; and there is every reason
to accept as broadly true the statement of the English
chronicler, who wrote in the days of Gregory XI,
that their unscrupulous negotiations and intrigues
were carried out *domino papa hec omnia ignorante*.[2]
Mere complaisance or even nepotism on the part of
the popes is not sufficient to explain the remarkable
influence which the fourteenth-century cardinals
exercised over the system of provisions: its basis was a
firm consciousness of political strength in their relations with the popes. In no connexion was their
strength more evident than in the unprincipled
accumulation of benefices. We must guard against
placing the main responsibility for this state of affairs
on the papacy itself; but this does not alter the fact
that the self-seeking attitude which the cardinals as a
body were able to maintain, was without doubt a
major factor in undermining respect for the curia, and
also in counteracting the reformatory efforts of popes
such as Innocent VI, Urban V, or above all, of Gregory
XI.

The main reason, however, why the popes were
never able to offer a determined resistance to the
growing secularization of the clergy and to the fatal
emphasis on the purely material value of ecclesiastical

---

[1] Cf. Mollat, *Les papes d'Avignon*, 92–93.

[2] *Chron. de Melsa* III, 169: 'Cuius tempore cardinales in diversis regnis
optima queque beneficia eligentes, sibimet ipsis petiverunt et obtinuerunt
abbatias, prioratus, diaconatus, archidiaconatus et alias dignitates ac prebendas necnon et ecclesias parochiales plurimas ubique terrarum, ut aliquis
eorum septem et octo abbatias et prioratus preter alias dignitates et beneficia
pariter possideret. Et cum tanta haberent, omnia que expedienda vel impet-
randa erant in curia predicta, vendebantur, ita ut, si quis aliquid vellet expedire vel impetrare, primo adiret aliquem cardinalium seu secretarios et
consiliarios seu familiares domini pape et cum eis componeret, quid daret
pro expeditione negotii sui, domino papa hec omnia ignorante'.

benefices was neither the constitutional issue with
the cardinals, pressure from outside, nor mere weakness and corruption—in other words, nepotism and
favouritism—but the very conception which had
gradually been defined and strengthened within the
canon law, of the nature of the ecclesiastical benefice.[1]
This conception consisted broadly-speaking in an
identification of the benefice, from a legal point of
view, with other non-ecclesiastical types of property.
There were, of course, certain obvious differences
between ecclesiastical benefices and ordinary secular
property; the complex of rights which were united
in the benefice included—in accordance with a
familiar principle of canon law[2]—definite spiritual
rights, indeed the material objects of possession were
logically merely *res spirituali annexae*;[3] and consequently
it was—and is—impossible to classify the *ius beneficiale* indiscriminately according to one or other of the
categories of civil law, Roman or feudal.[4] But the
whole endeavour of the canonists of the classical
period was to minimize the differences between the
benefice and secular property. They sought to apply
to it with as little modification as possible the familiar
rules of Justinian's jurisprudence. They regarded it—
and this is the most widely important point—as the
object of private rights, not of public interests,
precisely as rights in secular property are private
rights in regard to which the State's only interest,
right or duty is to do justice. This point of view is
radically different from that which obtains to-day.
According to modern conceptions, one of the foremost public interests of the Church is the safeguarding
of the *ius beneficiale*. The maintenance of rights in a
benefice is not left to the civil action of an interested
party: it is the business of the appropriate ecclesiastical

[1] On this question, Gross, *Das Recht an der Pfründe*, is of basic importance.
[2] Lega, *De iudiciis ecclesiasticis* I, p. 1, t. 3, c. 1, §. 7.
[3] Gross, cap. 3.
[4] Gross, cap. 1.

superior, and is enforced by him in his administrative capacity by administrative process.[1] It is essential to appreciate the contrast between the mediæval and the modern attitude in this regard; for in this contrast lies the main explanation of the weakness of the mediæval papacy in all those aspects of policy and administration which dealt with the disposal and distribution of benefices. The public interest was not placed first. The most cursory acquaintance with the works of the classical glossators shows that it received ample consideration;[2] but modification within the framework of the civil law was thought a sufficient safeguard against injury to the Church as a whole. The real question, however, was whether a particular process of administrative law was not more suited to the peculiar character of the *ius beneficiale* than the ordinary civil procedure; and this possibility was never seriously put to the test.

The effects of the mediæval legal attitude towards ecclesiastical benefices are well illustrated by the much censured practice of 'surrogation'. This practice (*subrogatio*) permitted the substitution of a new litigant in the place of the deceased, if one party to a *causa beneficialis* died *lite pendente*. It is therefore often regarded as a prime cause of the long suits for possession of benefices, of benefices standing vacant year after year until one party or the other had obtained judgement, and consequently of the neglect or ill-performance of the spiritual and religious offices wherever lengthy litigation was proceeding.[3] It is held up as an example of the cupidity of the papacy, which preferred the profits accruing to it from litigation, to rapid settlement in the interests of the due

---

[1]Gross, p. 228; Barraclough, *Execrabilis*, 214 (particularly n. 5).

[2]Cf. for example, Hostien., *Summa* ad tit. *De concess. preb.*, §. *Utrum beneficium non vacans conferri possit vel promitti:* 'Tamen ubi receptus fuit ad primam vacantem, potest iudex . . . de hoc inquirere et ipsum repellere *propter periculum anime*'.

[3]Cf. for example, Sauerland III, lvii; Fierens, p. 829.

performance of the duties pertaining to the benefice at issue. Yet the object of the decretal on which the practice was based was precisely to prevent a general injury to the Church arising in the given circumstances;[1] and granted the legal premise on which it was based, it is difficult not to share the enthusiasm which the glossators felt for it.[2] This premise was, however, that the differences between ecclesiastical benefices and secular property should, as already said, be minimized and that the legal relationships arising out of the possession of benefices should be brought within the framework of the civil law of property;[3] and so long as this was the orthodox point of view, there was no inconsistency in regarding the function of the canon law *de beneficiis*, like that of the civil law of property, as the prevention of injury to the rights of the individual. If A dies in *de facto* possession of a benefice, the title to which I am disputing with him, there is an obvious injury to me, if the ordinary collator confers the benefice as vacant *per obitum A*; for a new party with a new title is introduced and my difficulties thereby increased. On the other hand, the mere circumstance of the death (or cession) of my adversary is no reason that I should arbitrarily profit; and the pope is therefore prepared to surrogate a claimant with a colourable title in the place of the deceased.

The whole procedure is a notable example of the equitable principles which pervade the canon law.[4] But it was not always easy to combine this equitable principle of setting the parties to an action on a parity, with the safeguarding of the public interest. Thus

---

[1]Cf. van Espen, *Ius eccl. universum* II. xxiv. 5. §. 5: ' . . . relationem suam habet ad c. *Si ii* [c.2], *Ut lite pendente* [in VI° 2, 8], ubi statuitur, beneficia litigiosa non posse conferri per ordinarios collatores, lite adhuc indecisa, uno collitigantium decedente, *ne propter novos adversarios litigia in Ecclesiae dispendium prorogari contingat'*.

[2]Cf. *gl. ord. ad* c. 2 in VI° 2, 8 *v*. 'In illo statu'.

[3]Thus Johannes Andreae writes in the 'Casus' *ad cap. cit.*: ' . . . forte intentavi interdictum *Uti possidetis* vel *Unde vi* . . .'

[4]Cf. in general Wohlhaupter, *Aequitas canonica*.

although the popes in their Chancery Regulations and Extravagants made every attempt to guard against the surrogation of claimants lacking a colourable title, their efforts to check the abuse of the practice failed.[1] But they failed not because of the use of the practice by the papacy as an instrument of financial policy, but because the popes and their legal advisers failed to see that too extensive an application of equitable principles, too great a care for the rights of litigants, too complex a system of remedies and counterbalances, might work to the public disadvantage. In short, in the endeavour to prevent possible prejudice to one party or the other, the popes and lawyers who moulded the canon law of procedure went so far that they provided a weapon for those parties who were willing to grasp at every advantage in a spirit of chicanery and barratry.

These remarks apply to the canon law of civil procedure as a whole. In spite of Clement V's constitution *Saepe*[2] of 1306, which (in answer to strongly-felt needs) firmly established a special summary procedure for use in beneficial and other 'spiritual' litigation,[3] the canonical rules of civil procedure were marked, from the second half of the twelfth century onwards, by an excessive attention to the rights of parties, by the formulation of the minutest regulations for maintaining impartiality and by an exaggerated regard for forms, which justify us in expressing their spirit in the words: no prejudice, no injury to parties, though the heavens fall![4] It would, of course, be absurd to pretend that this was all to the bad. There is ample evidence that the legislators were convinced that, in safeguarding to the best of their ability the

---

[1] See the important historical survey of the regulations in Gomes, *Commentarius* ad reg. *De subrogandis collitigantibus* (fo. 125 sqq.)

[2] c.2 *in Clem.* 5, 11.

[3] Cf. the decretal *Dispendiosam* (c. 2 *in Clem.* 2, 1) of 1311.

[4] Important for the whole question is Briegleb's brilliant *Einleitung in die Theorie der summarischen Processe*, 15 sqq., 34 sqq.

interests of private parties, they were automatically providing the best safeguard for the public interest; and this is a theory which—revived by Bentham and other exponents of legal *laissez-aller*—still commands respect. The construction of a system of procedure which was as impartial and well-balanced as human ingenuity could contrive, made canonical process necessarily dilatory and complicated; but it was a great achievement, and probably an achievement which only a jurisprudence exercised with a consciousness of the nearness of God and of eternity could have produced. It was the characteristic result of the influence of thorough-going ecclesiastical conceptions of justice on jurisprudence, and was historically of the greatest importance for the legal development of Europe. Within the limits of ordinary civil litigation, moreover, it is probable that the ill-effects of the dilatoriness and complication which it engendered, were not seriously felt; but it is another question whether the complex system of canonical process was suited to the other types of litigation to which it was extended.[1] This doubt arises above all in regard to *causae spirituales*, of which matrimonial cases and suits over benefices were the two main branches.[2] Where only private rights were at issue, mere slowness was probably outweighed by the guarantee which the carefully staged and balanced procedure afforded, of

---

[1]Cf. Briegleb, p. 17: 'Mit der Zeit freilich musste dieser Formalismus doch als zu schwerfällig und lästig, ja für manche Fälle zweckwidrig befunden werden, und zwar um so eher, je mehr derselbe nach damaliger Ansicht und Sitte als eine allgemein giltige officielle Geschäftsform betrachtet, auf die Verhandlung eigentlicher Rechtsstreitigkeiten keineswegs beschränkt war. Es ist wesentlich derselbe solennis ordo iudiciarius, welcher in der Form des Accusationsprocesses auch in Criminalsachen galt, und von welchem die leichteren Formen des Denunciations- und Inquisitionsprocesses erst abgezweigt werden mussten. Ja es sind die Grundsätze derselben feierlichen Geschäftsform, welche für noch ganz andere Geschäfte, soweit nur irgend möglich, massgebend geworden waren; für allerlei Regiminalsachen, Disciplinarfälle, Streitigkeiten über die Berechtigung auf Kirchenpfründen, über die Grenzen kirchlicher Sprengel ...'

[2]Cf. for the moment, Barraclough, *Public Notaries*, 64.

G

impartiality and automatic impersonal control.[1] But
where public duties were combined with private
rights, as in the *ius beneficiale*, and the two could not
be dealt with separately, a procedure which may well
have made for the certain, incontrovertible delimitation of private rights, was not even in theory the best
means of safeguarding the public interests involved,
and in actual mediæval practice undoubtedly exposed
them to serious dangers and disadvantages.

It is thus a question of first importance, how and
why the predominantly 'spiritual' rights united in the
beneficium came to be classified as civil rights and
governed by the ordinary rules of civil procedure. To
this question, however, we must probably be content
with the general answer, that it was one effect of the
powerful influence exercised by Roman or civil
jurisprudence over canonists in the days of Alexander
III and thus during the crucial, formative period in the
development of the classical canon law. When canonists like Huguccio first concerned themselves in the
second half of the twelfth century with the problem of
the legal content and the legal enforcement of the *ius
beneficiale*, they proceeded immediately by comparison
with civil usufruct.[2] This was the earliest stage in the
legal construction of the *ius beneficiale*, and we have no
legal definition of the benefice in which the canon law
approached the question without reference to civil
law categories.[3] In other words, the legal definition of
the benefice was not made until the canon law was
under civilian dominance, and was perhaps a direct
consequence of the influence of civil law ideas. This
did not mean, however, that the *ius beneficiale* had been
treated from the earliest period, on the analogy of the
civil law of property, as a category of private law.

[1]The fundamental object of canonical process was to construct so rigid
an external system that the subjective intervention even—or perhaps
particularly—of the judge, was reduced to a minimum; Engelmann, *Der
Civilprozess* II. iii, 35.—With this compare Bentham's criticism of judicial
authority in English common law, e.g. as quoted by Vinogradoff, *Common
Sense in Law*, 205.   [2]Cf. Gross, *op. cit.*, 122–3.   [3]*Op cit.*, 124.

Peter of Blois, writing about 1180,[1] still regarded it as under the administrative authority of the hierarchical superior, and consequently withdrawn from the ordinary civil authority and civil procedure of the courts,[2] but this administrative authority was later revoked by Alexander III in favour of the *solemnis ordo iudiciarius*.[3] Alexander's practical decision (for the very reason that the law of procedure and the substantive law were much more closely interconnected then than now)[4] had almost immediate effects on the theoretical interpretation of the *ius beneficiale*. In minimizing the public aspects of the *ius beneficiale* and stressing its similarity to other categories of private law,[5] Goffred of Trano and Roffredus Beneventanus, the earliest commentators of the codified decretals of Gregory IX, were merely following theoretically in Alexander's footsteps. In the theoretical construction which they and their immediate successors created, the *ius beneficiale* was brought within the category of *iura in re*, which the civil lawyers of the day were engaged in defining.[6] But 'this classification and the implied identification of the right of the *beneficiatus* in all essentials with the *iura in re* of private law occurred not merely in theory or by analogy, but with full acceptance of all the practical implications and emphasis on all the necessary consequences of the classification.'[7] The *ius beneficiale* was thenceforward governed and safeguarded by the established actions and interdicts of the civil law of property. The procedure applied in maintaining it was (with certain modifications defined in the constitution *Saepe* of 1306) the unified civil-canonical system of procedure. 'That the *ius ipsum*

---

[1] Cf. Reimarus, *Petri Bles. Spec. iuris canonici*, xliii.
[2] *Op. cit.*, cap. 42, has the arguments both for and against this contention.— The *Speculum* was unfortunately overlooked by Gross.
[3] c. 7 X 2,13: I have no doubt that this is the decretal to which the important but ambiguous gloss in Peter's *Speculum* (p. 78) refers.
[4] Engelmann, p. 27.
[5] Gross, p. 125.
[6] Gross, p. 138; cf. Landsberg, *Die Glosse des Accursius*, 82–92.
[7] Gross, p. 139.

beneficiorum had a spiritual character and that, because
of its inseparable association with the *sacrum officium*,
the *ius in re*, expounded and interpreted in this way,
ought to embrace also—at any rate in principle—
the further, purely spiritual content of the office, was
not altogether ignored; there are indications that certain misgivings about the purely private-legal construction of the theory of the benefice and its sometimes
rather crued consequences made themselves felt;
but they were not weighty enough to prevent the continued maintenance and the amplification of the
construction.'[1]

It is to this legal construction of the *ius beneficiale* that
we must turn, if we want the ultimate explanation not
only of the lengthy and involved litigation over
benefices, which was without doubt the origin of
many disorders in the mediæval Church, but also of
the predominantly material conception of the benefice,
which obtained not merely among the admittedly
secularized clergy of the Germanic lands, but also in
the more strictly legalistic circles of the curia. As a
legal conception, it was gradually but logically and
firmly established by the usual process of legal development—that is, by the theoretical interpretation of
texts and by the decision of actual law-suits. It presupposed, naturally enough, a certain conception of
the law; but it did not presuppose on the part of the
papacy a fixed policy, good or bad, in regard to benefices or provisions. Even so outstanding a lawyer as
MAITLAND did not do justice either to the papacy or
to the law in this regard: if a bishop disputes the
'idoneity' of a nephew, he writes, an appeal lies to the
pope: how can such a discussion end?[2] . . . The obvious

[1]Gross, 140.

[2]*Canon Law*, 66–7: 'instead of the simple statement that the pope cannot
lawfully provide clerks with English benefices . . . we find this indefensible
distinction between use and abuse, and are at once led on to discuss the
demerits of the *nepotes*. How can such a discussion end? If the bishop disputes
the 'idoneity' of a nephew, an appeal lies to the pope. The bishop who makes
a stand against the pope at the line between use and abuse is indeed heroic;
but his is the heroism of despair'.

insinuation is that the pope would not scruple, whatever the legal circumstances, to carry his policy through, if it suited him to carry it through. But the presupposition which MAITLAND makes is that the bestowal of benefices, in this case by means of provisions, was an act of administration, not an act of law. Following GROSS, we have shown that this was not the case. An appeal lay, in a theoretical, verbal sense to the pope or (according to the usual formula) *ad sedem apostolicam*; but it was in fact an appeal to the pope's supreme central appellate court, to the Rota Romana,[1] and anyone who has read through the great body of fourteenth-century case-law, the *Decisiones dominorum de Rota*,[2] nine-tenths of which deals with beneficial litigation, will need no convincing that the decisions were based on fixed legal principles and reached by the ordinary rules of interpretation common to the case-law of all countries. It is, in short, not the good faith but the legal principles of the popes or of the papal judiciary which can be called in question. If we wish to criticize the attitude of the mediæval papacy to Church benefices, we must criticize not its single decisions and regulations, which evince to an altogether remarkable degree an anxious striving not only to do justice but also to achieve equity, but the principles on which those decisions were based.

It must be reiterated that the basis of these principles was the classification of the *ius beneficiale* as a private right of civil law. For this classification, it is perhaps superfluous to add, responsibility can be p aced neither on the popes nor on anyone else: it was the logical, necessary consequence of the legal conceptions of the age—particularly perhaps of the revival

---

[1]The Rota functioned also, under certain circumstances, as a court of first instance, cf. Schneider, *Die röm. Rota*, §. 18.

[2]I use the edition, Lugduni 1515, which contains, as well as the better known *decisiones nove et antique*, the decisions of Bernard de Bisigneto and of Thomas Falstoli. On these collections, cf. Göller, *Z. Gesch. d. Rota Romana*, and *Wilhelm Horborch u. die Decisiones Antiquae*; Pfaff, *Z. Gesch. d. Kanonisten Wilhelm Horborch*; Fliniaux, *Les anciennes collections des Decisiones Rotae*.

and broad influence of civil jurisprudence. That it resulted in a disregard for, and a slurring over of those aspects of the *ius beneficiale* connotated by the word, not *beneficium*, but *officium*, is beyond all doubt. The public interests involved did not receive due consideration. They were not of the sort which could be adequately safeguarded by the incidental intervention of a public official, such as the proctor-fiscal— an officer, in any case, of government rather than of society.[1] They could not in the long run be protected by the minute delimitation and regulation of private rights; for this very attention to equitable minutiae exposed them to the complication and dilatoriness of the law—the worst threat to which such interests could be exposed. Thus the limitations the popes imposed on the rights of the individual complicated the law without providing a final safeguard for the public interests involved. It is a superficial view, only rendered possible by the scant attention general historians have paid to the legal situation, to suppose that the complications introduced, for instance, by the Chancery Regulations were merely arbitrary means of exerting financial pressure. They represented as a whole an honest endeavour to build up a rigid, complicated system in which the rights of private parties were clearly and minutely fixed, and none could profit unduly at the general expense.[2] But they

[1] Cf. Göller, *Der Gerichtshof d. päpstl. Kammer u. d. Entstehung d. Amtes d. Procurator fiscalis*. For the intervention of the proctor-fiscal in a *causa beneficialis*, cf. Kirsch, *Ein Prozess gegen Bischof u. Domkapitel v. Würzburg*.

[2] Thus compare with the modern view of the *clausulae* included in letters of provision—namely, that they were an unprincipled method of depriving the ordinary collators of their rights (Haller, pp. 168, 172)—and particularly of the evil character of the *non obstantia* (cf. Stubbs, *Const. Hist.* III, 321; Mann, *Lives of the Popes* XIV, 254-5; Mackenzie, *Anti-Foreign Movement*, 202; Ellis, *Anti-Papal Legislation*, 59), the widely different contemporary attitude of Roffredus Beneventanus, for whom they were first and foremost a (from his point of view unwarranted) check on the rights of the providee; cf. Roffredus, *Opus libellorum*, tit. *De preb.*, §. *Quomodo concipiatur libellus* (fo. 89a): 'Verumptamen littere hodie, si conceduntur vel pro beneficio vel ut recipiatur quis in canonicum et in fratrem, cum tot clausulis conceduntur, quod non reportat quis nisi laborem et dolorem. Nam conceduntur ita sub hiis clausulis: "si pro

provided no final protection for the public interests involved in the *ius beneficiale* because these could not be safeguarded merely by careful modification and elaborate adaptation of the ordinary civil procedure. This was eminently a case—perhaps, indeed, an outstandingly exceptional case—where the public interest had to be placed first or placed nowhere at all. The civil procedure was not adapted to complex relationships of public and private interests, such as found expression in the benefice. A more speedy, more direct, less involved procedure was needed.

This was perhaps an ideal want. From the point of view of the law, if not from that of the Church, the decline of the administrative jurisdiction of the bishop and its replacement in a matter of such importance as the ordering of benefices by the *solemnis ordo iudiciarius* was without doubt at that time a definite progress. It offered, as Peter of Blois well realized,[1] a firmer guarantee of justice to the individual; and even from a wider standpoint, the substitution of a uniform regular system in the place of the earlier personal authoritarian procedure was an essential development in the law of the Church, and indeed in the law of mediæval Europe as a whole.[2] With particular regard to provisions, the very fact that they raised the broad constitutional issue of the respective rights of pope and ordinary was in itself a good reason that a fixed *ordo* should be established, and that this should be the widely known *ordo* of the Roman-canonical civil process. It is obvious—though the fact may not have been realized until the assimilation of the *ius beneficiale*

alio seu pro aliis vobis non direxerimus scripta nostra". Item apponitur etiam clausula: "nisi canonicum quid obsistat"; item: "si non scripserimus pro aliquo, qui huiusmodi gratiam prosequatur". Multe enim sunt exceptiones, que competunt contra istum impetrantem . . .'

[1] *Speculum*, 75: 'Et hoc ideo, ne detur episcopis occasio malignandi et auferendi subditis suis ecclesias vel prebendas legitime vel canonice collatas, cum forte sint legitimis probationibus destituti, quibus titulum et causam sue possessionis debeant demonstrare . . .'

[2] Cf. Fournier, *Les officialités*, 7, 288–9.

to the *iura realia* of private law was practically complete[1]—that the constitutional rights at issue made it impossible to expect the maximum of justice under a liquid administrative procedure in which the decisive factor was necessarily the judicial probity and conscientiousness of the *ordinarius*. For this reason, in the fixed executorial process which was rapidly formulated for dealing with provisions, it was made a rule in the expedition of *gratie communes* that—though ordinarily the executor commissioned was the bishop of the diocese to which the collator of the benefice in question belonged—three ecclesiastical dignitaries of the diocese should be commissioned, if the benefice to which provision was made happened to be one in which the rights of collation pertained to the bishop himself.[2] Even in these circumstances it was often difficult *propter metum episcopi* to get the commissioners to carry out their judicial functions.[3] It is obvious that the difficulties placed in the way of justice would have been greater still under an administrative procedure in which the main responsibility was left to the discretion of the bishop himself.

If, for the protection of the public interests involved in the *ius beneficiale*, an administrative procedure was ideally necessary, it is thus highly questionable whether the older administrative jurisdiction of the

[1] In other words, I do not assert that this was an operative reason for the application of the civil *ordo iudiciarius* to beneficial questions: there can, I think, be no doubt that this took place without any consideration of policy, as a purely internal legal development.

[2] Tihon, *Les expectatives*, 81.

[3] Cf. for example, Schwalm, *Das Formelbuch des Heinrich Bucglant*, no. 48. Here the impetrant seems to think he has no remedy at law and appeals *extraiudicialiter* to the pope for the appointment of executors *extra diocesim*. That there was (or was perhaps later devised) a remedy at law, is shown by *Coll. Regin. Oxon., Cod.* 54, fo. 371': 'Et nota quod quandocumque executor principalis sive subexecutor sint rogati, ut exequantur mandatum apostolicum eis directum, et recusant vel differant exequi, sive sint in gratia communi sive speciali, sive processus sit factus sive non, si habeant instrumentum requisitionis, legitime possunt acceptare provisi, ac si processus esset factus, et tunc possunt appellare contra executorem vel subexecutorem, qui negligunt vel recusant exequi mandatum . . .'

bishop was suited to the particular legal problem which the complex character of the benefice involved.[1] Nor does it serve a useful historical purpose to consider theoretically what form of procedure might have been devised to safeguard equally the private rights and the public interests at stake. Practically, there was no alternative to the civil procedure actually enforced. The most general knowledge of the history of the internal development of both the civil and the canon law at this period suffices to show that the assimilation of the *ius beneficiale* to the established categories of private law took place without ulterior object, and in good faith: for the generation of Accursius it was perhaps the only, certainly the most natural method of classification. Thus for the historian it is less important to weigh the question of alternatives, than to investigate in detail the procedure actually used: it may not have been ideally the most appropriate method of dealing with benefices, but it was certainly not without practical merits.

[1] This conclusion is not affected by the fact that, in modern times, the benefice has again successfully been brought within the administrative jurisdiction of the bishop; cf. *supra*, p. 78 (n. 1). First the Concordats with the various nations and then the settlement of Trent imposed statutory limits on the extent of papal provisions, as a result of which the relationship between papal and episcopal rights was defined, and the constitutional issue (at any rate in theory) solved; cf. Th. de Rosa, *De executoribus*, I. ii. §. 87. Yet even then there was a long period of difficulties in practice, before the modern equilibrium was reached; cf. Delannoy, *La juridiction ecclésiastique en matière bénéficiale sous l'ancien régime*, and (from the papal point of view) the interesting report printed by Just, *Quellen u. Forsch. a. ital. Arch.* XXIV, 266 sq.

CHAPTER VII

FROM THE POINT of view of papal provisions, the chief merit of interpreting the *ius beneficiale* according to the well-established principles of civil law, and prosecuting it in accordance with definite rules of procedure, was the guarantee provided that the exercise of the power of provision would be subjected to the rule of law. Instead of a loose, undefined practice of administrative intervention by the popes, the system of provisions was organized, from approximately the days of Innocent IV (1243–1254) onwards,[1] as a rigid, balanced, self-operative system of law, in which no room was left for papal caprice and very little for legitimate papal discretion.

This legal system still remains to be described, and can only be described and explained at length.[2] No historian either of the law or of the Church has as yet investigated the subject, and the view of provisions which, practically unchallenged, still holds the field, places more stress on arbitrariness than on system, on administrative freedom than on legal order. Even HALLER wrote that the Avignonese popes 'distributed offices and benefices purely by caprice and favour'.[3] As an actual historical fact, however, after an investigation of all the evidence in one particular church, this statement was categorically challenged by RIEDER: 'at Constance', he asserted, 'no overstepping of the generally recognized papal powers can be proved'.[4]

[1]Regarding the date, cf. my articles *Formulare f. päpstl. Suppliken*; *The Constitution 'Execrabilis'*, 213; *Bernard of Compostella*, 492.
[2]It is the subject on which I have been engaged for some years.—I have now collected and edited the abundant but hitherto unused MS. material, and hope to be able to publish the results of my investigations within a short time.
[3]*Papstt. u. Kirchenreform*, 25.
[4]*Röm. Quellen*, lxxx.

Which standpoint are we to adopt? Must we wait until RIEDER's examination of the position at Constance is supplemented by a wealth of similar investigations, before we attempt, from the point of view of the Church as a whole, to decide the question? In this way alone can the actual historical facts be determined; but for the understanding of the facts, whatever conclusions they point to, it is without doubt essential to study the system itself into which the practice of provision was organized.

The system of provisions, regarded from this point of view, fell into two divisions. There were, in the first place, those transactions which took place in the Papal Chancery; the preliminary negotiations for obtaining a letter of provision, which were essentially the same class of formal proceedings as were involved in any other chancery in suing out a writ. Secondly, there was the more strictly legal procedure in execution of the provision or (in the more technical but at the same time more suggestive phrase, almost invariably used by contemporaries) of the *rescriptum apostolicum*.[1] Here again it is essential to insist on the similarity to the contemporary English originating writ. Contrary to the accepted view of historians, a provision did not have *executio parata*; that is, it was not put through, as an administrative matter, without judicial cognizance, the function of the executor was not merely to carry out an order, but to do justice in accordance with the terms of his commission. Thus the procedure followed by him consisted not merely in a formal enforcement of obedience, but in a lengthy

[1] What is suggested is historical connexion—no doubt under modification —with the late Roman 'rescript procedure'. This question would repay further investigation: historians of judicial procedure at canon law have given too little attention to the influence of the late Imperial extraordinary processes on the legal institutions of the Church. Cf. Bethmann-Hollweg, *Der Civilprocess d. gemeinen Rechts* III, 333–341; Buckland, *Text–book of Roman Law*, 671; Andt, *La procédure par rescrit*; Collinet, *La procédure par libelle*.— Since this section was written, Steinwenter's investigations (*Zeitschr. d. Sav.-Stiftung, kanon. Abt.* XXIII, 1–116) have added considerably to our knowledge of the earlier phases of canonical 'rescript procedure'.

judicial investigation, in every way as interesting as and in many ways comparable with the older English procedure on the writ.

In form and in origin, the mediæval English procedure on the writ was an administrative procedure —the writ was the king's order, issued however with certain limiting clauses—but in intention it was judicial.[1] The same is broadly true of the ordinary papal rescript *de providendo*.[2] The various types of rescript need careful classification: special forms involved particular procedural modifications. The rarely used *forma motu proprio* perhaps always, certainly during the later period in the history of provisions, had *executio parata*;[3] but the ordinary rescript *in forma communi*, and certainly the majority of *forme speciales*, presupposed what came to be known technically as a *purificatio*—that is, the execution under judicial cognizance of the conditions laid down in the writ.[4] And this was not all: as the special treatises on procedure in the execution of a provision, composed in the fourteenth century, and the contemporary muniments of the Rota Romana prove, the way was normally left open for legitimate defence by the established

[1]Thus the well-known form *Praecipe* begins with an order: 'Praecipe X quod . . . reddat', and then continues: 'Et nisi fecerit . . . tunc summone eum . . . ostensurus quare non fecerit'. The preliminary order was not necessarily formal—the defendant may have obeyed, and had at any rate the opportunity to obey; but from a legal point of view, the stress falls on the second half of the writ. The chancery was proceeding on the *ex parte* statement of the plaintiff, and did not intend the defendant to obey if he had a valid defence— the administrative order was merely a formal method of bringing the law into play.

[2]Cf. Hostiensis, *Summa* ad tit. *De rescriptis*, §. *Quod iurisdictionem conferat*: 'sed hoc nota, quod regulariter quodlibet rescriptum cause cognitionem habere presumitur, in quo aperte quicquam facti narratur, quia semper subintelligitur hec clausula: "si preces veritate nitantur", *inf. eod.*, c. 2 [c. 2 X 1, 3], et quelibet exceptio rationalis admittitur . . .'

[3]Cf. Ridolfini, *Praxis recentior*, P. II, c. 8, §. 60 (p. 371).

[4]E.g. (according to *Reg. Vat.* 26 (*Urbani IV, a.* 1), fo. 2, nn. 3, 4): 'si est ita', 'si non est alias beneficiatus', 'dummodo in litteratura et vita reperiatur idoneus et vellit in illo personaliter residere', 'ita tamen quod dictus clericus ad ordines, quos requiret onus beneficii, de quo sibi duxeris providendum, se faciat statutis temporibus promoveri'.

procedure of exception and replication.[1] In other words, the papal rescript put the providee in the position of plaintiff, the bishop, patron or chapter, to whose benefice provision was made, in the position of defendant. More than this it did not do. The orthodox theory, accepted unquestioningly by historians, that the papal letters or even the pope's signature on a petition conferred a right in or to a benefice,[2] is in marked contrast with the explicit statements of the classical canonists.[3] A proprietary right in a benefice (*ius in re*) was only acquired by the formal act of collation or investiture; a right to a benefice (*ius ad rem*) was only acquired by the formal act either of acceptance or of reception. One right— a *tenue ius*—was imparted by the papal rescript: the right to demand a hearing, the *ius implorandi officium iudicis*[4] or the *impetrandi seu petendi facultas*.[5] Against a collator who ignored the papal writ a providee might perhaps occasionally resort to a personal action,[6] and punitive proceedings by the pope were also within

[1]Cf. Roffredus, *Opus libellorum* ad tit. *De preb.*, §. *Quibus ecclesiastica beneficia sunt conferenda* (fo. 88*b*): 'Illud autem diligenter attende, quod cum impetratur rescriptum ad beneficium optinendum, multe subintelliguntur conditiones, licet papa precise mandet, sine quibus rescriptum non valeat; puta, si est clericus, si est dignus . . . et in ecclesia sufficere potest tot . . . Licet enim dominus papa precise scribat, exceptiones tamen patienter admittit, ut *De rescr.* [1, 3], c. *Si quando* [c. 5] et *De off. del.* [1, 29], *Ex parte* [c. 13] et *De etate et qual.* [1, 14], c. *Accepimus* [c. 13], ubi dicitur quod quantumcumque dominus papa absolute scribat, exceptiones tamen admittende sunt . . .'

[2]E.g. Bresslau, *Urkundenlehre* (1889), 686: 'nach der geltenden Rechtsanschauung die Genehmigung der Petition durch den Papst die Rechtskraft der Bewilligung schon an und für sich bewirkte'.—This statement is somewhat amended, but not radically changed, in the 2nd edition, II, 23, 110.

[3]Cf. Gross, *Das Recht an der Pfründe*, cap. 2 (and Barraclough, *Execrabilis*, 206 sq.) where the authorities for the following are assembled. The evidence could be multiplied, but it would be out of place to discuss the question in detail here.

[4]Barraclough, *loc. cit.*

[5]Roffredus, *op. cit.*, *tit. cit.* §. *Quomodo concipiatur libellus* (fo. 88'*a*): 'Certum est quod iste ex rescripto nullam habeat actionem, licet rescriptum det sibi impetrandi seu petendi facultatem'.

[6]Innoc. IV. *ad* c. 27 X 3, 5 *v*. 'Recipi facias': 'Receptus in canonicum contra eum, qui eam [*sc.* prebendam] contulit alteri, non habet actionem, nisi *forte* de dolo vel in factum ad expensas'. Cf. *Id. ad* c. 17 X 3, 5 *v*. 'Resignatione': '. . . . ex mandato obligantur persone, non res vel prebende'.

the bounds of possibility, for 'papa non debet sustinere, quod sibi deludatur'.[1] But this does not alter the main fact: the papal letters in themselves gave no real proprietary right to a benefice,[2] and if a real right were acquired by a third party in contempt of the papal mandate, it was valid, and was not invalidated by the fact that a papal mandate had issued.[3]

This whole legal construction of rights and counter-rights is thus a remarkable proof of the force which the law accorded to *real* rights, both in comparison with personal rights and with mere claims such as papal letters of provision contained.[4] It is also a forceful indication of the true nature of the papal rescript. It was not a direct administrative order, which admitted neither qualification nor refusal,[5] but a statement of claim which could only be enforced with judicial cognizance. Modern writers have been deceived by its form into thinking that it was purely administrative in nature, without realizing that the administrative form was common to the contemporary English writ of the *Praecipe* class, although the judicial intention of the latter is not called in doubt. They have been led also by the doctrine that the pope's signature to a petition in itself made the 'grace' perfect, to suppose that this perfection was such that the 'grace' acquired immediate force of law.[6] But the doctrine of the *signatura*[7]—a doctrine, incidentally, which was only perfected in the later fifteenth and sixteenth century, and which therefore can only be accepted for the mediæval period in so far as it is supported by contemporary evidence—must be interpreted in connexion

[1] Innoc. IV. *gl. prox. cit. et ad cap. id. v.* 'Retractata'; Roffredus *ad tit. cit.* (fo. 90a).
[2] Bern. Parm. *ad* c. 27 X 3, 5 *v.* 'Conferendam': ' . . . nec solum mandatum pape sufficit ad hoc, ut ius habet . . .'
[3] Innoc. et Roffr., *locc. prox. citatis.*
[4] Cf. Bern. Compost., *notabilia ad* c. 30 X 1, 3, §. *Item quid si duo sunt recepti*: ' . . . in hoc ambiguo faveamus primo, qui ius habet, et non secundo, qui ius alterius voluit ambitiose habere . . .'
[5] Cf. Innoc. IV *ad* c. 4 X 1, 14 *v.* 'Litterarum'.   [6] Cf. *supra*, p. 93 n. 2.
[7] It is treated with great clarity by de Rosa, *De executoribus*, I. i. §. 37 et sqq.

with other important legal doctrines, such as that of *subreptio*.[1] The modifications and limitations to which it was subject, must be understood.[2] This is too technical a question to enter upon here. But even if the papal signature and subsequent registration of a petition 'perfected' a grace, 'adeo ut ius quaesitum esse dicatur gratiato',[3] there is no reason to conclude that the *ius quaesitum* was a real, proprietary right in the benefice. The *ius quaesitum* was the right to the benefits expressed in the petition which the pope had sanctioned, or alternatively in the papal rescript which was then drafted and which reproduced precisely the terms of the sanctioned minute;[4] and these benefits, as the mediæval legal authorities show, can be summed up as a right to a judicial hearing,[5] in which all interested parties were entitled to intervene and to show cause.

As a result of this judicial hearing, a proprietary right to or in a benefice might be acquired; but this depended on the circumstances of the case and on the action of the parties who appeared as defendants. If they had legitimate exceptions to propose, they had every facility for proposing them.[6] The defence

[1]Cf. van Espen, *Ius eccl. univ.* P. II, t. 24, c. 3, §. 6: 'Unde si quid falsi sit expressum, aut veri omissum, ratione cuius ipse Pontifex per *errorem* concessit alias non concessurus, ipsa provisio tanquam *sub* et *obreptitia* erit invalida; eo quod data censeatur provisio sub hac tacita conditione: modo omnia *sincere* ac *vere*, prout oportet, in supplica sint expressa . . .'

[2]Cf. Gomes, *Commentarius, Utr. signaturae compendium*, §. *Est tamen unum circa hoc valde notandum* (fo. 116'); Rebuffus, *Praxis beneficiorum*, cap. *De signat. gratiae*, §. *Secunda pars signaturae* (pp. 96–99); van Espen, *cap. cit.* §§. 12–15; de Rosa, *loc. cit.*

[3]van Espen. P. I, t. 23, c. 2, §. 21.   [4]Cf. van Espen, P. II, t. 24, c. 3, §. 4.
[5]Cf. further Bern. Parm. c. 13 X 1, 9 *gl. ad. v* 'Renunciasse iuri'.
[6]The *non obstantia* in papal letters of provision, which acted in some respects as a limitation on the defences of the ordinary collators, have been strongly criticized; cf. *supra*, p. 86 n. 2. But if we compare them with the clauses, for example, in contracts for loans, where the parties under obligation were deprived, in a long series of stipulations, of *omne iuris canonici et civilis auxilium* (cf. the example I have printed in the *Formularium notar. curie*, App. no. 7), their relative mildness becomes evident enough: there is nothing in letters of provision of any class, to compare with the stripping away of the legitimate rights of defence, which was common and even usual in contracts; cf. Sallustius Tiberius, *De modis procedendi in causis, quae coram Auditore Camerae aguntur*, l. I, c. 2 *et passim*.

usually put forward turned on the question either of the 'idoneity' of the providee or the correctness of his statement of claim. Of the latter type, an example among many is furnished by the case of the church of Mitton, referred to above;[1] of the former, no example is more curious than the detailed charge of sorcery and conversation with the devil brought by the chapter of Bremen against a providee of John XXII.[2] But the defences open to ordinary collators were in no way limited to imputations against the papal providees. Among the broader forms of defence the *exceptio paupertatis* is particularly worth mention. It was a legitimate pleading—'nam inanis est actio quam inopia debitoris excludit'[3]—to show that the limited revenues of a church did not permit the reception of a providee, that there was no means of supporting another canon;[4] and actual cases have survived in which the pope allowed the appeal of a chapter against commissioners who had either refused to admit the exception or to examine witnesses produced in its support.[5]

Thus the ordinary collators had the right—and, indeed, from the point of view of the public law of the Church, the duty[6]—of defending themselves both

[1] *Supra*, pp. 52–53.

[2] Selections from the acts of these cases are among the documentary evidence which I hope shortly to publish.

[3] *Cod. lat. Monacen.* 8011, fo. 86'*b* (*Questio disputata per Egidium de Fuscarariis*) citing D. 4. 3. 6 and c. 16 X 2, 13.

[4] *Vide* Bern. Parm. *ad* c. 16 X 2, 23 *v*. 'Sufficiebant': 'Hec exceptio legitima est, quia tot sunt ponendi in ecclesia, quot ex facultatibus ipsius possunt commode sustentari'. Cf. Innoc. IV. *ad* c. 10 X 3, 8 *v*. 'Nullatenus': 'Non debent habere beneficium de ecclesia, nisi offerat se facultas—non qualiscumque, sed talis quod honeste possint inde vivere, secundum quod consueverunt et secundum consuetudinem provincie'.

[5] E.g. in the formulary falsely ascribed to Marinus of Eboli, the vice-chancellor of Innocent IV, (ed. Schillmann) no. 1176.

[6] Cf. the important *questio* disputed by Egidius de Fuscarariis in *Cod. lat. Monacen.* 8011, ff. 107*a*-107*b* (also *ed.* Reatz, pp. 40–45, no. 8): 'Et ista tria debent in prelato concurrere, scilicet maturitas etatis, morum honestas et scientia litterarum. . . . Cum ergo hoc sit contra ius publicum, non poterant ei renuntiare. . . . Nemo ius publicum remittere potest aliquibus pactionibus, nec mutare formam antiquitus constitutam. . . . Eodem modo non potest quis facere, quod canones non habeant locum in electionibus et institutionibus ecclesiarum sive prelatorum, qui requirunt predicta tria in hiis, qui promoventur ad regimen animarum. . . . Preterea defectus talis non solum ab optinendo sed etiam ab optento repellit . . .'

against providees who were morally or intellectually unfit for their office and against overburdening with provisions. A fuller knowledge of the system would probably show that the papacy relied on the co-operation of the ordinary collators in this regard; for in any procedure based on the principles of civil law, justice necessarily depended on the mutual activity of both parties. In issuing a rescript the pope used the *ex parte* statement of one side; but the rescript, like the original writ, was only a means of setting the judicial machinery in motion, and the presumption on which the rescript was issued was that the defendant, in his own interest, would prevent any miscarriage of justice by forcing the impetrant to prove that his claim was justified. It was a system of legal *laissez-aller*, in which the initiative was left to the parties involved;[1] but if each side insisted on its rights, there was reasonable ground for presuming that, as a result of a formal judicial cognizance of the facts, neither party would be allowed to suffer injustice.

Thus a summary sketch of the main features of the procedure employed in the execution of papal provisions indicates that the charges brought by contemporaries against the system were exaggerated. The unworthiness of providees, the overburdening of churches—these were the main headings of complaint. Yet on both counts the exceptions and replications of the chapters and bishops and patrons were admitted with a freedom and a fullness which only the canon law of procedure knew, and appeal could be made on the smallest provocation at practically any stage of proceedings. It is too soon to decide how far the complaints of the ordinary collators were justified; but it is obvious that they had legitimate means of defence at law, and that if they had a real grievance against a provision, a regular legal method of venti-lating it was offered. Under the civil procedure, as

[1] Cf. Barraclough, *Execrabilis*, 213–216.

H

adapted to benefices and beneficial rights, the public interest found expression practically solely in provision *ne ad beneficia ingressus patere valeat vitiosus*;[1] and the only means that was left to the papacy of safeguarding this principle of public law, was to leave the chapters in possession of all legitimate weapons of defence. Investigation of the legal operation of provisions and of the legal procedure involved in their execution shows that the rights of the ordinary collators were not overridden, limited and circumscribed in the way that modern historians have supposed. In two ways the orthodox theory of the operation of provisions needs modification: on the one side, the rights acquired by providees in virtue of their letters of provision were relatively intangible and unsubstantial, on the other, the rights of the ordinary collators were varied, comparatively well respected and firmly rooted in the established routine of procedure. In short, the rules of procedure established a balance between the parties which went some way to safeguard the public interest, and prevented at any rate the most glaring infringements of the established rights either of the ordinary collators or of the papal providees. It was a system under which justice was done to both parties, no less to the bishops, chapters and patrons whose benefices were in question, than to the providees of the pope, and in which the rules of procedure gave each side ample opportunity for maintaining its proper rights and interests and traversing the claims of its adversary.

[1] c. un. in VI° 2, 7 (together with the gloss *ad v.* 'Vitiosus').

CHAPTER VIII

SUCH WAS THE bare framework of the procedure used in the execution of papal provisions, and even a summary sketch of the main features of the procedure shews beyond all doubt that a legal approach to the subject has many advantages. Provisions formed a system, organized on the basis of well-established legal principles. By defining the elements of this system, by seeking out the basic principles and investigating their application, we can reconstruct the regular, customary practice, which on pain of legal penalties it was essential to follow, and see just what effects the issue of letters of provisions produced. Analysis of the historical material, as undertaken by RIEDER, TIHON, BAIX and others,[1] shows conclusively that only a relatively small proportion of provisions had final efficacy: by investigating the legal operation of papal *rescripta de providendo* we can determine why and how their effects were limited.

Statutory enactments by the popes, the practice of the Papal Chancery as established by long custom[2] or by papal regulations,[3] and the interpretation and application of the same by lawyers whose methods were the objective, scientific methods of comparison, criticism and logical deduction, which are common to lawyers of all ages and places, produced by the middle of the thirteenth century a fixed practice, with the main features of which litigants and their notaries and proctors *in partibus* were well acquainted. To understand this procedure aright, it is often necessary

[1] *Supra*, pp. 32 sqq.
[2] Cf. Bonaguida, *Consuetudines curiae Romanae*; the second part (*consuetudines cancellariae*) also *ed.* Teige, *Mitteil. d. Inst. f. österr. Geschichtsforsch.* XVII, 44 sqq.
[3] Cf. Ottenthal, *Die päpstl. Kanzleiregeln.*

to consult the detailed, technical works of renowned canonists such as Hostiensis or Innocent IV; and in their works, encumbered with all the apparatus of legal learning, the system seems immensely involved and even unpractical—almost incapable of application and certainly beyond the understanding of the ordinary litigant or his local agents. But the short, anonymous, untechnical, practical treatises on procedure—'De agendis in partibus ut habeatur canonicatus et prebenda,' 'Modus procedendi auctoritate litterarum apostolicarum', 'Instructiones et diverse forme seu notule super prosecutione gratie' and the like—which exist in considerable numbers in fourteenth- and fifteenth-century manuscripts, show that the technical, disconnected glosses and commentaries of the famous exponents of the canon law were soon reduced to a form in which they were intelligible to the ordinary clerk or legal practitioner, who was involved in litigation either to enforce or to oppose a provision; and it is these works—hitherto singularly ignored[1]—which enable us to say that a well-recognized practice was soon evolved and consistently applied. By editing and comparing them, it is possible to discover what were the basic elements of the procedure actually applied by the courts; and once the broad practical outlines are established in this way, the detailed commentaries of the more renowned canonists provide ample material for filling out the picture, and determining what principles lay at the back of the established practice.

A legal study, executed according to this scheme, provides the essential background in which the history

---

[1]One is printed uncritically by Schmitz-Kallenberg, as an appendix to the *Practica cancellariae apostolicae*; cf. Barraclough, *Public Notaries*, 7 n. 4, 46, 121 n. 6.—Ignorance of the practical legal literature, as opposed to glosses and commentaries, was doubtless one reason that Gross, *Das Recht an der Pfründe*, §§. 64–66, 71, came to the conclusion that the benefice was never in fact treated as an object of civil rights in the courts, but remained throughout under the administrative authority of the bishop; cf. however, *Engl. Hist. Review* XLIX, 214 n. 5, and Briegleb, *loc. cit., supra*, p. 81 n. 1.

of papal provisions must be placed. Knowing not merely the abstract legal principles on which the practice of provision was based, but also the ordinary day-to-day procedure which the delegate courts followed, and were forced under pain of appeal to follow, we have an objective standard, by the light of which the value of the statements of chroniclers and publicists can be judged, and the ambiguity of the documentary material explained. Operated by the mutual activity of two legally opposed parties, regulated by the abstruse relationships between the rights of each, which the thirteenth-century canonists constructed, subject to the complicated balances and counter-balances devised by the subtlety of the law, the system of provisions was by its very nature confined in its practical operation within narrow, well-defined limits. What could be done, what could not be done, was in practice too well-established not to be thoroughly realized and understood by the interested parties. Only the foolhardy would attempt to transgress the rules of procedure: there was—as long as the adversary was vigilant of his rights—nothing to be gained thereby, for the law provided safeguards impartially for both parties, and the litigant who did not respect the law, only jeopardized his legitimate rights and claims. The same was true of the preliminary transactions involved in suing out a rescript. What could be asked, what could not be asked, was known—if not to the individual petitioner, then to the expert proctor in whose hands it was wise to place the conduct of business with the chancery officials.[1] The graduates of Oxford and Cambridge who between 1417 and 1421 regretted the suspension of the *consuetudo approbatissima scribendi*[2]—that is, the practice of sending in *rotuli* to the curia, in which the names of candidates for provision were inscribed—and

---

[1] Cf. R. v. Heckel, *Das Aufkommen d. ständigen Prokuratoren.*
[2] Wilkins, *Concilia* III, 384.

complained to the archbishop of Canterbury of the arbitrary way the ordinary collators disposed of benefices,[1] did so because the curia followed a fixed practice which they understood and appreciated. The bachelor or licentiate who petitioned for a benefice which, according to rule or custom, was obtainable only by a doctor or master, was wasting time and money: the *pauper clericus* who demanded a vacant benefice instead of an *expectatio in forma pauperum* had little reason to hope that the pope would sign his supplication. The detail of this system needs working out, the different gradations and classifications defining and explaining.[2] But there can no longer be any doubt that the whole process of provision by the pope—from the drafting of a petition to the issue of papal letters, from the presentation of the rescript to the commissioner or executor to the final act of collation, or alternatively to appeal, and from the sanctioning of appeal to the conclusion of the suit in the Rota Romana and the execution of the judge's sentence—operated as a settled, regular, duly observed system.

If the practice of provision, above all in the fourteenth century, has been regarded as arbitrary and capricious—without method regarding the persons favoured, without limit or balance regarding the number and value of benefices conferred, without scruple regarding the ordinary collators whose rights were 'prevented'—it is because the system has not been studied *qua* system. It is too often forgotten that even in the most complicated and involved legal transactions the needs of daily practice, the necessity for getting things done, forced men to perfect a practical routine, made rules and immutable customs inevitable, transformed variable practice into rigid system. Knowledge of the day-to-day practice—in

[1] Cf. the archbishop's ordinance on the subject (16 July, 1421), *op. cit.*, III, 401–402.
[2] Thomassin's chapter *De graduatis* (*Vetus et nova eccl. disciplina*, P. II, l. 1, c. 53) is still worth consulting.

other words, of the true system—was mainly taken for granted: statutory enactments and chancery regulations dealt for the most part with exceptional circumstances and abuses of the recognized and accepted system, which needed reform. They throw light on particular aspects of the system; but behind all these isolated points, and connecting them all together, there was a general scheme of administrative and legal procedure, and this it should be our object to lay bare.

Just as in describing the relations of Church and State the historian is too apt—because the contemporary material consists almost solely of the partisan writings of either side—to overstress the points of discord and difference, forgetting that, except at times of unusual stress and storm, the customary spheres of each were in practice clearly recognized by the men of the age, and a working arrangement was very consistently maintained, so in studying a system such as the system of provisions it is too easy to lay stress on outstanding points, to exaggerate the theoretical difference and the theoretical antithesis between the older method of collation by bishop, chapter and patron and the *collatio extraordinaria* by the pope, and particularly to overstress the element of freedom from restraint and even of arbitrariness, wherever and whenever the pope chose to intervene. The large interpretation which theologians and philosophers even more than lawyers put on the easy doctrine of *plenitudo potestatis* and of the superiority of the pope to the law, is too well known. It prejudices our attitude to the business and administrative activity of the papacy, though without doubt it represents much more the logical deduction of theory than the regular standard of practice. Like all bureaucracies, the centralized Church of the fourteenth century was built up on rules and regulations; its strength as well as its weakness was system; its life-breath was order and method. From this point of view, we should do well to forget the theoretical conception of papal rights and powers. Sentences such as :'de aliquo facit nihil et de nihilo aliquid, mutando etiam rei naturam . . . omnia regit, disponit et ordinat et iudicat, prout sibi placet . . . auferendo etiam ius suum, cui vult . . . nam apud eum est pro ratione voluntas, et quod ei placet, legis habet vigorem'[1]—are of little significance from the standpoint of administrative practice. If we could forget them and concentrate on the limitations and regulations which the popes of the thirteenth and fourteenth centuries had the good sense to establish, on the system by which they exercised their power and without which they could never have exercised so wide a power as they came to possess, we should better understand the Church and the papacy of the day.

Historically the doctrinal problem whether or not the pope was theoretically empowered to deprive an individual of his *iura quesita*, whether or not his will was law, is of little significance. The important question is how he regularly acted, and here all the evidence points to system and order. His provisions might disturb *de facto* possession; they did not affect *iura quesita*.[2] There was nothing, perhaps, in theory to prevent the pope overriding well-founded rights; but it has yet to be proved that he normally did so.[3] By

[1]Alvarus Pelagius, *De planctu ecclesie* I, 45 (cf. Haller, *Papstt. u. Kirchenreform*, 85 n. 4).

[2]I.e. if a benefice were 'reserved', and I obtained *de facto* possession on episcopal authority, I should have no answer—except an argument that there was no reservation—to a papal providee, for I had no legitimate title; if, on the other hand, the pope ordered A to provide to me in the church of B, and before I (or A on my behalf) had acted, the canons had elected C and installed him, my letters did not invalidate C's *ius quesitum*.—For an actual case in which it was argued that reservation had not taken effect, cf. *Arch. Vat. Collect.* 495, from which I hope shortly to print selected documents.

[3]Cf. Hostiensis, *Summa* ad tit. *De off. et pot. iud. del.* §. *Quis sit effectus recusationis:* ' . . . Nec dominus papa contra ius alterius scribit; unde appellare potest quilibet a iudice delegato, si sibi preiudicium faciat, quamvis in litteris appellacio sit remota'. When an actual case of the use of the plenitude of power to override legitimate rights appeared, the comments of the glossators were outspoken; cf. Bern. Parm. *gl. ad* c. 4 X 3, 8 *v.* 'De vacaturis': 'Ex hac decretali volunt quidam dicere, quod si papa mandat aliquem recipi in canonicum, et alius recipiatur, quod debet cassari, ut hic fecit Celestinus. . . . Sed hoc fecit Celestinus ex plenitudine potestatis, *et iniuriam fecit illi instituto, quem cassavit*, cum de iure teneret electio, ut hic colligitur'.

exercising his plenitude of power, he could, again, grant an archdeaconry to a mere child; but was this his normal practice? We can point to a certain number of isolated cases, which no modern writer would wish to defend, where important offices were conferred on young boys, papal nephews or members of the nobility; but what it is important to ascertain is the principle behind the provision of the hundreds of thousands of ordinary clerks who approached the pope in years like 1342—who had mostly no influence, of whom the pope knew personally nothing, but to whom he strove to provide *secundum merita sua*. Unless we realize that the question is one of thousands and tens of thousands, not of tens and hundreds, we shall not approach it as it must eventually be approached.

No question arising from the history of provisions is more important, and none more difficult to solve, than the question of numbers. What the historian to-day wishes first and foremost to know is the extent to which the system was used. The effort to achieve a vivid, realistic conception of the situation in the fourteenth century depends for its success on this very issue. The historian would like to know at least the average yearly number of letters of provision granted throughout the fourteenth century: it would help him even more to know the daily average of petitioners. And yet study of the historical sources has shown that this want is impossible of realization. The problem is one which only the registers in the Vatican could solve; and the Vatican registers, we have seen, do not give us a picture of the reality.[1] Moreover, even if a yearly average could be worked out, it would, in some directions at least, be necessarily misleading. The concession of ordinary graces was limited to special occasions, such as the coronation of a pope or the visit of royalty;[2] and on such occasions, which were far from frequent, the number of provisions granted may

---

[1] *Supra*, pp. 26 sqq.   [2] Tihon, *Les expectatives*, 63–64.

well have exceeded that for a whole year in more
normal circumstances. From three independent
sources the fact is reliably attested that between
80,000 and 100,000 petitioners were in the curia during
the period immediately following the coronation of
Clement VI (1342).[1] We can, and must, accept this
remarkable fact; but we must realize that such numbers
were exceptional—indeed, that they probably represent
the very peak of development. A yearly average which
included such figures would not help us to visualize
the historical reality. At the same time, it becomes
clear that, in the fourteenth century, papal provision
was the normal means of access to a benefice; and the
fact is borne home, that the historian who is concerned
with the *system* of provisions, has to think in terms of
thousands and tens of thousands. He must not let his
attention be distracted from the systematic elements by
individual cases and outstanding instances: his concern
is with the system as it affected the ordinary clerk in
ordinary circumstances. A numerical average is
unattainable; but this want can to some extent be made
good, if, in dealing with the legal aspects of the
situation, we keep our attention fixed on the average
man and refuse to be led away to the consideration of
abnormalities. There was a system, and it is with the
thousands and tens of thousands of cases which fit
into the system, not with the hundreds which are
exceptional, that we are primarily concerned. If in a
few isolated cases, the pope used his plenitude of
power to break through the customary limitations of the
system, he was putting to an exceptional use an exceptional right, which no one in that age doubted was his;[2]

[1] Cf. *supra*, p. 31 n. 2.

[2] "Die ganze Papstgeschichte des Mittelalters ist ein unverständliches,
unerklärliches Phänomen, wenn man nicht im Auge behält, dass die Päpste,
auch wo sie sich die weitgehendsten, vor dem Forum historischen Kritik
anfechtbarsten Rechte beilegten, doch nur aussprachen, was zum mindesten
ein grosser Teil ihrer Zeitgenossen schon glaubte . . . Die *plenitudo potestatis*
des römischen Bischofs ist nicht etwa eine unerhörte Anmassung Innocenz'
III., sie ist der Glaube des Jahrhunderts. . . .'; Haller, *op. cit.*, 39–44.

but the occasional use of a theoretically boundless prerogative[1] only served to throw up in greater relief the method and orderliness which were characteristic of the practice of provision as a whole. The methods and system used may not have been those which to modern eyes were best calculated to serve the needs of the Church as a whole;[2] but it was something that where in theory the pope was free to turn his veriest whim into law, in practice he proceeded in ninety-nine cases out of a hundred according to fixed rules and established methods.

This can be said, in spite of the fact that the pope himself, by his signature, personally sanctioned all provisions, except those *in forma communi pauperum*.[3] There is every reason to admire the conscientiousness of a procedure in which—in spite of the safeguards provided by the activities of a series of highly qualified officials[4]—the pope personally took over the final responsibility for each provision, and with it a weighty burden of daily administrative work. But it would be absurd to suppose that, except in theory, each

---

[1]Regarding the limits of the plenitude of power, cf. Hostiensis, *Summa* ad tit. *De fil. presb.*, §. *Quis possit dispensare:* 'Unum tamen non omitto, quod, quamvis papa sine causa dispensare possit de plenitudine potestatis, pro eo quod non habet superiorem in hoc mundo, nec est qui corrigat vel emendet, attamen, cum homo sit, peccare potest, et a dominorum domino et pontificum omnium pontifice, si sine penitentia decesserit, punietur: ideo noverit sibi terribilius iudicium quam aliis inferioribus imminere'.

[2]Cf. the criticism I have made in the *Engl. Hist. Review* XLIX, 215–217.

[3]Cf. Göller, *Rep. Germ.* I, 74*sqq. Provisions *in forma pauperum* were sanctioned directly by the examiners appointed by the pope; Tihon, pp. 71 sqq. —Less important business (broadly speaking *rescripta de simplici iustitia*) did not need the personal sanction of the pope, but was expedited on the authority of the vice-chancellor; cf. Tangl, *Kanzleiordnungen*, Const. IX (re-edited, Barraclough, *Quellen u. Forschungen* XXV, 192–250). For the process by which the pope was gradually relieved of signing even *rescripta de gratia*, cf. v. Hofmann, *Forsch. z. Gesch. d. kurialen Behörden* I, 72 sqq. Throughout the fourteenth century, however, the pope remained personally responsible, and the first really material change was only introduced about the time of Sixtus IV (1471–1484) with the creation of the *Signatura gratiae* and the *Signatura iustitiae*.

[4]Cf. *Cod. lat. Monacen.* 8011 (*Questio disputata per Wilhelmum de Petra Lata*), fo. 102'*b*: 'Item non presumitur, quod littere apostolice contineant falsitatem, cum per tot manus transiverunt, sic quod statim per aliquem eorum potuisset falsitas deprehendi'.

occurrence of the pope's signature represented an exercise of his arbitrary will. In an exceptional case, where an unusual petition was presented, there was room for an exercise of discretion—indeed, of ordinary residuary discretion, such as in England was saddled on the chancellor,[1] and which the pope retained not only in regard to provisions and other *littere gratiales*, but also in regard to ordinary letters of justice.[2] But such circumstances rarely arose. Where the petition belonged to a normal class—and the form of petitions had become practically stereotyped by the middle of the thirteenth century[3]—the pope himself, aided no doubt by his 'referendaries',[4] proceeded according to well-established rules and standards. He was clearly accustomed to sanction letters of an ordinary type without difficulty.[5] But when an unusual clause was asked for, when a special privilege, an incidental dispensation or certain *non obstantia* were desired, substantial grounds for specially favoured treatment had to be put forward. Even in the twelfth century before the construction of formulae and clauses had reached mature development, Stephen of Tournai complained of the difficulty in obtaining the insertion of the clause *remota appellatione*,[6] and frequent remarks

[1] Cf. Maitland, *Equity*, 3.
[2] Cf. *Kanzleiordnungen*, Const. IX, §. 87: 'item in premissa generalitate litterarum, que iustitiam continent, hoc servetur, ut, si quando emergat seu occurrat forma, que non contineatur inter supra expensas, legatur domino nostro forma que occurrit, ut ipse mandet, quod velit in litteris eiusdem forme servari . . .'
[3] Barraclough, *Formulare f. päpstl. Suppliken.*
[4] On these officials, cf. Göller, *Rep. Germ.* I, 71*sqq., v. Hofmann, *loc. cit.*, and Barraclough, *Public Notaries*, 35 (with references to more recent literature).
[5] So much is already implied in c. 20 X 1, 3 (1208); cf. *gl. ad v.* 'In forma communi', 'In utroque casu'.
[6] *Ep.* 50: ' . . . in petitionibus nostris, que nec multe nec magne domino pape offeruntur, difficiles expertus sum tam eos, qui petitoria porrigunt, quam eos, qui admittere debuissent communes litteras illas, quas "de iustitia" appellant, in quibus Grecus et Latinus et Barbarus et Scytha adiectionem "remota appellatione" sese consequi gratulantur—nos, qui speciales filii Romane ecclesie dicimur, non potuimus obtinere. O modica adiectio "remota appellatione", quam speciosa facta es, que sic es difficilis filiis, sic facilis alienis!'—The tendentious side of these remarks can well be ignored.

of thirteenth-century canonists show that it was not regarded as easy to get special consideration in any direction.[1]

'Papalis littera cum magna maturitate conceditur.'[2] Solid reasons for special privileges and concessions were demanded; but the ordinary grounds on which preference could reasonably be claimed and was regularly conceded were clearly a matter of common knowledge. Academic rank and grades clearly carried weight; long service and administrative distinction carried weight; the recommendation of well-known ecclesiastics and of secular princes carried weight. Any of these factors would act as an inducement to the pope to grant letters containing some particular privilege. On the other hand, the clauses and types of letter were themselves classified. It was easier to obtain a general provision *in civitate vel diocesi* than a special one, even in a small chapel.[3] It was easier to obtain dispensation from the taint of illegitimacy where the father was an unmarried layman, than where he was a clerk in minor orders.[4]

These are isolated instances which tell us little. Before we can begin to understand the system of provisions, as it operated in the fourteenth century, the whole scheme of regulations and gradations, of which they were a part, needs careful investigation. It is not sufficient to know that a clerk with a university degree received more effective letters than one without, that a master had a claim to preferential treatment as compared with a bachelor: we must try to determine as

[1] E.g. Hostien., *Summa* ad tit. *De preb.*, §. *Cui sit conferenda:* ' . . . nisi a papa obtineret dispensationis gratiam, quod tamen non est facile'.

[2] *Quaestiones Bononienses* fo. 103a.

[3] Bonaguida, *Consuet. cancellarie*, no. 14.

[4] Cf. *Reg. Vat.* 26 (*Urbani IV, a.* 1), fo. 28, n. 115: 'Nam cum idem abbas fuerit genitus de clerico constituto in minoribus ordinibus et soluta, hoc suppresso, suggessit eidem Innocentio, quod de soluto fuerat genitus et soluta, ut dispensationem facilius obtineret'.—For further distinctions on questions of illegitimacy, cf. *Cod. Ottob. lat.* 747, fo. 26'.

precisely as possible what particular preference each class of petitioner could demand, what particular qualifications each special clause or each particular letter-type implied.

CHAPTER IX

MODERN STUDY of the Papal Chancery in the later Middle Ages, from the days of Innocent III onwards, has been concentrated above all on the business side of the organization. Its results, as summed up, for example, in GÖLLER'S valuable introduction to the *Repertorium Germanicum* for the pontificate of Clement VII (1378–1394),[1] enable us to depict the routine to which a petitioner had to submit in suing out letters of provision. We can see that little scope was left for the initiative of the petitioner himself,[2] that each petition underwent the same fixed operations, was subject to the same automatic controls: 'et aliter transire non sinuntur, et per multas manus transeunt, et quasi per ignem et aquam currunt ad refrigerium, et ad magnam maturitatem decoquuntur'.[3] But this was only one side of the business. It is important to see how, and under what conditions and safeguards, a rescript was obtained; but it is more important to understand the meaning of the rescript and the principles on which it was granted. As yet this side of papal diplomatic—in which legal principles and administrative practice interworked and the rules by which the system was operated sprang less from orderly business routine than from positive legal stipulations—has received scant attention;[4] yet from the point of view of pro-

---

[1] Part II; 'Die Grundlagen d. päpstl. Benefizialwesens u. die Praxis d. Stellenbesetzung z. Zeit d. grossen Schismas', pp. 43*–98*.

[2] In this connexion, cf. v. Heckel, *Beiträge z. Kenntnis d. Geschäftsgangs d. päpstl. Kanzlei.*

[3] Bonaguida de Aretio, *Summa Introductoria*, 332; cf. Hostiensis, *Summa* ad tit. *De rescr.*, §. *Que possint obici contra rescriptum:* ' . . . rescriptum pluries scribitur, per plures manus transit, moderatur, magna maturitate decoquitur, magnoque libramine ponderatur.'

[4] Lux's remarks, *Die Besetzung d. Benefizien*, 34–48 (§. 3: 'Aussere Form u. Interpretation d. Benefizialreskripte') are of small value, since he has not consulted the mediaeval legal authorities. Göller, *Rep. Germ.* I, 60*–64*, 89*–91*, hardly does more than suggest the broad outlines of the problems awaiting solution. Cf. further Lang, *Acta Salzburgo-Aquilejensia* I, xxiii sqq., lviii–lix, lxviii sqq.; Jackowski, *Die päpstl. Kanzleiregeln*; Göller, *Zur Gesch. d. kirchl. Benefizialwesens.*

visions, it is of inestimable importance. In this place we cannot investigate any of the problems in detail; but it is perhaps worth while to suggest some lines of investigation which would throw light on the operation of the system of provisions, and indeed on the legal and administrative operation of the canonical 'rescript-procedure' as a whole, in the centralized Church of the thirteenth and fourteenth centuries.[1]

From this point of view, primary importance attaches to the classification and interpretation of the different forms in which letters of provision were issued, and of the various clauses which these letters contained. Many different types of letter are known: common forms and special forms, *forme gratiose* and *forme commissorie*, expectations and direct conferments of *beneficia reservata*, letters issued *ex certa scientia* or *motu proprio*. From an historical standpoint, it is important to try to gain some impression of their relative numerical proportion.[2] How often were letters granted *motu proprio*? What was the relative proportion, in the fourteenth century, between direct conferments of reserved benefices and *mandata de providendo*, either in special or in common form? From a legal standpoint, it is important to distinguish precisely and categorically between the different forms. In the first place, we must determine what were the characteristic clauses of the different letter-types; in the second place, we must discover under what conditions, in what circumstances, to what class of petitioner, the different forms of provision were granted.

The first step in the detailed study of the papal rescripts themselves is the tracing of their historical development and the gradual emergence of fixed forms—a process which was practically completed

[1] Cf. for the moment the brief but suggestive remarks of v. Heckel, *Das Aufkommen d. ständ. Prokuratoren*, §. 2 ('Das neuere päpstl. Briefwesen').
[2] Cf. *supra*, pp. 26–28.

during the thirteenth century.[1] With the help of the documentary material the precise period at which each different clause made its appearance, can be determined; with the help of the contemporary legal material, the object of the new clauses and their significance can then be discovered. The next step is to discover in what circumstances the different clauses were employed; and here the customs and regulations of the papal Chancery offer ample material for incisive results. On what grounds could a petitioner claim exceptional advantages, special clauses, a differentiation in short from the basic *forma communis*? On what grounds did the pope sanction such demands for preferential treatment? Taking the two lines of investigation together, we can discover not only the principles on which different classes of letters were conferred, or particular clauses inserted, but the advantages which the petitioner hoped to gain thereby; and a careful analysis of the documentary material should indicate as well the frequency of special types of letter, and thus help us to determine with what degree of regularity, in what circumstances, and with what effect, the ordinary legal procedure for the judicial discharge of the terms of the papal rescript was in practice modified by the operation of special clauses, such as *remota appellatione* or *denuntiantes irritum et inane*.

This question is, in one sense, the crux of the whole problem. The legal position in regard to provisions in common form is reasonably clear, and the brief remarks which have been made above,[2] are in themselves probably sufficient to indicate that the judicial procedure in the execution of such provisions was so fashioned that, as a method of disposing of benefices, it was as innocuous as the older method of disposal by the ordinary collator. Every safeguard against

[1] Cf. Fierens, *Ons Prebendenwezen*, 823, 846; Barraclough, *Archiv f. kath. Kirchenrecht*.
[2] Cap. VII.

I

dishonesty on the part of the impetrant, or against the accidental use of the papal power to the manifest disadvantage of the Church as a whole, was supplied.[1] But the papal registers themselves are an indisputable witness to the frequency of letters in special form, in which exceptional clauses were incorporated—clauses by which the defences which could ordinarily be raised against a rescript of provision might be limited or in some cases even nullified. Thus it is essential to know how frequently such clauses were employed, on what grounds they were employed, and what effects they had.

Were letters of provision ever so drafted that the commissioner appointed was deprived of judicial functions and acted simply as executor of an administrative order, *merus executor*? And if such letters were issued, in what circumstances was their use regarded as justified? It is obvious, for example, that a definitive provision, after an appeal to the central courts from an earlier provision, might (like any other sentence) reasonably be given *executio parata*. Similarly, where letters of provision had been contumaciously ignored and the providee could get no legal response from the collator to whom the original writ was directed, or from the person in *de facto* possession of the benefice, there was ground for commissioning an executor simply to secure obedience, and not to try the case on its merits.[2] But were such legally justifiable cases the only ones in which judicial cognizance—the fundamental safeguard for the rights involved—was dispensed with? What was the legal position when the pope provided *ex certa scientia*, and when did he provide *ex certa scientia*? What again was the situation in regard

---

[1]Cf. c. 17 X 1, 3: 'cum adeo scripta sedis apostolice moderemur, ut ex certa scientia nihil in eis faciamus apponi, quod de iure debeat reprehendi, miramur non modicum et movemur, quod, quotiens ad te vel ad aliquos tibi subiectos nostras litteras destinamus, te super eis mirari rescribis, ac si mandaremus aliquid inhonestum.'

[2]Cf. in this connexion, Barraclough, *Public Notaries*, 81 sqq.

to 'reserved' benefices, which the pope alone could legitimately confer? They formed a class apart; for in this case the providee obtained an immediate *ius in re*, instead of the mere *officium iudicis ad petendum beneficium secundum tenorem litterarum pape*.[1] But for the very reason that the public law of the Church stipulated *maturitas etatis, morum honestas* and *scientia litterarum* on the part of all beneficed clergy, and a defect in any of these matters was adequate ground for rejection *ab obtento* as well as *ab obtinendo*,[2] even the pope's disposal of 'reserved' benefices was not a simple matter of administration, but could be met by legal exceptions against the person of the providee; and an equally valid and legitimate defence was to show that the 'reservation' itself was legally null.[3]

At the same time, the providee who was invested immediately by the pope, had important advantages. If the benefice to which he was provided was 'reserved', he could not be 'prevented' at any time by an episcopal nominee, for the bishop had no right to confer 'reserved' benefices and could not give his nominee even a colourable title; and even if the benefice in question was merely vacant without actually being reserved to the disposition of the Holy See, the papal providee could not be 'prevented' by an investiture,

---

[1] Cf. Innoc. IV. *ad* c. 39 X 1, 3 *v*. 'Monitorias': 'nam nec ex monitoriis nec ex preceptoriis nec executoriis [litteris habet ius ad prebendam], sed habet officium iudicis ad petendum beneficium secundum tenorem litterarum pape. Si autem papa contulisset, tunc haberet ius in re'.

[2] Cf. *supra*, p. 96 n. 6.

[3] E.g. if the pope conferred on A the church of B as vacant and reserved by the death of C, an *auditor* of the Rota, in accordance with the tenor of c. 2 in VI° 3, 4 (or later of c. 13 *in Extrav. commun.* 3, 2), and it was shown that the proprietary rights in the church were vested in D, C having merely detained it *de facto* without title: in this case A, although invested by the pope himself, had no right to dispossess D (supposing that D had taken actual possession on the cessation of C's occupation)—indeed, he had no right of any sort in the church of B, for the pope had conferred it, not absolutely, but as vacant and reserved *per mortem* C, and this it was not.—But D, of course, would have to prove his rights in court, and have them approved by sentence, before A's claim was disposed of.

episcopal or other, subsequent to his own.[1] Certain exceptions he might well still have to face; but in comparison with the petitioner who received a provision in common form, and who had to undertake lengthy judicial proceedings before he obtained not a full but merely a partial proprietary right, he found himself in a favourable position.

Such distinctions, created by clauses which were the subject of meticulous interpretation and definition by the canonists of the day,[2] were the stuff out of which the finely graded and carefully balanced system of provisions was built up. Through a clear understanding of the precise legal meaning and operation of each separate clause, and of the circumstances in which each

[1] On this subject Roffredus' careful distinctions, although he was writing (c. 1240–1245) before the promulgation of the first general Reservation, are of sufficient interest to be quoted at length. Cf. *Opus libellorum*, tit. *De preb.*, §. *Quando prebenda sit conferenda*: 'Item queritur: pone quod papa concedit alicui prebendam vacantem, postea concedit prelatus, vel econverso, sicut sepe de facto vidi contingere in curia. Nam multi habent beneficia vel prebendas in Anglia, qui sunt in curia. Moritur aliquis illorum, statim dominus papa confert. Postea prelatus, in cuius dyocesi habebat ille prebendam, audita morte eius, similiter confert: cuius collatio valet? Respondeo, tenet collatio illius, qui primo contulit. Si primo dominus papa contulit, illius collatio tenet; si primo contulit episcopus, collatio episcopi potior est, et sic qui prior tempore, potior est iure. . . . Sed queritur: ecce dominus papa contulit hodie prebendam Titio. Titius fuit piger; non misit illi prelato litteras, qui debebat conferre, in cuius diocesi erat prebenda. Prelatus ille, ignorans domini pape concessionem, contulit alii: quis erit potior? Respondeo, ille cui dominus papa contulit, sicut dixi superius. Item queritur, sicut vidi de facto in questione magistri Guidonis de Palerno, amici mei: dominus papa, mortuo magistro Palermo, capellano suo, conferri mandavit prebendam, quam habebat predictus capellanus in ecclesia Salernitana, filio magistri Guidonis. Magister Guido fuit negligens, nec misit cito litteras de concessione facta a papa, sed litteras tales misit archiepiscopo, viz. quod dictus archi episcopus Salernitanus illi prebendam conferret, amoto quolibet illicito detentore. Archiepiscopus vero primo contulit, antequam mandatum apostolicum ad ipsum perveniret: quis erit potior? Respondeo ad hoc, dico illum, cui archiepiscopus contulit. Dominus enim papa non contulit sed mandavit conferendam; unde ex rescripto non habet accionem, licet habeat impetrandi facultatem, ut ff. *De rel. et sump. fun.* [D. 11. 7], l. *Si quis sepulchrum* [12]. Sed nunquid propter illamclausulam: "amoto quolibet illicito *etc.*",poterit ab illo prebendam avocare, cui legitime per archiepiscopum est collata? Respondeo, non; nam non est illicitus ille detentor, cui legitime collata fuit, cum iuste possideat, qui auctore pretore possidet, ut ff. *De acquir. possess.* [D. 41. 2], l. *Iuste* [11]'.

[2] Cf. the interpretation of the clause *amoto quolibet illicito detentore* in the previous note.

was employed, the biggest step towards a real understanding of the system can be achieved. To this end, however, the study of the actual formulae of letters of provision—not merely in the Papal Registers, but above all in the great formularies employed in the Chancery itself[1]—together with their interpretation in the glosses and commentaries of the canon lawyers, is not sufficient. It must be supplemented by a thorough analytical and historical study of the thirteenth-century customs and fourteenth-century regulations of the papal chancery.

The chancery regulations supplied the most directly operative check on the petitioner in the public interest. Thus the *regula de idiomate beneficiatorum*[2] was designed to prevent clerks obtaining a benefice with cure of souls, if they could not speak the language of the parishioners; and from the time of its promulgation the chancery officials regularly inserted a clause to this effect in provisions to *beneficia curata*.[3] No special mention was necessary to secure inclusion of this clause: it was inserted as a matter of routine, in pursuance of the terms of the regulation, and the only way to get it omitted was to obtain explicit papal sanction to a request for its omission. In this way the chancery regulations acted as a constant check, in the public interest, on the extent of the benefits conferred by papal letters, and it was impossible to obtain any unusual advantage unless the pope specifically acknowledged it by his signature. Here again, moreover, by setting a close interpretation on the intentions

---

[1] On these, cf. in summary Barraclough, *Public Notaries*, 9–11. They are important because they offer examples of all the manifold letter-forms in use: in the Registers, on the other hand, certain important classes of rescript were regularly omitted (cf. *supra*, p. 27–28).

[2] Cf. Nelis, *L'application en Belgique de la règle de chancellerie apostolique: de idiomate beneficiatorum*. Gomes' commentary (fo. 101 sqq.) is also still well worth consideration.

[3] E.g. Rieder, *Röm. Quellen*, no. 1865: ' . . . dummodo ipse Iohannes de provincia, in qua ecclesia in Hiltzingen consistit, vel de alia provincia prefate provincie contigua oriundus existat, et intelligat ydioma, quod parrochiani eiusdem ecclesie loquuntur'.

of the pope, the chancery regulations supplied a salutary limitation. A cursory glance through the regulations of Pope John XXII—the first regulations in a long unbroken series—shows that the papal 'Fiat' in no wise implied the absolute sanctioning of the unrestricted demands of the petitioner.[1] The pope's signature was interpreted restrictively, and a petitioner who desired sanction for wider benefits than those normally granted, had to put each particular claim explicitly before the pope, and could only hope for ratification by convincing him that his claims were supported by substantial qualifications.

There is thus no ground for characterizing the system of provisions, as administered in the fourteenth-century curia, as capricious, erratic, inequitable or unsystematic. The chancery regulations—regulations which really affected points of substantive law, and were in no wise concerned with the detail of chancery procedure[2]—kept it, at every stage, within well-defined limits; and the only means of overstepping these limits was to acquire the explicit consent of the pope himself to special, individual demands. In these circumstances the personal character of each individual pontiff was doubtless of some importance. Some popes, like Benedict XII or Innocent VI were very cautious in their use of provisions and suspicious in their attitude towards petitioners; others, like Clement VI, were noted for liberality and for their accommodating disposition.[3] But there was at no time any possibility

---

[1] E.g. §. 10: 'Item si quis secularis supplicet pro uno vel duobus aut tribus vel pluribus beneficiis usque ad certam summam, nunquam per simplicem responsionem 'Fiat B' intelligitur dominum nostrum fecisse gratiam nisi de uno dumtaxat, nisi de manu propria de pluribus declararet'. Similarly *Reg. Innoc. VI*, §2: 'Item quod in ecclesiis ubi sunt maiores et minores prebende quantumcumque petatur maior, non detur per simplex 'Fiat', nisi de manu pape concedatur expresse, sed de stilo cancellarie detur minor prebenda, quamvis petita non fuerit per eundem'.—Cf. more generally, v. Hofmann I, 41 sqq.

[2] Cf. Ottenthal, pp. vi–vii: Chancery procedure, on the other hand, was governed by the Chancery Ordinances.

[3] The remarks of the chroniclers in this connexion are usefully summarized by Rieder, p. xxxvi.

of the purely personal standpoint or disposition of the pope becoming the decisively important factor. Beyond and above the free use of papal discretion, there was the permanent, objective expression of papal will and policy, as expounded in the chancery regulations—regulations which existed and developed as an organic whole, and on which the personal inclination or disposition of any particular pope had (as far as I can at present determine) little or no effect. Despite the outstanding personal differences in character between the popes of Avignon, the regulations drawn up by John XXII (1316–1334) continued in use with no modification and but few additions under Benedict XII (1334–1342), Clement VI (1342–1352), and Innocent VI (1352–1362). Urban V (1362–1370), on the other hand, added considerably to the collection; but even Gregory XI (1370–1378), who reviewed the previous regulations and issued a revised version under his own name, remained under weighty obligation to, and acted in strict dependence on, the enactments of John XXII, and his more immediate predecessors. In these circumstances the permanent, organic elements in the system were of more importance than the varying character of successive pontificates: as in all bureaucracies, the element of continuity, the acceptance of established rules and methods, the continuance of old traditions, was more powerful and more determinative a factor than the transient, temporary influence of changing personalities and policies.

CHAPTER X

WHEN WE UNDERSTAND not only the precise legal operation of provisions, but also the fixed and accepted administrative tradition (already deeply rooted before the fourteenth century began), which permeated the centralized bureaucracy in which the system was formulated, then—and then alone—will it be possible to gauge and to explain the effect, for good or for evil, of the system of provisions on the Church as a whole in the later Middle Ages. But this method of approach can only be fruitful, if we make one assumption: the assumption that the disposal of benefices by the pope was in itself in every way as capable of meeting the needs of the Church as the disposal of benefices by bishop, chapter or patron. In the Middle Ages, as now, it was possible to carry out any act of administration either through a centralized organization and by centralized machinery, or through local agents by means of a localized administrative organization. If the historian is prepared to condemn any particular institution of government for the sole reason that it is, or was, 'centralized' in character, then no defence can be put up either for the system of papal provisions or for the centralized papal administration of the Church as a whole from the days of Innocent III till the Council of Trent. But such an historical attitude savours more of the age of 'philosophical historians' than of the twentieth century. What historian to-day is prepared—even in regard to the Church—to base his arguments and theories on the presupposition that one form of government, be it stark centralization or be it federalism, must in all times and under all circumstances be wrong, can only have evil results, is worthy only of condemnation? It is no part of our plan to discuss the ultimate object of historical writing. But if we wish to approach the history of the Church in the later Middle Ages with open mind, we must do so on the assumption that both a centralized and a localized system of government had its weaknesses and its advantages, and that neither can be condemned out of hand for no other reason than its inherent tendency to one form or the other of governmental activity. Thus, as GERSON recognized no later than the beginning of the fifteenth century, the point of cardinal importance in regard to papal provisions, as in regard to so much else in the mediæval Church, was not whether the bishops or the pope should have the power of conferring ecclesiastical benefices, but in what spirit, on what principles their conferment was carried out.[1]

For this reason it is of the utmost importance to understand beyond all possibility of controversy the legal procedure and administrative methods by which the power of papal provision was put into practice. Papal provisions were one method of conferring benefices, episcopal collation was another: that the one was necessarily, fundamentally, inherently better than the other is a possibility which the philosopher or the student of political theory might be prepared to decide, but which the historian can only approach by an empirical inquiry into the actual historical working of each. For him they exist, in the first place, simply as alternatives: it is by studying the operation, and after the operation the effects of each—and in this way alone —that he can attempt to decide the question whether the influence exerted by the one on the character of the Church was good or was bad, whether the practical supersession of the older method of disposal by the system of papal provision was one of the factors which led to disorders in, and subsequently to the decline of, the Church. Like most other methods of administra-

[1] The passage is cited by Haller *Papstt. u. Kirchenreform*, 13.

tion, the system of provisions was capable of functioning well or of functioning badly. What in some circumstances was bound to lead to abuse, was equally likely in other circumstances to work as an instrument of order and good government. The question which faces the historian is how it did actually work; and to this end no line of investigation offers more definite and objective results than the study of the system of provisions *qua* system.

Even then another question forces itself forward for consideration: the question whether the gradual supersession of the ordinary methods of collation by papal provisions was at that time and in those circumstances to all practical purposes inevitable. Walter Mapes' well-known remark to Glanvil in discussing the difference between the justice and expeditiousness of English temporal and spiritual courts in the days of Henry II—'if the king were as far from you as the pope is from the bishops, I think you would be equally slow'[1]—goes far to explain the centralization of Church institutions which was taking place at that very date. The English Crown may have been ahead of the Roman See in developing its machinery of centralized government; but centralization was as necessary to the Church of that day as it was to the realms of England or of France—as necessary and as natural a development. The constitutional development of the Church in the twelfth and thirteenth centuries would be much better understood, were it treated by comparative methods as a parallel movement to the growth of centralized power in France or England, and indeed more closely parallel to the former than to the latter. The Empire, where the central authority always remained weak, represented one end of the scale: the Church represented the other.

[1] *De nugis curialium*, 241: '"Certe nos hic longe velocius causas decidimus quam in ecclesiis episcopi vestri." Tum ego: "verum est; sed si rex noster tam remotus esset a vobis, quam ab episcopis est papa, vos eque lente crederem". Ipse vero risit'.

Among the popes of the thirteenth century, though there was a Celestine V, there was no John; though there was determined constitutional opposition to Boniface VIII, there was no Magna Carta. The centralizing movement which ran throughout thirteenth-century Europe—a movement which deserves independent treatment as a whole, apart from national bounds and national associations[1]—was nowhere more successful than in the Church. But its very success, the rapid uniform development which it underwent, makes it difficult to judge it aright, and particularly difficult to view the early, formative period without seeing it in the light of later developments which, inevitable as they may appear in the broad outlines of mediæval history, were not inevitable in the parallel growth of central authority in England, and which men in the age of Alexander III or Innocent III could not foresee. Walter Mapes' remark to Glanvil shows that there were real reasons for the transference of the bulk of litigation from the 'ordinary' to the 'delegate' courts[2]—reasons which in England, in different but parallel circumstances, led to the institution of the 'eyre', and to a rapid extension in the use of the king's writ, which was paralleled in the Church by the similar extension which Alexander III gave to the use of the papal rescript. But whereas in England the use of the king's writ was checked, in one direction, by the clause of Magna Carta directed against the *Praecipe*,[3] in another by the inability (which the growing parliament jealously maintained) to create new forms to meet new cases,[4] the pope was free to invent new

[1] Petit-Dutaillis, *La monarchie féodale en France et en Angleterre*, and Mayer *Deutsche u. französische Verfassungsgeschichte* cover part of the ground; but a more comprehensive study of the whole European development, including that in the Church, is needed.

[2] This question has been dealt with in some detail by Maitland, *Canon Law*, 103 sqq., and need not detain us here.

[3] §.34: to what degree this clause was effective is another question, which does not however affect our argument.

[4] This disability was in no wise removed by 13 Ed. I., c. 24 (Stat. of Westminster II, 1285); cf. Maitland, *Forms of Action*, 300, 345.

rescripts at will, and met no vested opposition from the bishops regarding the rapidly extending jurisdiction conferred on delegate judges. Thus the centralized judicial machinery in the Church developed and expanded, practically without check, over an exceptionally wide range, and possibly grew to such an extent that, at the end of the Middle Ages, its disadvantages were more manifest than its advantages.[1] But we must not judge the twelfth-century history of the delegate courts in the light of fourteenth- or fifteenth-century evidence. The development may, for constitutional reasons, eventually have gone too far; but there was no inherent reason that it should not be held within moderate limits, that a balance should not have been maintained between the local jurisdiction of the bishops and the centralized jurisdiction conferred on delegate justices. In the earlier period, at any rate, there were as many and as potent grounds for an increased centralization of justice in the Church as in the secular states of Europe where parallel tendencies obtained.[2]

Much the same can be said of the development of papal provisions. *Abusus non tollit usum.* What, in the days of Boniface IX, might lead to excesses and disorders, was equally capable, at another time, of serving as a means of betterment.[3] I would not argue, and can see no evidence, that provisions were consciously devised (in the early, formative period of their history) as a means of reform, that the object of papal intervention was to check abuses in the disposal of benefices by the ordinary collators,[4] even though

[1]'Usurpation we see wherever we turn . . .' 'What we shall look for and what we shall not find is any formula, or even any well-directed effort to construct a formula, for the delimitation of those causes which, since some federal interest is involved in them, ought to come before a federal court'. Maitland, *Canon Law*, 103, 120.

[2]Cf. also Maitland, *op. cit.*, 120-122.

[3]Cf. Haller, p. 160.

[4]This view has been tentatively suggested by Mollat, *Collation des bénéfices,* 43, 44, 324, *Jean XXII*, 529, is, however, a product of his apologetic tendencies.

practically all the abuses ascribed to provisions at the end of the fourteenth century in the famous *Speculum aureum de titulis beneficiorum*, for example, can be paralleled in similar descriptions of ordinary collation at the end of the twelfth century.[1] But if we ask ourselves how this extraordinary change in the method of bestowing benefices took place—a change which gave the papacy control of thousands of livings every year—we shall not approach within sight of the truth if, with our eyes on the acts of Clement V or Boniface IX, we see in it nothing but illegal encroachment and violent usurpation.[2] It is too easy to take our stand at the turning-point in the pontificate of Innocent III, and to point to the revolution in Church government which appears before our eyes as we look first backwards, then forwards. At the beginning of one century, the bestowal of benefices was still uniformly in the hands of the local ecclesiastical authorities; at the beginning of the next, it had been gathered together into the hands of the supreme pontiff.[3] Within three or four generations the constitutional position was entirely reversed. And yet it was reversed without constitutional struggles, open hostility or violent resistance from vested interests at the very time when the same constitutional issue between the central and local power in secular government was destroying the peace of Europe. It is scarcely possible to discover the faintest murmur of discontent with the use to which papal authority over Church benefices was being put, before the English complaints in the days of Gregory IX and Innocent IV.[4] But if the extension of papal administrative activity to the disposal of benefices had been nothing but encroachment and usurpation, would it have been met in so passive a way? If there had been a veritable revolution, a sudden

[1] Cf. for example Giraldus Cambrensis, *Gemma ecclesiastica*, 293–304, 334–339.
[2] Cf. Haller, p. 39.　　　　[3] Cf. *loc. cit.*, *supra*, p. 10 n. 1.
[4] Cf. Baier, capp. IX and X; *supra*, pp. 10–11.

upheaval in Church government, would the opposition, with its ancient canonically recognized rights, have given way without a struggle, or still less a protest? There are many questions which must be asked and answered before the growth of papal provisions and reservations, from the middle of the twelfth century onwards, becomes intelligible. A mere description of expansion does not explain the causes of development. The statement that the papacy began to intervene in the bestowal of minor benefices, tells us nothing of the reasons which led to direct papal action. More interesting, in short, than the facts, are the motives, grounds, influences, principles, ideas, which produced the facts. Such questions are worthy of brief discussion.

The common answer to these less immediate questions is expressed in the one word: Policy. We survey the Church at the beginning of the twelfth century and we find that it is characterized by institutional arrangements which are broadly-speaking federal. We find, above all, that the bishopric is for most purposes a self-governing unit, and that the bishops take a very active and reasonably independent part in Church government. We survey the Church at the beginning of the fourteenth century, and we find that it is a highly centralized organization, that the pope 'is not merely the supreme but the sole ruler of the Church, the prelates are no longer his vassals but his servants'.[1] What has caused this change? The answer that is given is: Policy. For two centuries a centralizing policy has been pursued. The popes have sought to depress the influence of the bishops. First the action of legates from Rome, then the grant of exemption, the *visitatio liminum sanctorum apostolorum*, the limitation of episcopal powers of dispensation, the growth of appeal judicial and extra-judicial direct to Rome, the formulation of papal legislation, the creation of a

[1]Haller, pp. 25–6.

system of taxation for the Church as a whole, and finally provisions—all are regarded as part of a conscious anti-episcopal policy.

Provisions thus fall into line with parallel developments in all spheres of ecclesiastical administration. Clement IV's basic reservation *Licet ecclesiarum* appears as the first general denial of the bishops' right to dispose freely of the benefices in their dioceses. And yet if we turn to the contemporary authorities, we find an entirely different point of view. Duranti (followed by Johannes Andreae)[1] regarded the constitution *Licet ecclesiarum* simply as a remedy for abuse. 'Ante constitutionem Clementis', he wrote, 'prelati habebant suos procuratores in curia, qui quamcito contingebat vacare aliquod beneficium ad eorum collationem spectans, illud conferebant, et sepe dominum papam in conferendo preveniebant, et sibi illudebant, propter quod ipse dominus Clemens motus fuit ad promulgandum constitutionem illam *Licet*'.[2] Exactly parallel was the position in regard to the devolution of the right of election to bishoprics. Compostellanus tells how, more than once in his day, the question was raised of conferring this right, in case of devolution, on the metropolitans; 'sed finaliter deliberatio in contrarium resedit . . . et fuit ratio, quia prompti essent archiepiscopi in cassandis electionibus, ut provisionum potestas rediret ad eos'.[3] So also Peter of Blois urged the restriction of the administrative powers of the bishops, the insistence on the observance of legal procedure in their relations with their subordinates, 'ne detur episcopis occasio malignandi et auferendi subditis suis ecclesias vel prebendas legitime vel canonice collatas';[4] and in the same way Bernard of Parma noted that the right to permit the holding of two or more

---

[1]c.3 in VI° 3, 4 *gl. ad v.* 'Per seipsos'.
[2]The text is printed, with an excellent commentary, by Göller, *Zur Gesch. d. 2. Lyoner Konzils*, 85.
[3]I have printed the passage in question, *The Making of a Bishop*, 292.
[4]*Supra*, p. 87 n. 1.

cures of souls was taken away from the bishops 'on account of their indiscreet and stupid dispensations'.[1]

Unless we are determined to convict these writers either of deceiving or of being deceived, it will be well to reconsider the conception of the thirteenth and fourteenth centuries—as far as internal Church history is concerned—as a period devoted to the carrying out of a conscious anti-episcopal policy. It is easy to judge by results; and in the same way it is easier, looking back on the past, to discern a continuous scheme of high policy, than it was for contemporaries to perceive the trend of events which they were helping to create. If we consider each act of what appears to be anti-episcopal policy separately, we are bound to admit that their nature is more that of independent measures *against* specific abuses, than of co-ordinated efforts to carry out any preconceived policy. It is curious how the conception of continuous policy dominates mediæval ecclesiastical history. In studies of the political aspects of Church history from the days of Gregory VII onwards, there is the same tendency to regard the feudal monarchs of Europe as merely upholding, in a conservative way, what they regard as the long-standing customs of their realms, against an aggressive papacy. On the secular side, there is a determination to maintain the old law: on the papal side, an endeavour to put through a radical policy, which is sometimes not altogether without reason summed up as Ultramontanism.[2] But this conception is not beyond criticism. In the first place the royal attitude, even if conservative, was progressive. In England, for example, there was marked development of the royal position from William the Conqueror to

---

[1] c. 28 X 3,5 *gl. ad v.* 'Per.sedem apostolicam': 'Olim enim per antiqua iura bene dispensabant episcopi, ut aliquis haberet plura beneficia curam animarum habentia. Sed illud hodie recipit immutationem per hanc constitutionem; et hoc mutatum fuit propter indiscretas et stultas dispensationes episcoporum'.

[2] Cf. Brooke, *The English Church and the Papacy.*

Henry I, from Henry I to Henry II. On the other hand, what of the popes? Was Hildebrand[1] the conscious innovator of a new radical policy, or was he setting out to restore what he regarded as the ancient law and order of the Church? 'Wiederherstellung des Rechtes —das ist der Titel, unter dem sich alle Revolutionen vollziehen'.[2] But restoration of the old order of things though in course of time it may proceed in a definite direction, is not the same as a conscious policy towards a definite object. Reform of abuse, where abuse was evident, was an obvious course for a man like Hildebrand; it was, indeed, his pontifical duty. But it does not follow that he—or any of his successors—was acting in accordance with any definite scheme of high policy, because the concrete actions taken by him are susceptible of a particular explanation. In short, it is dangerous to insinuate that the motives of the popes were any different from the motives of the kings and princes who opposed them. We shall be nearer the truth if we suppose that they, like the secular potentates had a definite conception of what was customary and accepted and therefore right, and that their actions were very simply and very naturally directed towards applying this conception in concrete cases. That there should be a marked discrepancy, not only between the papal and the secular standpoint, but also between the papal standpoint and that of a large section of the clergy, was not a question of principle, but simply the result of a different view of what constituted ancient law and custom, what merely long-standing but none the less insufferable abuse.

[1] There is, it will be readily admitted, good reason to regard him as a 'test case'; in other words, it is less difficult to trace a common line of policy running through all his acts, than in the case of any of his successors, not excluding Innocent III.—The question is, of course, too big to open up here; but it is worth pointing out that, even if the more or less contemporary Yorkist pamphleteer—to take as an example the most outspoken contemporary critic of Gregory's régime—discerned an all-pervading anti-episcopal policy in Gregory's actions (Böhmer, *Kirche u. Staat*, 240–255), the mere existence of this view is in itself no adequate ground for accepting it as valid. [2] Haller, p. 288.

K

In short, therefore, the idea that the popes of the
twelfth and thirteenth centuries pursued a definite
and conscious anti-episcopal policy, of which provisions were one of the later but at the same time
the more radical aspects, is too simplified a view of
events. Gregory VII could not foresee Alexander
III; Alexander III could not foresee Boniface VIII;
Boniface VIII could not foresee John XXII. Slowly,
however, the idea of the customary part of the papacy
in the ecclesiastical constitution changed. What was
not customary at the time of Gregory VII was ancient
usage to Alexander III, what was an innovation in
1150 was self-evident to Boniface VIII in 1300.[1] We
may well assert that the only policy the popes of the
twelfth and thirteenth centuries pursued, as regards
the internal government of the Church, was to perform
their ordinary duties in concrete day-to-day action.
But, if we insist that the facts of papal activity do not
hide ulterior motives, that administration was not
subjected to a scheme of 'high policy', this must not be
interpreted as a denial of historical continuity or of
the domination of the whole period by very definite
ideas. Such a development as provisions would have
been impossible for an age which did not regard the
papal office as comprising an active, direct participa-
tion in local Church affairs, the Roman pontiff
himself as more than *primus inter pares*, the Church
more as a monarchy than as a federation of dioceses.
If a decisive personality like Alexander III had
been convinced of the fundamental necessity of
diocesan autonomy, had regarded his office, as St.
Bernard regarded it, as merely ultimate superin-
tendence, *super universum ecclesie statum consideratio*,[2] a

---

[1] The point is well worked out in various directions by Sägmüller, *Tätigkeit
u. Stellung d. Cardinäle.*

[2] 'Superest, ut generaliter super universum ecclesie statum intendat
consideratio tua: si plebes clericis, si clerici sacerdotibus, si sacerdotes Deo in
ea, qua oportet, humilitate subiecti sint; si in monasteriis et religiosis locis
servetur ordo, vigilet disciplina; si super prava opera et dogmata censura

development such as provisions, which acted eventually as a solvent of episcopal authority and of diocesan autonomy, would have been impossible. If the supplicants who approached the pope, begging him to provide for their sustentation, had been categorically told that that was not a papal concern and that they must apply to their bishops, if the pope had been firmly convinced that the disposal of benefices lay under no circumstances within his sphere of action and that nothing should induce him to interfere with it, the history of the Church would have known no system of provisions or reservations.

So much is obvious. Provisions presupposed a certain conception of papal powers and of the papal office. What is mistaken is to characterize this conception as definitely 'papalist', and to think of papal action as designed to realize a theoretical 'papalist' end, to materialize a 'papalist' idea.[1] 'The whole history of the papacy in the Middle Ages is an incomprehensible, unaccountable phenomenon, unless it is borne in mind that the popes, even where they attributed to themselves the most far-reaching—and from the point of view of historical criticism, the most assailable—rights, were only expressing what at least the greater part of their contemporaries already believed. . . . The *plenitudo potestatis* of the bishop of Rome was not, as we might say, an exorbitant pretension of Innocent III, but the creed of the century'.[2] And the *plenitudo potestatis* is the fundamental conception without which the centralized monarchy, which the Church became in the fourteenth century, could not have been constructed. Even St. Bernard, who told the pope to keep the *cura* and yield *possessio* and

ecclesiastica vigeat; . . . si demum vestra ipsorum apostolica mandata et instituta ea, qua dignum est, sollicitudine observentur, ne quid in agro Domini tui aut neglectu incultum aut fraude subreptum inveniatur' (*De consid*, III. v).

[1] In this connexion Macdonald, *Authority and Reason*, cap. IV, is suggestive.
[2] Haller, p. 40.

dominium—a 'futile distinction', it has been called[1]—
who dared to say, in regard to the confusion of ecclesiastical order by papal exemptions: 'sic factitando
probatis vos habere plenitudinem potestatis, sed
iustitie forte non ita: facitis hoc, quia potestis, sed
utrum et debeatis, questio est'[2]—even he addresses
the pope thus:[3]

Quis es? Sacerdos magnus, summus Pontifex. Tu princeps
episcoporum, tu haeres Apostolorum, tu primatu Abel,
gubernatu Noe, patriarchatu Abraham, ordine Melchisedech,
dignitate Aaron, auctoritate Moyses, judicatu Samuel,
potestate Petrus, unctione Christus. Tu es, cui claves
tradite, cui oves credite sunt. Sunt quidem et alii coeli
ianitores, et gregum pastores: sed tu tanto gloriosius,
quanto et differentius utrumque prae ceteris nomen here-
ditasti. Habent illi sibi assignatos greges, singuli singulos:
tibi universi crediti, uni unus. . . . Ergo iuxta canones tuos,
alii in partem sollicitudinis, tu in plenitudinem potestatis
vocatus es. Aliorum potestas certis arctatur limitibus: tua
extenditur et in ipsos, qui potestatem super alios acceperunt.
Nonne, si causa exstiterit, tu episcopo coelum claudere, tu
ipsum ab episcopatu deponere etiam et tradere satanae
potes? Stat ergo inconcussum privilegium tuum tibi tam in
datis clavibus quam in ovibus commendatis.

As far as the origins of papal provisions are bound
up with the penetration and prevalence of ideas such as
these, their history takes us back to the days of
Hildebrand and further. But provisions did not
emerge in actual practice until half a century and more
after Hildebrand's death, and it is essential to try to fix
more closely the circumstances in which the practice
arose. To accomplish this in detail, would be to write
the constitutional and administrative history of the
twelfth-century Church. But the main facts are

---

[1]A. L. Smith, p. 175—though he does not realize whence Matthew Paris,
of whom he is writing, derived his idea. St. Bernard, it is worth noting,
meets the objection (*De consid.* III. i): 'Quid, inquis? non negas preesse et
dominari vetas? Plane sic . . . nam nullum tibi venenum, nullum gladium
plus formido, quam libidinem dominandi'.

[2]*De consid.* III. iv.   [3]*Ibid.* II. viii.

reasonably clear. In the first place, the age of Eugenius
III or Alexander III was not merely a logical development of the age of Gregory VII. This fact is strikingly
evident in St. Bernard's opposition to the latest
developments of papal activity.[1] There is no need to
consider Bernard's attitude in detail. The fact itself of
hostility, or at any rate contradiction, between the
party of monastic reform and the papacy, which had
worked hand in hand at the time of Hildebrand, is
striking enough. The same contrast is seen in the
statement that Alexander III would have allowed the
marriage of priests *more Graecorum*—the very practice
which Hildebrand fought so hard to eradicate—had
it not been for the opposition of Albert of Morra,
later pope Gregory VIII, 'qui vir erat singulari quadam
austeritate notabilis.'[2] If we attempt to trace back the
centralizing movement which was already under way
in the days of Alexander III, directly to the 'Hildebrandine Reform', we must not overlook these contrasts. The immense reforming activity of Gregory
VII was undoubtedly a stimulus, the effects of which
persisted long after Gregory's death. But there was
definitely a cleavage between the two periods, the
existence of which has been admirably demonstrated,
for example, in the history of the canon law. 'In the
first quarter of the twelfth century, the work of unify-
ing the law of the Church, vigorously undertaken
under Gregory VII, found itself once more at a halt'.[3]
It was another influence, outside the purely ecclesiastical sphere, which worked on men of the type of
Alexander III, and led to the essentially practical,
finite, concrete developments in Church law and
government, which are characteristic of the second

---

[1] In his *De consideratione* and certain of the letters.
[2] Giraldus Cambrensis, *Gemma*, 187.
[3] Fournier et Le Bras, II, 357; cf. *ibid.*, 360: ' . . . et plus tard, après l'effort
beaucoup plus energique du pontificat de Grégoire VII, des tendences
divergentes se font jour dans les recueils de la fin du XIe siècle et du premier
tiers du XIIe; elles révelent des fissures singulièrement menaçantes. . . .' Cf.
also Fournier's article, *Un tournant de l'histoire du droit*.

half of the twelfth century. I refer to the re-discovery, the renaissance of Roman law.

The legal renaissance was more than a revival of Roman jurisprudence. Like the scholastic philosophy, with which it interacted, it exerted a powerful influence on the mental processes of the men of the age, parallel to its more specific effects on jurisprudence, but not to be identified with the latter. It permeated the minds of men, who perhaps never had read a legal work. It directed not only the course of jurisprudence, but the canons of thought. Thus we do not need to dwell, on this occasion, on its place in legal history, or even on its effects—in stimulating the idea of a sovereign papacy, for example—on the theory of political philosophy. It is little more than incidental that Alexander III and many of his outstanding successors were trained lawyers, though it would be valuable to possess a precise study of the effects of civilian conceptions, working through a man like Alexander III, on Church institutions.[1] It was as an intellectual discipline, moulding the shape of mental processes, that the revival of Roman law immediately affected the general history of the age. Not so much any particular Romanist conception as the legal state of mind guided the popes, for example, in allowing the growth of appeals which did so much to extend the jurisdiction of Rome. It was the specific legalistic outlook, engendered by the revival of classical jurisprudence, which made such a development thinkable; and its being thinkable was a precondition of its coming to pass.

Very little is known of the specific effects of the new Romanist outlook on the development of ecclesiastical institutions. The extent to which it had penetrated into things ecclesiastical, the place legal considerations

---

[1]Macdonald, p. 124, describes the 'reviving study of Roman jurisprudence' as 'a parallel movement with the development of the canon law'. It was more; for it determined the actual course which that development took.

filled in Church affairs, is nevertheless obvious from the questionings and complaints which appear, in logical form in the *De consideratione* of Bernard of Clairvaux, but already before him in the epistles of Hildebert of Le Mans,[1] and later in the writings, to take the notable examples, of Peter of Blois, Stephen of Tournai, John of Salisbury, Ulrich of Steinfeld, and in the canons of more than one provincial council.[2] Bernard, writing to Eugenius III of the state of the Roman curia, noted how 'quotidie in palatio perstrepunt leges, sed Iustiniani non Domini'.[3] This was, for him, the crux; and Peter of Blois, using Bernard's own words, also distinguishes between the 'immaculate law of the Lord, converting souls', and the Justinian law, which 'perdit multos et gehenne filios facit'.[4] But with Stephen of Tournai the condemnation was extended from Justinian to Alexander—or rather to those who worked in Alexander's name.

Rursus, si ventum fuerit ad iudicia, que iure canonico sunt tractanda . . . profertur a venditoribus inextricabilis silva decretalium epistolarum, quasi sub sancto nomine sancte recordationis Alexandri pape, et antiquiores sacri canones abiciuntur, respuuntur, expuuntur.[5]

In this way, at the end of the twelfth century, the same complaints were made of decretal law, which two or·three generations earlier had been made of the Novels, Code and Digest. The development is interesting. It points to the growth in canon law of a legislation similar in spirit to that of the civil law, and

---

[1] *Epp.* 41, 82.
[2] E.g. *Conc. Rem.* (1131), c. 6; *Conc. Lateran.* (1139), c. 9; *Conc. Turon.* (1163), c.8 (Labbé, X, 984, 1001, 1421).
[3] *De consid.* I. iv.
[4] *Ep.* 140; cf. *epp.* 26, 123.
[5] ' . . . Hoc involucro prolato in medium ea, que in conciliis sanctorum patrum salubriter instituta sunt, nec formam conciliis nec finem negotiis imponunt, prevalentibus epistolis, quas forsitan advocati et conducticii sub nomine Romanorum pontificum in apothecis sive in cubiculis suis confingunt et conscribunt', *ep.* 251.

equally repugnant to the ancient canons.[1] It indicates that new—and to some critics, undesirable—elements were entering the law of the Church, and through the law, the ecclesiastical institutions. It is not uninteresting to find a cardinal like Guala, who was the first, immediately after the introduction of the principle of *Schriftlichkeitsverfahren* in canonical procedure, to put together a *Libellus petitionum* for use in the curia,[2] counselling Hamelin, bishop of Le Mans, to allow canons going to study at Bologna, Montpellier and other universities, to retain most of their revenues.[3] Thus the very person who was instrumental in laying the foundations of the new procedure at the curia, worked in the same direction in the provinces; and while the local church councils opposed the penetration of Roman law and conceptions,[4] the agents of the Roman curia helped it on.[5]

[1]As late as the beginning of the fourteenth century Petrus Iacobi stressed the same point; *Libellorum tractatus*, tit. *De statu curie Romane* (fo. 82'): 'iura decretorum et dicta sanctorum patrum, quibus sancte et honeste poteramus vivere, dimittuntur ex quibusdam subtilitatibus iuris, et conditi sunt plures decretales, et litigia multiplicata . . .'

[2]Cf. Göller, *Rep. Germ.* I, 61*–62*; the *Libellus* has been printed by v. Heckel, *Arch. f. Urk.-forschung* I, 500 sqq.

[3]*Gallia christ.* XIV, 390.

[4]Cf. *supra*, p. 135 n. 2.

[5]The attitude of the curia, as is well known, was modified from the days of Honorius III (cf. c. 10 X 3, 50); but curial opposition to the penetration of Roman law, even in the thirteenth century, must not be exaggerated. The bull *Dolentes* (c. 1253–1254; Potth. 15570) is a forgery. Cf. Digard, *La papauté et l'étude du droit romain*; Fournier, *L'église et le droit romain*.

CHAPTER XI

THIS IS THE background out of which the practice of papal provision emerged; and it is important to insist on the background, because without it the development of provisions would have been unthinkable and impossible. It presupposed conceptions of papal authority which derived not only from Hildebrand but also from Justinian, and it was the legal development of the papal supremacy on civilian lines which was the more immediately effective of the two elements. Were we, however, to follow the process by which these elements gradually transformed a practice which began simply as recommendation into a legal right to dispose of any benefice in the whole Church, it would be necessary to write the history of provisions in detail for the first hundred years from Alexander III to Clement IV, and such is not our object in this place.

But one phase in this history it is essential to make clear. The turning-point in the transformation of what we call provisions from mere extra-legal recommendations into writs which were backed by legal sanctions, was marked—as has long been recognized[1]—by the practice of following up the original recommendation, when it was not acted upon, by further letters in which a *monitor* and then an *executor* (or a number of executors) were appointed, whose ultimate object was to compel the ordinary collator of the benefice in question either to provide to the papal nominee, or to show cause why provision should not be made. This practice began in all probability during the pontificate of Alexander III and was already fully developed before Innocent III was elected to the Holy See.[2] The different types of

[1] Cf. for example, Febronius, *De statu ecclesiae*, 462.
[2] Cf. Hinschius, *Kirchenrecht* III, 116; of interest are Steph. Torn. *Epp.* 92, 114.

letter (*rogatorie, monitorie, preceptorie* and *executorie*) were
granted consecutively in the first place. This was the
law;[1] and Innocent IV noted that even if the pope
granted *monitorie*, it was not necessarily implied that he
would grant *executorie* subsequently.[2] But during
Innocent's own pontificate the practice of the curia
changed. In spite of the strict ruling of the law, the
practice was gradually introduced of granting all
categories simultaneously,[3] and with this innovation
we can regard the legal nature of the papal provision
as finally and definitely established. From this time
forward, the commissioning of an executor was
regarded as an integral part of the process of making a
provision, and the commissioning of an executor, as
we have seen,[4] implied a judicial cognizance of the
facts of the case and of the legal issues which a papal
provision involved.

In spite of the early growth of the practice of granting all categories of letter (including *littere executoriales*)
simultaneously to a petitioner, it remained down to
modern times the orthodox theory that the commissioning of an executor was only conceded as a remedy;[5]
and although this qualification may appear at first
sight to be merely theoretical in nature, it serves to
show that, even after the construction of legal
machinery for executing provisions, papal intervention
still took, in its first stage, the form of request or
recommendation. This distinction was not insignifi-
cant. It meant that, before an impetrant appealed to
his executor or monitor, he had to request the ordinary

---

[1]c. 37 X 1, 3.

[2]*Gl. ad c.* 27 X 3, 5 *v.* 'Assignari proventus'.

[3]Bonaguida, *Summa*, 331; repeated by Egidius de Fuscarariis, *Ordo iudiciarius*, 246.—Wunderlich's dating of Bonaguida's work (1249) is more correct
than Schulte's ('nicht vor 1263'); but I cannot produce the evidence in this
place. Actually composition probably took place c. 1250–1255.

[4]*Supra,* pp. 91 sqq.

[5]Thus it is compared by Ridolphini, *Praxis curiae Romanae*, P. II, c. 8, §. 1,
to the remedy provided for an heir in C. 6. 33, 3.—To this important analogy
I hope to return on another occasion.

collator to carry out the terms of the papal mandate,[1] and that the executor's functions only began after a *denegatio* on the part of the ordinary.[2] If the papal request were ignored or refused without legitimate grounds, a *denegatio iustitie* had taken place with regard to the impetrant, with regard to the Holy See a grave contempt:[3] and the papacy had therefore the right and the duty to grant a remedy by commissioning an executor.

The very fact that the appointment of an executor was regarded theoretically as a remedy, shows that it was originally looked upon as an unusual expedient— an attitude which no doubt persisted, even in practice, until it became normal to appoint an executor at the beginning of proceedings, at the same time as the originating *littera rogatoria* was issued. In other words, the development towards the end of the twelfth century, of machinery to carry out provisions did not signify that the original conception of the papal letter as a recommendation was lost. It did not signify that the papacy was setting its intervention on an entirely new basis of force and incontestable right.[4] Once the practice of appointing an executor became established, his functions were no doubt rapidly defined and by definition developed and made specifically juridical in character; but in the first place it is probably more correct to regard him, in

---

[1] Thus we find (*Cod. Cap. metrop. Pragen.* I. xxvi, fo. *2a*; cf. *infra*, p. 150 n. 2) the following exception raised against a providee: 'Item obicio procuratorio nomine dictorum dominorum meorum contra prefatum dominum *talem*, quod tempore denunciationis et presentationis dictarum litterarum ipse neque per se neque per alium procuratorio nomine suo petivit se admitti et recipi a capitulo *tali* in canonicum et in fratrem in ecclesia *tali* predicta'.

[2] I am speaking in this connexion of the *executor ad faciendum provideri* or *ad compellendum*: if an executor was commissioned *ad conferendum*, the position was obviously modified. It was, however, only in special circumstances that such powers were granted to an executor, e.g. if a benefice were reserved to the disposition of the Holy See. In this case there was no reason for addressing a request to the ordinary at all.—On the different classes of executor, Bern. Compost. *notabilia ad* c. 30 X 1, 3 are of fundamental importance.

[3] Cf. *supra*, p. 94 n. 1.

[4] For the contrary standpoint, cf. Baier, pp. 204–209.

a broad non-technical sense, as a *tutor*—a word which the popular legal writers sometimes used—that is, as a guardian and protector of the interests of the providee, rather than as an officer of the law. Thus we must beware of making any marked division between the 'extra-legal' and the 'legal' periods in the history of provisions. The appointment of monitors and executors was, in the first place, only a small, logical step forward: we can characterize it best by saying simply that it represented the wish of the papacy to give provisions more effect than they had been having. Moreover, it was not an expedient used by the papacy alone. The bishops also followed up their *littere rogatorie*, where necessary, by *littere monitorie, preceptorie* and *executorie*.[1] The point has not, so far as I know, been noted before; but it is a valuable indication of the normality of the step which the papacy was taking.[2]

Thus there was no sudden break, no markedly new phase in the history of provisions at this period. It is impossible to say how often the papal recommendation was acted upon in the first place, how often it was necessary to depute executors or (if executors were deputed immediately at the beginning of proceedings) how frequently they were called upon to perform their functions. But there is no reason to suppose that acceptance of the papal request, willing or unwilling, was not as frequent as, and perhaps at an early period more frequent than, execution under legal compulsion.

[1]Cf. the interesting formulae in Boncompagno, *Rhetorica antiqua*, ff. 122*b*–122'*b*, under the rubrics: 'Littere quibus archiepiscopus vel episcopus rogat aliquos, quod aliquem scolarem in fratrem et canonicum recipiant', 'Responsio quod non possunt in electione ipsius esse concordes', 'Littere indignationis, quibus precipitur, quod eum recipiant', 'Responsio, qua dicitur, quod non possunt esse concordes, et quod contra consuetudinem aggravantur', 'Littere quibus precipitur districte, ut eum recipiant', 'Littere quibus negatur, quod eum recipiant', 'Notula, qua doctrina datur, quomodo possunt super hiis materie infinite oriri'.

[2]And this would be hardly less the case, were it to prove that the archbishops and bishops were following papal example.—It is the cardinal weakness of a work such as Churchill, *Canterbury Administration* I, cap. 2, that the precise functioning of episcopal rights and powers, in this as in other respects, is not made clear.

The attitude of the chapter of Châlons-sur-Marne, which alleged a statute, 'quod neminem in vestra ecclesia potestis, *nisi compulsi*, admittere in canonicum et in fratrem, donec recepti in dicta ecclesia prebendas sibi debitas fuerint assecuti', was to all appearance exceptional, for it practically invoked executorial action.[1] Normally the attitude of the ordinary collator was conciliatory; the papal request was approached with an open mind. At the least, there was a readiness 'super dicto processu deliberare velle';[2] and then, even if there were ample protestations 'quod non intende-bant iuri, si quod habet in ipsa prebenda capitulum, in aliquo derogare',[3] even if there was a certain amount of unwillingness and prevarication,[4] the probability of immediate compliance with papal demands, even in the fourteenth century, still remained considerable. Thus in a characteristic document in the *Formularium notariorum curie* it is narrated how a chapter, 'super premissis inter se communicato consilio et diligenti deliberatione prehabita', received a providee unani-mously as canon, 'dicentes quod multum placebat eis, quod predictus executor faceret quidquid vellet et quidquid ad officium suum spectabat'.[5] In some cases

[1] *Reg. Vat.* 25, fo. 16', n. 127 (Loye-Cenival, n. 1713). Similar statutes were of course common, e.g. *Reg. Vat.* 9, fo. 76', n. 293 (Pressutti, n. 380), but without the clause *nisi compulsi*, on which in this connexion the stress naturally lies. They merely expressed the common law of the Church, which incidentally the pope was prepared to maintain by vigorous measures—cf. the very sharply worded writ in *Reg. Vat.* 13, fo. 113, n. 202 (Pressutti, n. 5821). But such statutes were understood to be *salva sedis apostolice auctoritate* (cf. c. 19 X 1, 3 in the restored version *ed.* Friedberg); and thus if the pope demanded 'reception', *non obstante statuto*, the canons were free to receive his nominee, in spite of their oath or statute (cf. *gl. cit. infra*, p. 144 n 2). The introduction of the clause *nisi compulsi*, on the other hand, put a different colour on the whole matter, ignored the special position of the pope, and necessitated executorial action whenever an expectancy was granted by papal letters.—On the clause 'salva sedis apostolice auctoritate', cf. Thaner and Sägmüller.

[2] *Cod. Marcian. Venet. lat.* IV. 98 (letters of the bishops of Volterra, 1301–1348, collected for use as a formulary), fo. 42.

[3] *Loc. cit.*

[4] Cf. Steph. Torn. *ep.* 92: 'Homo ille obedienter, ut solet, respondit, et mandatum domini pape sese completurum promisit, canonicis murmu-rantibus et obicientibus....'

[5] No. 106; cf. nos. 107–111.

it is possible that this accommodating attitude was due to the realization (in the words of Stephen of Tournai) that 'acceptius est spontaneum beneficium quam involuntarium, gratuitum quam extortum'.[1] But there is ample evidence that this was not always the case, and that there was often not only willing reception of the papal request, but also good reason for immediate compliance.

In the first place, there are a large number of provisions in which co-operation between the pope and the ordinary collator is unmistakably revealed by the papal letters. This element of co-operation, though it has been stressed by such writers as RIEDER and KOTHE,[2] has hardly received due consideration from the bulk of historians. It was occasioned, in the first place, by the prohibition of elections to non-vacant benefices, which was part of the positive law of the Church.[3] The broad principle of this legislation was clear enough; but it could be, and was, circumvented in a number of ways, and the trend of legislation was to interpret the prohibition with increasing laxity.[4] A chapter which deliberately elected a canon in contravention of the law, lost the remedies which the law provided[5]—a result which may have been just from the private standpoint of the parties, but which from a public standpoint practically meant that the law could be abrogated at the will of the individual; and consequently elections *ad vacatura* were of all too

---

[1]Ep. 114.

[2]Cf. *supra*, pp. 40–42.

[3]Cf. *Decr. Greg. IX*, l. 3, t. 8 *De conc. preb. vel. eccl. non vacantis*.

[4]On the other hand, the statutes which practically every chapter issued on the subject (cf. *supra*, p. 141 n. 1), were clearly drawn up with the object of maintaining as far as possible the old canonical rule.

[5]Cf. Goffredus de Trano, *Summa*, ad tit. *De conc. preb.*: 'Et quod dixi, recipientes recepto obicere non posse, quod contra concilium sit receptus, ideo contingit, quia, cum sit in possessione canonie, in pari casu turpitudinis peior est conditio agentis et melior possidentis. . . . Si vero in possessione non esset, sed ageret ex promissione, ut reciperetur, tunc illi, qui promiserunt contra concilium, possunt excipere contra eum, et in hoc casu in pari causa melior est conditio rei. . . . Circa idem et commune delictum in hoc casu non daretur agenti replicatio contra doli exceptionem. . . . '

frequent occurrence from the middle of the thirteenth century onwards. Similarly from a theoretical point of view, it gradually became established that only the promise of a certain named benefice, not of a future vacancy in general, fell incontestably within the ruling of the statute. It would, however, be mistaken to suppose that the ever-widening interpretation of the principles at stake was due merely to growing laxity: it was undoubtedly very difficult to administer the law in such a way that the basic ruling of the Third Lateran Council[1] was maintained in its integrity, and at the same time no injustice done to the individual.[2] Like much reformatory legislation, the canon of 1179 was more perfect in theory than in practice. But the fact remains that, to writers at the turn of the twelfth and thirteenth centuries, the legal position was confused, and many regarded it as wilfully confused;[3] and it is of the greatest interest to trace the slowly and hesitatingly changing attitude of the canonists to the question throughout the hundred years which ran from the Lateran Council of 1179 to the Lyons Council of 1274.

In this place, however, we must confine our attention to the broad principle and to its practical consequences. The prohibition of election to non-vacant benefices meant that in collegiate churches where there was a *numerus clausus* or *certus numerus canonicorum* and *distinctio prebendarum*—and by the beginning of the thirteenth century most chapters were in the process of fixing the number of canons by statute[4]—it was illegal for the canons to elect or to confer prebends *extra numerum*. Whatever modifications either in theory or in practice were introduced,

---

[1] c. 2 X 3, 8.
[2] As a typical case, cf. c. 14 X 3, 8 in the restored version, *ed.* Friedberg.
[3] Peter of Blois' criticism, *Speculum*, cap. 23, is particularly noteworthy.
[4] Cf. Hergenröther-Kirsch II, 642.

this basic principle remained clear.[1] But the pope was
not bound by any of the legislation in this connexion,
local or general;[2] and it was therefore, time after time,
to the advantage of all parties, was indeed the only
licit course, either to petition the pope to provide a
candidate of the ordinary collator, or to sue out *littere
facultatis*, by which the ordinary was empowered to
collate *auctoritate apostolica, non obstante statuto* or *non
obstante certo canonicorum numero*. The position is seen
very clearly in two petitions under the rubric:
'Quando canonici supplicant pape, quod provideat
cuidam de canonicatu et prebenda in eorum ecclesia',
which appear in the formulary drawn up, during the
pontificate of John XXII, for the notaries of the
curia;[3] and it needs no particular proof that canons
petitioning in this way were not likely to put obstacles
in the way of the execution of the papal letters.

In other cases, local conditions may have worked in
the same direction. In some places the bishop was sole
collator of benefices in the cathedral church; in others

[1]The position is well summarized by Roffredus, *Opus libellorum*, tit. *De
preb.*, §. *Quando prebenda sit conferenda:* 'conferenda est autem prebenda,
quando vacat. Nam si non vacat, conferenda non est. . . . Quid si concedatur
primo vacatura, vel promittatur, vel iureiurando se astringat prelatus ad
concedendam primo vacaturam: nunquid tenet obligatio talis vel concessio
vel iuramentum? Respondeo, non: *solus enim papa hoc mandare potest* . . . ab
alio autem facta promissio de non vacante non valet . . . Sed quidam tam
decretalem quam legem intelligere voluerunt, quando de prebenda alicuius
certi fit promissio. . . . Si in genere prelatus promittat primo vacantem, tunc
dicunt quod valet. . . . Sed in veritate reprobatur, quia nec concessio nec
promissio facta valet, sive in genere sive in specie. . . . Sed opponitur de eo,
quod habetur ex. *De preb.* [3,5], c. *Relatum* [c. 9], ubi dominus papa compellit
episcopum, qui promisit primam prebendam, cum in ecclesia vacaret,
assignare illi, quem episcopus ille in ecclesia instituit, et cui promisit. Respondeo: ibi papa precepit provideri, non ratione promissionis, sed intuitu
pietatis . . .'
[2]*Loc. prox. supra cit.*; cf. also c. 19 X 1,3 *gl. ad v.* 'Iuramento': 'Sed in omni
tali iuramento, semper intelligitur auctoritas maioris excepta. . . . Ergo non
facerent contra iuramentum, si ad mandatum domini pape illum reciperent.
. . . Si papa mandat aliquem recipi in canonicum, non obstante tali iuramento,
tunc licite eum recipiunt, quia sic apparet, quod papa iuramentum factum
quasi de re sua non vult ratum habere, cum administratio sola commissa
est capitulo, et non dominium collatum, et hoc iuramentum servare tenentur
canonici quantum in se est, nisi papa contrarium mandet'.
[3]Barraclough, *Form. not. curie*, nos. 269, 270 (printed in full as *Appendix*,
nos. 1 and 2); cf. also *ibid.*, 270 n. 1, 271 n. 2, 273 n. 2.

the chapter alone, to the exclusion of the bishop; in others both co-operated.[1] The result was often that the one or the other—and this seems to have been particularly true of the prelates—had not as many benefices at his command as he deemed requisite,[2] and was willing, to gain his ends in opposition to the other party, either to sue out *littere facultatis* from the pope, by which he was authorized to provide a certain number of additional clerics, or else to ask the pope himself to provide to such persons as he nominated.[3] Thus Honorius III wrote to the bishop of Limoges on 21 May, 1226: 'Presentata nobis ex parte tua petitio continebat, quod licet magister Gaufridus clericus et procurator tuus apud sedem apostolicam et alibi tibi diutius servierit fideliter et devote, nondum tamen prebendale beneficium aliquod, cum ad te alicuius ecclesie tue diocesis collatio non pertineat prebedarum, potuit obtinere; quare nobis humiliter supplicabas, ut eidem in aliqua ecclesiarum tude iocesis in prebendali provideri beneficio faceremus',[4] and other similar cases are frequent.[5]

It would nevertheless be mistaken to overstress the element of co-operation between the ordinary collator and the pope. The papal registers of the thirteenth century are the best proof that there soon arose a

---

[1]Cf. Sägmüller I, 344, and notably c. 5 X 1,10 *gl. ad v.* 'Communiter'. In other collegiate churches, what follows is equally valid of the appropriate superior (either dean or provost, according to local circumstances).—We can ignore *beneficia ad collationem laicorum spectantia* because it is well known that the Holy See did not normally interfere with these; cf. *supra*, pp. 43–44.

[2]Thus the bishop of Laon complained that 'preter prebendas nichil habet in sua donatione conferre', *Reg. Vat.* 9, fo. 260', n. 1137 (Pressutti, n. 1388).

[3]Cf. Rieder, *Röm. Quellen*, lxxxix: 'gerade dem Bischof gab das Provisionswesen die Mittel in die Hand, in die immer mächtiger werdenden Domkapitel Personen zu bringen, welche die bischöflichen Interessen vertraten'. Numerous examples of letters of the type referred to are preserved in the Marinus formulary, nos. 1423–1426, 1428–1430, 1466, 1468, 1470–1475, 3135, 3136, 3139, 3140, 3156, 3162, 3192, 3199, 3503–3505.

[4]*Reg. Vat.* 13, fo. 133', n. 293 (Pressutti, n. 5949).

[5]*Reg. Vat.* 9, fo. 153, n. 623 (Pressutti, n. 770); *Reg. Vat.* 21, fo. 264, n. 376 (Berger, n. 1725), fo. 522, n. 752 (Berger, n. 3800); *Reg. Vat.* 27, fo. 103' (Guiraud, *Reg. Caméral*, n. 371), fo. 129 (*ibid.*, n. 452).

growing and determined resistance to provisions.[1]
Already in 1232 a case is mentioned, where bishops had
been demanding oaths from all whom they ordained,
that they would not seek preferment by means of
papal provisions.[2] On other occasions they extorted
oaths from providees, by which their rescripts were
rendered useless.[3] At the same time a certain amount
of legal chicanery occurred, as in a curious case at
York in 1272, in which the archbishop claimed to have
conferred a prebend one day, and even one hour,
after the death of the occupant in Viterbo, and thus to
have forestalled the papal providee.[4] More usually,
of course, the papal mandate was simply ignored, or
the providee threatened with violence if he attempted
to make use of his rescript. Such a case occurred at

[1]These points are well summarized by Baier, *Päpstl. Provisionen*, cap. 10.
[2]*Reg. Vat.* 16, fo. 48', n. 150 (Auvray, n. 939): 'Quanto fratres et coepiscopos
nostros sincerioris amplexamur brachiis caritatis, tanto fortius contristamur,
quotiens ea de ipsorum aliquibus nostris auribus intimantur, per que deus
offenditur, ecclesie deformatur honestas, fama denigratur apud homines
eorundem, et apud deum conscientie maculantur. Ad nostram siquidem
audientiam, quod dolentes referimus, noveris pervenisse, quod quidam
episcopi infra tue legationis terminos constituti, sue fame prodigi pariter et
salutis, a clericis sue diocesis ordinandis, antequam eos promoveant, ne
occasione promotionis huiusmodi super provisione sua per litteras apostolicas
molestent eosdem, in sue salutis dispendium et scandalum plurimorum,
iuramentum exigunt et extorquent. Cum igitur ex iniuncto nobis apostolatus
officio de regno ecclesie omnia scandala colligere teneamur, mandamus,
quatenus omnibus episcopis infra tue legationis limites existentibus auctoritate
nostra districtius inhibere procurans, ne a clericis de cetero promovendis
huiusmodi iuramentum exigere vel extorquere presumant, cum non careat
vitio symonie, illos, quos tibi constiterit extorsisse ab ordinatis consimile
iuramentum, ad relaxandum illud qua convenit districtione compellas, eos
sublato appellationis obstaculo taliter castigando, quod ipsi et alii attemptare
talia de cetero non presumant'.
[3]E.g. *Reg. cit.*, fo. 55, n. 178 (Auvray, n. 972): 'Ad audientiam nostram
noveritis pervenisse, quod cum ad mandatum nostrum dil. fil. G. clericum . . .
in fratrem et canonicum duxeritis admittendum, vos, ut huiusmodi gratiam
inutilem redderitis, iuramentum de parendo mandatis vestris, quod alii
prestare non solent, exegistis ab ipso; qui, credens quod id pro utilitate
ecclesie peteretur, illud prestitit confidenter. Cui postmodum iniunxistis, ne
iure canonicatus vel loci competentis eidem usque ad annum et dimidium
uteretur, non minus in hac parte nobis quam cui gratiam fecimus, illudere
molientes. Cum autem mandatum huiusmodi fuerit indiscretum, mandamus,
quatenus illud sine difficultate qualibet revocetis. . . .'
[4]*Reg. Vat.* 37, fo. 25, n. 79 (Guiraud, n. 81): ' . . . absurdum tamen et potius
per rerum naturam impossibile videbatur, ut de tam extensa longinquitate,
utpote de Viterbio, ubi dictus P. noscitur decessisse, ad quamvis partem dicti
regni una die vel potius una hora cuiusquam rei geste notitia pervenisset . . .'

Coblenz as early as 1233.[1] But even the most forcible endeavours to prevent the execution of a papal provision in no way implied a challenge to the pope's right, as such, to provide. This is a well-known fact, and needs no stressing here.[2] On the other hand, it is well worth considering how far the *de facto* opposition which was aroused, and of which the papal registers provide ample evidence, was merely opposition to the single concrete provision, and especially to the particular person provided. The chapters drew up statutes regulating the admission of canons, by means of which the *pauperes clerici* whom the pope had provided, were extruded; but it is questionable whether the same attitude was maintained towards members of rich and powerful families.[3] When a chapter, like that of Orvieto in 1253, refused to receive a providee, 'quia ipsorum ecclesia gravata erat onere debitorum, nec suppetebant pluribus eiusdem ecclesie facultates',[4] and then promptly received others at the mandate

[1] *Reg. Vat.* 16, fo. 93, n. 311 (Auvray, n. 1116): 'iidem decanus et capitulum non solum denegarunt mandatum apostolicum adimplere, verum etiam comminari sibi mortis periculum, si prebendam ipsam peteret, presumpserunt; propter quod idem clericus non sine multo pudore et magno expensarum gravamine a loco ipso discedere ac redire ad propria est coactus'.

[2] Cf. Maitland, *Canon Law*, 66–67.

[3] Cf. *Reg. Vat.* 29, fo. 79', n. 203 (Guiraud, n. 1154): 'Ad audientiam nostram non sine admiratione pervenit, quod prepositus decanus et capitulum ecclesie s. Floriani in Confluentia . . . motu proprio statuerunt, quod duo et duo canonicorum ipsius ecclesie . . . unum pro sua voluntate nominare valerent, ac dicti prepositus decanus et capitulum, ad quos canonicorum institutio et collatio prebendarum ibidem pertinet, nominatos huiusmodi tenerentur recipere in canonicos et in fratres, de hiis observandis prestito nichilominus iuramento. Porro iamdicti prepositus decanus et capitulum, huiusmodi temerarii statuti pretextu, quamplures eorum consanguineos et affines nullis prebendis vacantibus in predicta ecclesia in canonicos receperunt, quorum quidam minoris etatis, aliqui vero ydiote, nonnulli etiam minus ydonei prorsus existunt. Iidem quoque prepositus decanus et capitulum quosdam divites et potentes ex eis, quos taliter receperint, in prebendis, quas in ipsa ecclesia vacare contingit, pro eo instituere propria temeritate presumunt, ut, divitibus et potentibus ipsis eas propter impotentiam dictorum pauperum et ydoneorum clericorum violenter detinentibus, recepti prefati per eos illis leviter in prebendarum ipsarum assecutione succedant, dictis pauperibus et ydoneis clericis in ipsa ecclesia remanentibus omnino provisione fraudatis' (1263, XI. 12).—A practically identical letter against similar fraudulent reception *statuti nepharii occasione* at Zürich appears in *Reg. Vat.* 29, fo. 158, n. 658 (Guiraud, n. 1608).

[4] *Reg. Vat.* 22, fo. 296, n. 864 (Berger, n. 6724).

both of the pope and of his legate,[1] there is every reason to suppose that their opposition was directed not against the provision as such, but against the particular person provided. As we have seen, the ordinary collators were willing to use the system of provisions on behalf of persons who were acceptable to them. 'Illos totis precordiis nostro desideramus adiungi consortio et collegio sociari', they wrote to the pope, 'qui morum nobilitate litterarum scientia amicorum potentia radiantes, ecclesie nostre possint esse multipliciter fructuosi'; and if the result was to acquire a colleague 'de potentibus et valentibus parentibus', by whom 'et eius amicos, dicta nostra ecclesia poterit multipliciter relevari', they were indifferent as to the method by which this result was achieved.[2]

For this reason, the significance of mere *de facto* opposition is to be discounted. It implied less a radical hostility to papal intervention than an objection to the particular direction that intervention took in a certain proportion of cases. Far from being the period at which direct opposition to papal provisions was gradually formulated, the thirteenth century really represented the moment at which the proposition: *omnes ecclesie et res ecclesiarum sunt in potestate pape*—a proposition which might well, had it been set out a century earlier, have been challenged—gradually became a commonplace of everyday thought, for the very reason that it was so self-evident in fact as to become self-evident in theory.

In the same way, it is clear that the antithesis, so palpable in theory, between the ordinary methods of collation and papal provisions, was practically of small importance. Throughout the first hundred years of papal intervention, few men realized that a constitu-

---

[1]'Nonnullos quoque tam nostra quam legatorum sedis apostolice auctoritate in canonicos receperunt, postquam idem Iacobus nostras super hoc litteras presentavit'.

[2]*Form. not. curie*, App. I.

tional issue of some magnitude was involved. According to Alexander III, Bishop Simon of Meaux gloried in the fact that he had never conferred a benefice at the pope's request;[1] but his attitude was individual and expressed a challenge to papal power rather than to papal right. When again in 1266 a prelate adopted a similar attitude, it was in express reliance on the support of the secular power at the height of the political difficulties which faced Clement IV.[2] For the majority of churchmen from the days of Alexander III to those of Innocent IV episcopal collation and papal provision were simply and solely two methods of disposal which existed side by side, and to either of which recourse could be had. It would take us too far to try to discover, by an analysis of the material in the earlier papal registers, in what circumstances it was a usual practice to seek preferment from the pope rather than from the local prelate.[3] In general, however, we can say that those who used papal provisions were men who, owing to their particular situation, had small expectation of preferment at the hands of the bishops; clerics, for example, who had no bishop except the Roman pontiff, converts, members and officials of the curia who had left their dioceses to work in the central bureaucracy, and above all clerks who had left their homes and gone to the universities in search of knowledge. On the other hand, we find the pope

[1] Jaffé, n. 13622; cf. Baier, p. 189 n. 1.

[2] Jordan, *Reg. de Clément IV*, n. 863 (from the formulary of Berard of Naples): 'porrectas tibi nostras deprecatorias litteras pro dilecto filio magistro Iacobo . . . super eo, quod ecclesiam s. Mauritii . . . canonice apostolica sibi auctoritate collatam de facto Iohanni clerico tuo presumpsisti conferre, non erubuisti surdis auribus obaudire. Suntne ista gratitudinis argumenta et grate devotionis indicia, que sedi eidem pro receptis beneficiis recompensas? Que, fili, de tua gratitudine nobis spei reliquie relinquuntur in posterum, dum te in ipsa quasi beneficiorum perceptione tam patenter experimur ingratum—presertim cum dicaris frequenter ad verba satis inconsulta prorumpere, asserens quod de principum auribus, quorum te consiliarium et familiarem intitulas, sic confidis, ut illis salvis tibi de aliis superioribus non sit cura'.

[3] I hope to be able to deal with this question on another occasion: the evidence for the following statements will there be produced in full.

writing in a surprisingly large number of cases on behalf of clerks who had laboured faithfully and devotedly in their churches for many years, and were still without preferment. It is right to insist on the frequency and importance of this class of letter. The chapters and prelates neglected to provide for their ministers and agents, and the latter, very naturally after long years of service, turned to the papacy for what they doubtless regarded as but their due.

Once it became the established practice, in circumstances such as these, for a clerk to seek from the pope the preferment which he despaired of obtaining from bishop or patron, there was every reason, within these orthodox and accepted bounds, for a rapid increase of papal intervention. The preference which the nominees of the pope could claim over those of the ordinary collator—a preference which was accorded long before the legal position was ultimately defined by Boniface VIII[1]—was a powerful inducement to seek promotion from the pope rather than from the ordinary. When one person had recourse to papal help, others were led to do likewise. A clerk received as canon in a certain church without a prebend, approached the pope, for example, and was granted letters providing him to a prebend, 'cum indignum sit, ut idem inane canonici nomen gerat'.[2] Thus he obtained a preference over others in the same position. We might well ask what right he had to preferential treatment; but it is more important to note that others in a like position, if they wished to hold their own, had no alternative

---

[1]c. 12 in VI° 3, 4; cf. *gl. ad id. v.* 'Hii qui', where Johannes Andreae says: 'probatur hoc olim per decr. *De accus.* [5,1], *Accedens* [c. 23]', which was a decretal of Innocent III.—The ruling was expressed again in Alexander IV's constitution *Execrabilis*; cf. *Engl. Hist. Review* XLIX, 193, and further the so called Marinus formulary, n. 60.

[2]*Cod. cap. metrop. Pragen.* J. xxvi (1130), fo. 1', §. *De forma littere provisionis domini pape* (temp. Clementis IV.)—On this formulary, cf. for the moment Schulte, *Abhandl. d. k. böhmischen Gesellsch. d. Wissensch.* (Folge VI) II, 79, n. 200.

but to follow his lead.[1] Thus, apart from actual confirmations *auctoritate apostolica*, which were common enough,[2] anp which were often hardly distinguishable from provisions,[3] papal action frequently had a confirmatory character.[4] In other words, it represented not the initiation of proceedings, but the final step by which a clerk strove to assure himself of a benefice which inferior authorities had already explicitly or tacitly granted or promised.[5] It was safer to go to the supreme authority in the Church—once that authority had shown itself willing to deal with these matters—than to the immediate collator, who might be overridden. There is no need to insist on the fact; but it is essential, particularly since the position is rarely manifest in the documents, to realize that it was precisely in this way that papal provisions became normalized. It was natural to go to the highest authority available, to the collator who offered the greatest privileges. As soon as it became an established fact, first that papal provisions were more than mere recommendations on which the ordinary could act or not at will, and secondly that the candidate of the

[1] Cf. Bern. Compost. *notabilia* ad c. 30 X 1, 3: 'sed pone quod primo receptus per capitulum . . . impetrat litteram papalem ad executorem, *sicut sepe fit*, in qua papa, facta narratione de receptione ipsa, eam approbat, mandans sibi conferri prebendam . . .' The whole passage is important regarding the provision of the clerk who, in Compostellanus' words, 'habet auctoritatem capituli et consensum'.

[2] E.g. *Reg. Vat.* 9, fo. 34, n. 139; Marinus-formulary, nos. 1414–1417, 3354, 3357.

[3] Cf. *Reg. Vat.* 26, fo. 96', n. 144 (Guiraud, n.281). The bishop of Palentina conferred a canonry and expectation of a prebend on a certain Gutterius, who then applied to the pope for confirmation. The pope wrote in confirmation: 'provisionem et reservationem predictas, sicut per eundem episcopum provide facte sunt, ratas habentes et firmas, easdem auctoritate apostolica duxerimus confirmandas'. But he went further, continuing: 'discretioni tue per apostolica scripta mandamus, quatenus eundem Gutterium . . . in canonicum ecclesie predicte recipi facias et in fratrem, stallo sibi in choro et loco in capitulo assignatis, eique de prebenda huiusmodi, si vacat ibidem ad presens, vel quamprimum ad id se facultas obtulerit, provideri procures'. —It needs no particular proof that, in this case, the position was henceforth the same as if the pope had made a provision in the first instance.

[4] Cf. Lux, *Besetzung d. Benefizien*, 28 sq.; Rieder, *Röm. Quellen*, lxxxiii; and see also Haller, pp. 174–175.

[5] As a particularly clear example, cf. *Röm. Quellen*, n. 708.

papacy, supported by the highest authority in the Church, had a right to privileged treatment, the advantages of papal rather than episcopal provision became manifest. Thus already in the twelfth century we find Stephen of Tournai recommending a youth 'in Aurelianensi nutritus ecclesia' for provision in the same church, not to the bishop of Orleans, but to the pope;[1] and it has been shown that the persons who supplicated for papal provisions were the very ones whose families had always within memory had an interest, whose relations or ancestors had always been beneficed, in the church in which they sought a place.[2] They worked by means of papal provisions because this was the most effective means, not because they had no local influence; they approached the pope because his authority was more effective than the ordinary collators', not because it was out of their power to obtain preferment from the local prelate or chapter. The question was one of outward procedure, not of fundamental differences. But the result, as soon as the practice became fixed, was a rapid increase in the numbers of provisions made by the Holy See.

[1] *Ep.* 12.
[2] Cf. *supra*, pp. 39–42.

CHAPTER XII

WITH THESE FACTS before our eyes, it is possible to explain the rapid and at the same time natural growth of papal intervention in the disposal of benefices. They indicate—and it is for this reason that we have dwelt on them at some length—the correct line of approach. Historians have been too prone to ask: what had the papacy to gain thereby? To what end was this policy directed? They have assumed too readily that the initiative came from the papacy, working for its own ends—ends which hostile critics have summed up as little more than sordid material gain, and more favourably-minded historians have regarded as increased constitutional power. It is time that this whole conception was criticized. If we ignore all external influences, such as the political struggle between Innocent IV and Frederick II or the financial needs of the curia, the history of provisions still shows uniform progress from decade to decade, culminating in the formation of a mature system at the middle of the thirteenth century; and this progress can only be explained and understood if we transfer our attention from the papacy and the curia, which formulated and operated the administrative machinery, to the petitioners, who set it in motion. It was from the petitioners, impetrants, or providees, who sought to make use of the papal right of intervention, not from the papacy, that the initiative came; and it is therefore from the standpoint of the petitioner that the history of provisions during the formative period extending from Innocent II to Innocent IV has to be approached.

The cardinal fact which we have to bear in mind, is that the papacy only intervened at the instance of the interested party. When a petitioner could produce *prima facie* grounds for papal intervention—and we must remember throughout that the broad principle: *provisio clericorum opus in se continet pietatis*, was never called in question[1]—the pope might be induced to issue letters; but there is no suggestion, in the legal or the documentary evidence for the period in question, that the pope intervened of his own accord, or even that he acted without *prima facie* evidence that, owing to special circumstances, his intervention was necessary.[2] The fact that he was prepared to intervene at the instance of a party clearly indicated a general persuasion that such action was within his legitimate powers; and without this, as we have seen,[3] the practice of provision could never have developed. But there is no reason to think that the popes, in exercising this residuary power, were striving to build up for themselves an organization which would give them constitutional strength in relation to the bishops, political strength in their struggle with the Empire, and that financial stability in which the central government and the curial bureaucracy were notably lacking. We must remember that it is impossible to discover any financial motive weighty enough to have influenced the papal administration of minor benefices, before the first levy of Annates by Clement V at the beginning of the fourteenth century.[4] Similarly I find no evidence of political influences until the pontificate of Innocent IV,[5] and this was probably only a tem-

[1] *Reg. Vat.* 9, fo. 228', n. 936 (Pressutti, n. 1146); cf. *Reg. cit.*, fo. 185', n. 774 (Pressutti, n. 934): 'Debitam officii nostri prosequimur actionem, cum hiis, qui clericali militie sunt ascripti et ecclesiasticorum sunt beneficiorum expertes, de Christi patrimonio providemus'.
[2] Cf. *supra*, pp. 149–150.   [3] Cf. *supra*, pp. 130 sqq.
[4] Göller, *Repert. Germ.* I, 55*.
[5] Cf. Berger, *Reg. d'Innocent IV*, nos. 1350, 1597, 1598, 1600, 1602, 1612, 1691, 1704, etc. Moreover, it is not improbable that Innocent was following imperial example. Already under Gregory IX (1232. X. 7) the chapter of St. Servatius in Utrecht told a papal executor, 'quod mandato regis nec volunt nec possunt contradicere'—Frederick's eldest son, Henry, having conferred the benefice in question 'de facto, cum de iure non posset', in striking contempt of the papal providee; *Reg. Vat.* 16, fo. 36', n. 106 (Auvray, n. 893).

porary result of Innocent's individual attitude to the
Church and to the problems which faced him.[1] It is
more difficult to fix the time at which the constitutional importance of papal provisions was recognized.
But it is certain that Clement IV's constitution *Licet
ecclesiarum*[2] of 1265 had not the importance in this
regard which has generally been attributed to it. Far
from marking a determined attack on the rights of the
ordinary collators, it really only expressed definite
legal recognition of an established practice. As the
pope himself said, it was a long-standing custom that
the collation of benefices vacated *apud sedem apostolicam*
should be reserved to the papacy;[3] and there is every
reason to accept his statement at its face value.[4]
Licet ecclesiarum therefore only represented a stage in
the familiar process of the adjustment of law to fact.
The change it introduced was one of method or
form, rather than of practice; and it is thus not surprising that it caused no evident increase in the
number of provisions as compared with the period
before 1265.[5] In itself the constitution was of minor
(or, we might perhaps say, of only technical) importance. Its real historical significance was in relation
to the future. In other words, the formulation of the
principle of reservation in 1265 was merely a normal
step in legal definition; and it was only when it was

---

[1]Cf. Smith, *Church and State*, caps. IV, VI; Barraclough, *Execrabilis*, 211–
213.

[2]c. 2 in VI° 3, 4.

[3]'Collationem tamen ecclesiarum personatuum dignitatum et beneficiorum
apud sedem apostolicam vacantium specialius ceteris antiqua consuetudo
Romanis pontificibus reservavit'.

[4]Cf. Haller, p. 31 n. 2; Barraclough, *Formulare f. päpstl. Suppliken.*
See further Roffredus, *loc. cit. supra*, p. 116 n. 1.

[5]Fierens, p. 819: 'De *reservatio generalis* van 1265 deed dan ook niets anders
dan aan dit gebruik kracht geven van wet: zii ondervond noch beknibbeling
noch tegenstand en bracht in de praktijk geen de minste verandering: het
getal der toepassingen van het pauselijk begivingsrecht schijnt zelfs na haar
uitvaardiging veeleer te verminderen dan te vermeerderen. Ten onzent zijn
meer dan de drie vierden van de apostolische benoemingen der dertiende
eeuw ouder dan het jaar 1265: op de zes en zestig aanstellingen die ons bekend
zijn voor het bisdom Luik vallen er vijf en vijftig vóór en slechts elf na de
afkondiging der *reservatio*'.

realized, from the days of Boniface VIII onwards, that the principle of reservation, as formulated in 1265, was capable of manifold expansion and extension, that it became a factor of constitutional importance. It is possible enough that Boniface VIII, Clement V, and John XXII, in expanding the system of reservations, had constitutional (and other) objects in mind; but there is no reason to suppose that similar motives influenced Clement IV when he made the first step in the historical process in 1265. His enactment was a practical alteration not of the actual, but of the legal situation, with adequate practical reasons to explain it,[1] and there is no need to search for ulterior motives behind the objects which he openly alleged.

It is thus possible that, by the end of the thirteenth century, the papacy had come to see the financial, constitutional and political advantages of central control in the disposal of benefices; but these factors did not come into play until the system of provisions was maturely developed, and in so far as it was influenced by them, the papacy was only turning to incidental use an organization which already lay fully developed at its hand.[2] There is no evidence that ulterior motives of this sort played any part in the early development, or even that the papacy sought to develop and extend the system of provisions (in contrast to the older methods of collation) for its own sake. The popes were convinced—so convinced, indeed, that the question appears never to have been debated—that they were entitled, by reason of their very position and function in the Church, to intervene in the disposal of benefices; but as we have said, they only intervened at the instance of the interested parties.[3]

[1] Cf. *supra*, p. 127 n. 2.
[2] When I say 'fully' or 'maturely' developed, I am speaking from the point of view of system: the practice, of course, and above all the scope of the general Reservations, continued to expand.
[3] This is no less true where the pope provided (from a legal point of view) *motu proprio*, or made special reservation of a benefice before the death of the occupant; cf. Riede *Röm. Quellen*, lxxxi n. 1.

It was the pope's duty, his function, according to the conception of the papal office which prevailed at the time, to listen to the pleas of petitioners, to provide remedies for their grievances, and to satisfy their demands, in so far as they were consonant with reason and positive enactment;[1] and in so doing, he was not overstepping the bounds of his normal recognized activities.

On the other hand, it is evident that the papal power of provision was very quickly put to such extensive use that it cannot be regarded simply as a residuary prerogative power, which could be used as a supplement and corrective to the ordinary powers vested in the ordinary collators. But it would be difficult to prove that the papacy itself directly or intentionally fostered the use of provisions, and at the same time the gradual replacement of ordinary by prerogative action. As we have seen, there were definite and weighty reasons for an ever-extending recourse to provisions:[2] they had the backing of the highest authority in the Church, and their efficacy was correspondingly great. The popes themselves, during the early formative period in the history of provisions, showed no evident inclination to encourage clerks to seek provision at their hands, by granting their providees manifest advantages over the nominees of the ordinary collators.[3] It is obvious, from all we know of his character, that a man like Innocent III was not likely to suffer his mandates to be lightly disregarded: provisions issued *auctoritate apostolica*, and a pope with a high ideal of apostolic authority had every reason to see that it was respected. But such an attitude was consonant with the most restricted as well

[1]Cf. *Reg. Vat.* 22, fo. 293, n. 837 (Berger, n. 6697): 'Ad provisionem cunctorum, qui gratiam nostre provisionis exposcunt, intendere teneamur.'

[2]*Supra*, pp. 150 sq.

[3]Cf. *supra*, p. 150 n.1; but the decretal there referred to was not issued till 1215 (Potth. 5018), and even then the conclusions drawn from it were only tentative, and had to be reasserted both by Alexander IV, and by Boniface VIII.

as with an extending use of papal prerogative: when the power of the Holy See was used, it was of importance in itself that it should be accorded due respect, and a determination to employ the full weight of papal authority to secure respect for the papal writ in no way implied an endeavour to make the use of papal provisions so attractive that they would be increasingly sought after. Mere willingness on the part of a higher authority to perform acts of administration which could also be carried out by a subordinate authority was in itself sufficient to attract interested parties, without any definite policy for undermining the influence of the local functionaries being brought into play. The same tendency for recourse to the centre was, for example, a familiar feature of administration in late Imperial times.[1]

The popes, in short, did not reject the opportunity for centralized action (and ultimately for central control) which the constant recourse of petitioners to the Holy See afforded them—and what we have said of the background from which the practice arose, is sufficient to show that there was no inherent reason that they should reject it.[2] But they simply responded to a need which the increasing use of the central, instead of the local, administrative machinery shows to have been real and urgent. The initiative came from the impetrants. It was in response to their needs that the practice of papal provision arose, it was in response to their needs that the practice was transformed, about the middle of the thirteenth century, into a fixed and regularized system. The reason that papal intervention increased and extended from year to year during the century which divided Alexander III from Alexander IV was that there was a real demand from certain if not from all sections of the clergy, for a new, revised method of collation. If papal provisions had not

---

[1]Cf. Wenger, *Institutionen d. röm. Zivilprozessrechts*, 313–314.
[2]*Supra*, pp. 132 sqq.

suited the needs of large numbers of clerks better than the older forms of preferment, they could never have developed and extended as they did. The final explanation of their growth is, and can only be, that they supplied a need which was new, but at the same time deeply felt. The older methods of collation were no longer adequate, no longer satisfied the majority of clerks seeking preferment; a new procedure was necessary, and this new procedure was—as in that age it could only be—the disposal of benefices by the pope and a central administrative organization.

It would be difficult to set out with anything like certainty the factors which led to this change of attitude, this gradual movement from the local to the central administration. In the first place, it would be necessary to know how the ordinary methods of collation functioned during the twelfth century; and though the literary authorities suggest with some force that they were far from perfect,[1] there is little possibility of checking the statements of writers like Gerald of Wales by reference to documentary authorities. On the other hand, there is good reason to suppose that the growth of papal intervention and the contemporary growth of the Schools were not unconnected. It has often been remarked that in the centralized administration of benefices by means of papal provisions, the personal touch—acquaintance with the man and knowledge of his suitability for the post selected—was sacrificed; that the pope had no means of judging the character of the thousands of providees who approached him during his pontificate.[2] But it is well worth suggesting that under the ordinary procedure the personal factor played too dominant a

---

[1] *Loc. cit. supra*, p. 125 n. 1. Cf. also Hergenröther-Kirsch II, 643, where the canons of certain provincial councils are cited; but the objective value of evidence of this class is very difficult to appraise.

[2] It has already been shewn that this criticism tends to exaggeration, and that the legal procedure in use provided other safeguards against the promotion of persons of unsuitable character; *supra*, pp. 97–98.

part; that the bishops and patrons were too prone to regard personal service and personal connexion as the foremost qualification, and paid too little attention to other less immediate but no less weighty recommendations. To clerks who had attended the Schools for years, who had put knowledge of theology and law before parochial or administrative experience, who could with reason regard their academic qualifications as a recommendation for spiritual office, there were obvious advantages in a system of collation in which the importance of learning and university training was duly recognized and personal factors only exceptionally played any part. The pope viewed the arguments of the ordinary providee objectively, and had no reason to view them otherwise. He had an appreciation of the qualities produced by university training which only a fraction of his brother bishops shared.[1] He understood the point of view of the university man, valued the *margarita scientiae*, had high standards of education and scholarship. The clerk who looked to his scholastic attainments and intellectual training to bring him preferment had more to expect from the pope, in the period preceding the Fourth Lateran Council (1215), than from the majority of local prelates, and it is no accident that one of the first to profit by papal intervention was the *magister sententiarum*, Peter Lombard, whom Eugenius III recommended to the bishop of Beauvais.[2]

The appearance of a growing class of university-trained men among the clerics seeking preferment was one of the main factors which necessitated a new

[1] This is indicated also by their failure to provide theological teaching in their own churches. Honorius III wrote (c. 5 X 5, 5): 'volumus et mandamus, ut statutum in concilio generali de magistris theologis per singulas metropoles statuendis, inviolabiliter observetur'. But to the word *observetur* Bern. Parm. appends the gloss: 'nec tamen servatur, et ita nullus est fructus illius statuti et aliorum'.—On the other hand, cf. Gibbs and Lang, p. 1, c. 4; but the period there discussed (*post* 1215) is subsequent to that with which we are here predominantly concerned.

[2] Jaffé, n. 9534.

attitude to the question of benefices, new standards in judging the qualifications of clerks, and at the same time a new procedure of conferment. The bishops and local prelates could, and no doubt gradually did, adapt themselves to the new situation; but the papacy was from the beginning, and always remained, the main standby of the university-trained clerk. The popes had used all their influence to foster the growth of the Schools: it was a natural and necessary corollary for them to lend their support to the learned clerks whom the Schools turned out. Among all the different classes seeking preferment none could with greater reason complain of the localization and preponderance of personal influence in the disposal of benefices than the graduates of the universities; and it was because they—and others whose claims the older methods of collation were equally ill-adapted to meet—called in the central authority to redress the balance in their favour, that the papacy was led to intervene in the disposal of benefices. The determining factors were new forms of education, a change in standards, a new approach to the clerical career, and a new attitude on the part of the clergy themselves. Circumstances in the second half of the twelfth century were widely different from any that had obtained in previous ages;[1] and in new circumstances clerks turned to the central authority for preferment, where previously the local machinery for the distribution of benefices had satisfied their demands.

This change of attitude was remarked, as early as the days of Hadrian IV (1154–1159), by Ulrich of Steinfeld, in a letter to a friend who had asked his advice on the problem, whether to seek preferment by papal letters or to rely on the good will of the canons at Bonn, where he was in hope of obtaining a benefice. 'Fideliter vobis consulo', was the reply, 'ut humilitate et servicio vestro per amicos vestros potius apud eos

[1] Cf. infra, p. 172.

M

agatis, quam per superiorem potestatem'.[1] In these words Ulrich reached the core of the question. The one way to preferment was service and humility; the other superior power. Ulrich himself obviously favoured the ordinary, established road to preferment; but what of the clerk who, instead of devoting himself to lowly service, had spent his youth at the Schools? It is noteworthy that Ulrich made no mention of learning or of academic training: *humilitas* and *servitium* were the qualities the ordinary collators sought, and the word *humilitas* itself was often used to imply the very opposite to the qualities of independence of mind, initiative, and clarity of judgement, which it was the object of the Schools to foster. In any case, the decision was one for the interested party himself. The initiative lay with him, and the pope and the central bureaucracy were merely an instrument by which provision could be effected. It was not a question of the pope intervening on his own initiative, but of the interested party intervening *per superiorem potestatem*; and it was because an increasing number of clerks found that their qualifications were better appreciated, their ends better served, at Rome than in the provinces, that step by step the practice of papal intervention grew.

Thus the development towards the creation of a fixed legal system, which began under Alexander III,[2] proceeded by hardly perceptible degrees, not in accordance with a definite policy of the papacy, but in response to the needs of the petitioners who made use of the central administration. Of the popes themselves, we cannot say that any put forward a radically different conception of his rights and powers from that adopted by his predecessor. We cannot say, even of Innocent III,[3] that external influences—among which

[1] Ep. 41.—Baier's interpretation of this letter (p. 206) is bewilderingly incorrect.
[2] Göller, *Rep. Germ.* I, 61*.
[3] Cf. Baier, p. 12.

political or other outward circumstances come much less in question than definite conceptions of papal authority, new ideas of the ecclesiastical constitution, or tendencies to reconsider governmental problems from a 'papalist' standpoint—produced a new, markedly legal, and somewhat intransigent attitude to the papal power of provision. We cannot say even that the formulation of legislation on the subject in the Decretals of Gregory IX marked any decided step forward in practice, that it provided a legislative basis which allowed immediate and unparalleled development of papal rights.[1] As we trace the progress of provisions, the growth and expansion of the practice appear as an independent process, conditioned not by external factors, but by the course of its own development. The main fact forcing development forward was that all classes of the clergy showed an appreciation of the advantages, a desire to make use, of the papal willingness to intervene and to collate, that provision by the pope was the method of obtaining a benefice which was preferred. Papal initiative—if the word can be used in this connexion—is seen solely in an endeavour to meet the demands of petitioners: the share of the papacy in the growth of its powers was hardly more than negative, the motive force derived from the people who demanded papal intervention on their behalf. Their increasing use of provisions transformed papal intervention from an occasional exercise of directive powers into a normal procedure for obtaining a benefice. There is no evidence that the papacy itself set out either to derogate from or to delimit episcopal powers, except by not refusing to act; and it stretches probabilities to the uttermost to see in a mere unwillingness to refuse assistance a positive anti-episcopal policy. Similarly in regard to insistence on obedience to its requests—the most striking development of the later twelfth century, represented

[1]Cf. Barraclough, *Arch. f. kath. Kirchenrecht.*

by the creation of an executorial procedure[1]—it is easier to believe that the pope was convinced of the merits of a particular case, was firmly confident of the justice of the plea on which he had been asked to intervene, than that his action arose from a broad conviction of the inherent rights of the Holy See, or a claim to put his demands as such into execution. Until a comparatively late date, we shall be well advised to regard every case as decided on its merits, and not to attempt to draw from a series of concrete actions systematic rules and broad principles. If, in any particular case, the pope made reiterated requests and threatened executorial action, his attitude was probably based on a belief in the urgency of that particular concrete case, without special regard to the constitutional position. As far as that was concerned, the orthodox and accepted ideas of the time allowed such scope to the papacy that in concrete action constitutional issues hardly needed consideration; and in practice the actual circumstances of particular cases were often such as to demand every papal exertion to secure satisfaction and to justify in the eyes of contemporaries the completest use of all the powers the papacy could summon.

Thus the practice of provisions grew and extended without the papacy advancing any special pretensions, and when in 1265 Clement IV asserted that the plenary disposition of all benefices was recognized to appertain to the Roman pontiff,[2] he was only asserting what the continuously growing practice of a century had already, without direct papal initiative, made a patent fact. Very different are the pronouncements of earlier popes which find a place in the *Decretales Gregorii IX*.[3] Forced by the growing recourse to provisions to systematize and regularize their use, they gradually estadlished what we may well call a system by process of concrete and individual judicial definition. Thus

[1]Cf. *supra*, pp. 137 sqq.   [2]c. 2 in VI° 3, 4.   [3]L. III, tt. 5, 8; l. I, t. 3.

while the initiative and the impetus came from the side of the petitioners and the users of provisions, the part of the papacy in the development was essentially conservative.[1] By a series of decisions based on equity and precedent, it strove to bring growing practice into line with the main principles of the *ius beneficiale*. The earliest schedules or manuals of curial practice which deal with the subject, were merely declarations of what the pope would or would not do in certain concrete circumstances, and normally the course he took was decided by judicial precedent.[2] The active papal part in the development was thus to formulate, by judicial means, a mass of rules on small concrete points, and to see that they were observed in practice. Thus a settled practice was produced, a system was co-ordinated—a system in which provisions were established as a normal method of collation, and the rights of the papacy were set as high as and even higher than those of the ordinaries. But the very means by which the system was co-ordinated—the progress from precedent to precedent, the solving of one practical problem after another, the gradual accumulation of a series of judicial decisions—indicate the way in which the system was gradually formed by purely internal development; and the fact that it was not by legislative enactment but by judicial decision that the legal position was defined, shows that the only policy pursued was the application of the normal legal and constitutional ideas of the time, when precedent was lacking and a new judgement had to be promulgated.

Thus we can fairly conclude that the system of provisions, as it existed about the middle of the thirteenth century, produced itself; that precedent worked on precedent, that one logical step in legal definition followed another, until a formidable system was consolidated. It was not created by the popes,

[1] Cf. Barraclough, *Engl. Hist. Review* XLIX, 493.
[2] Cf. Bonaguida, *Consuetudines*.

though it may have been created through the papacy. Once established and legally grounded, indeed, it became an instrument which the papacy could use, and already Innocent IV turned it to political ends; but the origins of the system were purely practical. There is no question of gradual encroachment or violent usurpation on the part of the papacy.[1] The powers which popes like Innocent IV, Clement V, and John XXII were able to use for political, financial and constitutional ends, were placed in the hands of the papacy for practical reasons and by process of practical development. They resulted from a growing practice of recourse to the Holy See, not from papal encroachment on the rights of the ordinary collators, or from a sudden determination of the papacy to 'revindicate' and to exercise, in this regard as in others, its primatial rights.[2] They were not powers taken by the papacy, but powers given to the papacy.[3] When Grosseteste said: *scio, et veraciter scio, domini pape et sancte Romane ecclesie hanc esse potestatem, ut de omnibus beneficiis ecclesiasticis libere possit ordinare*, he was proclaiming the ordinary belief of the age; and it was on this firm basis of common belief that the practice of papal provision was built.

Yet Grosseteste's position has been severely criticized. 'He had conceded to the apostolic see a power of freely dealing out ecclesiastical benefices all

---

[1] Cf. Haller, p. 39.

[2] Cf. Mollat, *La collation des bénéfices*, 189: 'Si, pendant de longs siècles, la Papauté n'exerça pas effectivement le droit de collation, il ne s'ensuit pas qu'elle acquit celui-ci en vertu d'impiétements progressifs sur les privilèges des collateurs ordinaires ou des électeurs. Elle le possédait originairement. Les circonstances politiques et religieuses l'empêchèrent longtemps d'en faire usage, autant qu'elle l'eût voulu. Quand le moment favorable fut arrivé, le Saint-Siège revendiqua avec fermeté son pouvoir de juridiction universelle et le développa méthodiquement, surtout à partir d'Innocent III'.—This argument is, of course, fundamentally theological, not historical; and its validity depends on the assumption of inherent papal primacy. But it makes the same presumption of papal initiative in the development of the practice of provisions as the (protestant) theory which it attacks, and is therefore equally repugnant to the views put forward here.

[3] Cf. Smith, *Church and State*, 56.

the world over, and then had to contend that this power should be used, but not abused. Instead of the simple statement that the pope cannot lawfully provide clerks with English benefices, and has no more right to appoint a canon of Lincoln than the bishop of Lincoln has to appoint a patriarch of Antioch, we find this indefensible distinction between use and abuse, and are at once led on to discuss the demerits of the *nepotes*'.[1]

It is hard to follow MAITLAND's argument. If the validity of legal powers and rights is dependent on the precedents that can be adduced in their support, then the power of provision which the pope exercised was (from a historical, if not necessarily from a theological point of view) unconstitutional or even illegitimate. When, a few decades after Grosseteste, Egidius de Fuscarariis in his turn made the proposition: *omnes ecclesie et res ecclesiarum sunt in potestate pape*, the authorities he cited in support of the statement were patently inadequate,[2] and if there had been any doubt on the matter at all, could have been challenged without fear of contradiction by the other disputants who took part in the discussion. The very fact that such a statement, deduced from such authorities, was allowed to pass in the foremost Law School of the day, is proof that the pope had the best authority for the powers he was exercising; namely, general consent. Not generally admitted, but disputed powers need the support of precedent; and it is because the papal power to dispose of benefices was as axiomatic to a lawyer like Egidius as to a theologian and bishop like Grosseteste, that it was even more secure than if it had been derived from incontrovertible legal principles. The pope could lawfully appoint a canon of Lincoln,

---

[1]Maitland, *Canon Law*, 66.
[2]*Questiones Bononienses*, fo. 86'a. He cites cc. 10, 16, 17, C. IX, q. iii; but as these canons all refer to the right of the Holy See to hear appeals *de qualibet mundi parte*, and to the duty of submitting to its appellate jurisdiction, they have small bearing on the question of provisions.

because no one questioned his lawful right to appoint
a canon of Lincoln; but who—even the bishop of
Lincoln himself—would have admitted the right of the
bishop of Lincoln to appoint a patriarch of Antioch?
MAITLAND's argument is a *reductio ad absurdum*, but it is
a *reductio ad absurdum* of his own attitude, not of Grosseteste's. The safest and best-founded rights are those
which no one challenges; and such, at any rate for the
first century of its exercise, was the right of papal
provision.

What MAITLAND really wished to imply, and what
no one would seriously deny, is that the intervention
of the pope in the disposal of benefices was radically
opposed to the spirit of the ancient canon law. This is
true enough. But, as HALLER has already remarked,[1]
we should have to ignore all possibility of normal
legal change and development, were we to conclude
from this undoubted fact alone, that the practice of
provision represented nothing but illegal usurpation.
To be bound by precedent is the weakness as well as
the strength of the law. Its concern is with the present,
not with the past, and a break with tradition is a
salutary change, when it brings the law into closer
agreement with current conceptions and contemporary
tendencies. What is of primary importance is that the
legal situation shall correspond to generally accepted
ideas, not that it shall be based on firm precedent; and
the enactments in the *Decretales Gregorii IX* and the
Liber Sextus, by which the practice of papal provision
was set on a permanent legal basis, only reflected an
established practice, which in its turn expressed the
ruling conceptions of ecclesiastical government.

It was fully realized, both in the thirteenth and in the
fourteenth century, that the power of conferring
benefices appertained *de antiquo iure et dispositione
ecclesie* to the bishops.[2] But this was the *antiquum ius,*

[1] p. 159.
[2] c. 18 in VI° 1, 6 *gl. ad v.* 'Devolvetur'; cf. *Cath. Hist. Review* XIX, 291.

and no one thought to apply it to contemporary circumstances. It is easy to criticize Grosseteste's 'logical position' in admitting a right which no contemporary denied;[1] but the attitude he actually took up was not lacking in good sense. To have criticized the power of provision the popes were exercising, by reference to the ancient law of the Church, would have been mere antiquarianism. A right was not necessarily good because it was ancient, or invalid because it was new. What was important was the way it was exercised and its effects. Grosseteste was a bishop and administrator: he was not concerned with logical attitudinizing, but with the good government of the Church. If the effects of papal intervention in the distribution of benefices were wholesome, he had no quarrel with the system of provisions as such. The question was simply one of ways and means. Grosseteste was not so doctrinaire as to condemn a practice which was potent for good, for the sole reason that it was an innovation; but even if he had been, would he in his day have been led to challenge the papal right to dispose of benefices? In the thirteenth century the inherent primacy of Rome, with all its legal consequences, was an admitted fact, untouched by historical criticism.[2] MAITLAND himself was one of the first to protest against reading the history of the mediæval Church through Protestant spectacles; but the mere application to Grosseteste of 'the simple statement that the pope cannot lawfully provide clerks with English benefices', is anachronous. Had Grosseteste thought this, he would have been, if not the first Anglican, at any rate a forerunner of Gallicanism. It was an attitude impossible for a churchman in the thirteenth century.

This is, however, only a secondary consideration.

---

[1]'The more we make of Grosseteste's heroism in withstanding Innocent IV, the worse we think his logical position', Maitland, p. 66.
[2]Haller, pp. 39–44.

The important fact is that MAITLAND's 'simple statement' is patently false. The pope could lawfully
provide clerks with English benefices, and no one
challenged the legality of his provisions. He would
have been hard put to it to justify his intervention by
the ancient law of the Church; but no one expected
him to seek justification from canons which recent
legislation and recent constitutional changes, including
the consolidation of the legislative power in papal
hands,[1] had rendered obsolete. The right the pope was
exercising had other foundations, other justifications.
The phases in the early history of provisions which we
have briefly surveyed, show what these were; and
they show also the solid historical reasons for Grosseteste's insistence on the distinction between the use
and the abuse of the papal power. The practice of
papal intervention, as we have seen, had originated
and developed in response to certain practical needs.
The power of provision had been placep in the hands
of the pope for certain practical reasons. In regard to
benefices, as in many other regards, the tendency to a
centralization of Church administration was not an
uncalled-for encroachment on the part of the central
power itself, but the result of definite historical
circumstances—circumstances which at the same
period were affecting the forms of secular government
in the same way as they were affecting the constitution
of the Church.[2] No explanation of the growth of
provisions can meet the facts which does not place the
greatest stress on the practical need for more centralized methods of distributing benefices. Provisions
came into existence because they suited the needs and
circumstances of the day, and could never have
developed as they did, if they had not had definite
practical advantages to recommend them. In short,
they represented an administrative development which

[1]Hinschius III, 734 sqq.
[2]Cf. *supra*, pp. 122 sqq.

was of service to the Church; they gradually supplanted the older methods of collation, decause from a practical point of view they introduced a preferable administrative procedure.

It would be hard to state briefly what the precise advantages of the newer procedure were; but, as we have seen,[1] one factor of importance was probably objectivity in regard to the providee, and with it regularity and system. Further, the ordinary methods of collation were probably at that time on the decline. Not only were they ill-adapted to meet the circumstances of certain classes of the clergy, whose careers no longer kept them in touch with their dioceses,[2] but also they left too great a scope for secular influence. Whether such influence was increasing at this period, is beside the point; it was (as from the days of Hildebrand onwards it was bound to be) more keenly felt. If we turn to the reports on diocesan conditions drawn up for the consideration of the Council of Vienne in 1311, we find that they deal to the exclusion of all else with the aggression of the secular power, with the 'gravamina, que ecclesiis et personis ecclesiasticis inferuntur'; that is, outside interference.[3] In such circumstances, as HALLER has said,[4] there is every reason to suppose 'that many a bishop was willing to surrender his rights to dispose of the benefices within his jurisdiction, in favour of the pope, if only to avoid the pressure of magnates and royal officials, and that a Duranti or a Lemaire, who wished to abolish or to limit the papal right of provision, was a rare exception. A bishop who held his spiritual office in serious esteem, and did not regard himself merely as an agent of state authority or a hanger-on of the court, could not, in the realm of Philip le Bel or Edward II, dispense with the standby which the papacy provided. The pope might

[1] *Supra*, pp. 159 sq.
[2] *Loc. cit.*
[3] Cf. Göller, *Die Gravamina auf dem Konzil v. Vienne.*
[4] *Papstt. u. Kirchenreform*, 73.

be no easy master, might often interfere too freely in diocesan administration and levy too frequent taxes; but he was and he remained the natural and the only refuge against a State which still exercised more might than right.'

The relations of Church and State, and their practical consequences, were only one factor among many in forcing forward the process of centralization, and we must not exaggerate their effects. More important in all probability were the changing conditions of the internal life of the Church and the corresponding constitutional developments. The collapse of the old dependence of a clerk on his diocese, the rise of the universities, the growth of 'absolute' ordination and the breakdown of the rule that ordination should only be conferred *ad titulum certum*,[1] the appearance of a rapidly growing class of churchmen whose lives were focused in the central bureaucracy, away from their dioceses, ordination by the pope himself,[2] increasing facility in the grant of *littere dimissoriales*: all these were factors which helped to make the older forms of collation obsolescent, circumstances which the older procedure had not contemplated. They were factors which made a more centralized, more regular, in some ways more automatic, and above all less personal method of distributing benefices of real benefit to one class after another of the clergy.

It has been too often said, and where not said implied, that the practice of provision was foisted on

---

[1] Cf. Fuchs, *Ordinationstitel.*—Ordination could be either *ad titulum beneficii* or *ad titulum patrimonii*, but it could not canonically be conferred unless the ordained had some permanent means of support. 'Non liceat ulli episcopo ordinare clericos et eis nullas alimonias prestare' (c. 2 X 3, 5). From the middle of the twelfth century onwards, however, the canonical rule was transgressed with increasing frequency, and there arose a class of clerks *sine certo titulo ordinati*, on whose behalf the papal chancery created the writ *Cum secundum apostolum*. A history of this writ—which was issued *de iustitia* and should therefore in no wise be confused, as e.g. by Baier, 130, 221–222 and *passim*, with the provision *in forma pauperum*—may be expected in the near future from R. von Heckel (München).

[2] Baier's remarks on this subject (pp. 96 sq., 107 sq.) are of considerable importance.

the Church against the best interests of the Church itself, and even against the private interests of the mass of the clergy, for the sole benefit of the papacy and the officials of the curia. There is no evidence to support this view.[1] Provisions grew because they were of real benefit to a steadily increasing number of clerks and to the Church as a whole. A further measure of centraliza-tion was what the Church needed about the time of Alexander III or Innocent III. Increased control from the centre was the most promising, and at that time the only practicable, means of tightening up ecclesiastical administration.[2] 'The papacy was the greatest poten-tiality for good that existed at the time',[3] and an increasing use of papal powers was the best guarantee of a steady progress in the efficiency, independence and conscientiousness of the Church organization. Even after the middle of the thirteenth century, after the disillusionment of Innocent IV's pontificate, the welfare of the Church was held to depend on the leadership of the pope, on papal initiative and central organization in face of the stolid impassivity and indifference of the local prelates. This was the cardinal thought, for example, of the memorials drawn up by Humbert de Romanis[4] and Gilbert of Tournai[5] for the guidance of the Council of Lyons in 1274. Historians of the reform movement within the mediæval Church

[1] I.e. no evidence from the period during which the practice was in process of formation (*circa* 1150–1250): it depends on an argument *post hoc ergo propter hoc* from the evidence of the succeeding age.

[2] The Fourth Lateran Council (1215) can be regarded as the last great attempt to introduce wholesale measures of reform by orthodox established methods: for the very reason that the local prelates made no firm endeavour to put the decrees of the Council into effect (cf. Gibbs and Lang, P. III), the urgent necessity for direct papal action in the administrative sphere became palpable.

[3] Smith, *Church and State*, 6, 133.

[4] *Opus tripartitum*, 1003: 'Quia plurimi prelati, proh dolor, sunt tepidi circa ea, que Dei sunt, immo etiam contrarii fere omni bono, non videtur modo aliquo expedire, quod de illis, que papa potest sine eis expedire, cum eis habeat tractatum; sed ante concilium vel post illa expediat sine ipsis, et maxime de pertinentibus ad mores'.

[5] *Collectio de scandalis ecclesie*, 62: ' . . . non potest sine summi pontificis providentia consilium et auxilium efficax adhiberi'.

have given too much attention to the phases of the movement directed against the papacy and the curia, to the *reformatio in capite*: it is time that the reform movement of the thirteenth century, in which the papacy, working with every means in its power, took the trenchant, directive part, was studied in detail: the methods of the papacy and their relative importance analysed, the causes of failure explained, the personal efforts of different popes, cardinals, prelates and notably of leading friars, critically appreciated.[1] The effort to make the most of the principle of papal leadership and of the machinery of central government was not lukewarm: the forces at the pope's command were directed with vigour and with talent as an instrument of good government: the potentialities of the strong centralization were not turned to unworthy ends. We know that the attempt at reform and efficient high-principled government from the centre failed, and can surmise that the struggle of Empire and Papacy and particularly the ruthlessly political attitude of Innocent IV were weighty causes of failure. But the attempt made by the popes of the thirteenth century from Gregory IX to Gregory X was not foredoomed. Natural causes brought about the striking centralization of Church government, natural causes led men to turn in one connexion after another to the Holy See and to papal leadership. A strong central government was necessary to the welfare of the Church; and the centralization nearly succeeded in its objects. It failed eventually but it justified itself for the time. It introduced real benefits to the Church; and as long as it was beneficial, it was worthy of wholehearted support.

The improvements in government which centralization brought could only be welcomed. But, as St. Bernard realized, centralization and the pre-eminence

[1] The scope of the problem is brilliantly indicated by Dufourcq, p. 674.

of the Holy See had their dangers.[1] *Praeesse* and *dominari* were hard to distinguish; the greater the potentiality for good, the greater also for evil. What could be used, could be abused. But the mere possibility of evil was no reason to forgo the possibility of good. As Grosseteste saw, the ideal course was to welcome the advantages of centralization and to guard against its abuse. If papal provisions led to the preferment of a better trained and educated class of clerk, if they operated more systematically and impersonally than the older forms of collation, they had, from the point of view of the administrator and of the prelate whose first interest was the good government of the Church, much to recommend them. They might not be perfect; but they were in certain directions an improvement, and they were essential for certain sections of the clergy. The providee recommended by the pope might not always be suitable; but were the ordinary candidates for preferment always properly qualified? And again there was such a thing as *subreptio*; the pope might have been deceived or misinformed;[2] 'omnium habere memoriam et in nullo peccare est potius divinitatis quam humanitatis';[3] 'papa numquam intendit dare litteras preiudiciales';[4] and if he were better informed, he might, as many an example showed, alter his intentions. The bishop who had the welfare of the Church and not the exaltation of his own rights at heart, would not challenge the practice of provision where it resulted in praiseworthy preferments, but would use his influence to prevent its abuse—not by the papacy (for it was a constant and basic legal presumption that the *intentio pape*[5] or

---

[1] *De consid.* III. i.

[2] Cf. Innoc. IV *ad* c. 4 X 1,14 *v*. 'Litterarum': 'non enim semper litteris pape obediendum est, quia decipi potest papa. . . . Sunt enim littere aliquando contra ius vel publicam utilitatem, unde non valent'.

[3] Hostiensis, *Summa*, tit. *De const.* §. *Qualiter constit. derogetur.*

[4] Innocent IV, *Apparatus ad* c. 38 X 1, 3 *v*. 'Prosequi.'

[5] Innoc. ad *cap. cit. v.* 'Si pro alio'.

propositum principis[1] was, and could only be, the good of the Church),[2] but by unscrupulous petitioners using the machinery of central government for their own ends. The distinction between use and abuse was not 'indefensible'[3] or 'futile';[4] it was fundamental. The right use of the authority of the pope and of the machinery of central government might be of inestimable advantage to the Church. It was the duty—and moreover the firmly established legal privilege—of the conscientious prelate to co-operate in the work which the papacy and the central bureaucracy had undertaken,[5] and to see that the central administrative machinery for preferment, which every clerk could invoke if it suited his purposes, was used for the benefit of the Church as a whole, and not abused in favour of particular individuals.

With the arrival of the fourteenth century and the growing importance of external influences, financial, constitutional and political, in the administrative organization, the situation necessarily changed. The interest of the papacy in the administration of the Church was no longer necessarily purely administrative. The popes were not necessarily interested alone in the proper performance of their duties as the heads of the ecclesiastical administration. It may have suited their purposes from time to time to make use of the powers which had been concentrated in their hands, for extrinsic or even illegitimate purposes. Good and efficient government may no longer have been pursued as an end in itself. The machinery of provisions may have been directed arbitrarily as an instrument of papal power, instead of operating systematically as a regular, immutable procedure of normal administration. This

---

[1]Hostien. *Summa*, tit. *De rescript.* §. *Que pena male impetrantium.*

[2]'Non enim credendum est Romanum pontificem, qui iura tuetur, ea, que multis sunt excogitata vigiliis, subvertere voluisse', *Arch. Vat. Collect. 495*, fo. 29'.

[3]Maitland, *Canon Law*, 66.

[4]Smith, *Church and State*, 175.

[5]Cf. *supra*, pp. 96–97.

is not yet, I think, proven. A careful investigation of the historical evidence shows that the evil effects of the centralized disposal of benefices have been exaggerated. A brief indication of the salient features of the legal arrangements suggests strongly that the safeguards and systematic elements in the procedure have not received sufficient attention. What it is necessary to investigate now is the precise legal operation of provisions, and following this, the actual historical effect of papal intervention in single churches and ecclesiastical districts. It is evident that in origin the practice of provision responded to definite needs within the Church, and was full of potentialities for the good and efficient government of the Church. Whether the power which gradually accumulated in the hands of the popes was too unlimited, whether it was open to abuse and was abused, whether provisions were too freely employed and without sufficient safeguards against misuse: these are questions which still remain undecided. It is certain now that much of the old criticism was unjustified; but we cannot be satisfied with a verdict of Not Proven. The evidence, both legal and historical, can be approached objectively, once its relative worth and character is known, and this must be the next step; for what holds good of the history of papal provisions, is valid in regard to many of the more important features of centralized Church government in the later centuries of the Middle Ages. Not merely ecclesiastical antiquities are at issue, but the very character of the administration of the mediæval Church, the qualities of its constitution, and its potentialities through three centuries and more as a moral and spiritual power.

N

BIBLIOGRAPHY

CONTEMPORARY AUTHORITIES

I

CODICES MANUSCRIPTI

Monachii, Bibliotheca nationalis: Codd. lat. 24, 741, 3892, 4111, 6350, 6904, 6905, 8011, 9549, 14011, 23499.
Oxonii, Bibliotheca collegii Reginae: Cod. lat. 54.
Pragis, Bibliotheca metropolitana: Cod. I. xxvi (1130).
Romae, Archivum capitulare S. Petri: Cod. H. 13.
    Archivum Vaticanum: Regg. Vat. 9, 13, 16, 20–22, 24–27, 29, 31, 32, 37, 38, 52; Collect. 417 A, 495.
    Bibliotheca Vaticana: Codd. Vat. lat. 2548, 3980; Codd. Ottob. lat. 448, 747; Cod. Palat. lat. 798.
Venetiis, Bibliotheca Marciana: Cod. lat. IV. 98.

II

DOCUMENTARY

Auvray, L: *Les Registres de Grégoire IX* (1227–1241). 12 fasc., Paris, 1890–1910.
Berger, E: *Les Registres d'Innocent IV* (1243–1254). 4 vols., Paris, 1881–1919.
Berlière, U: Suppliques de Clément VI (1342–1352). *Analecta Vaticano-Belgica*, vol. I. Bruxelles, 1906.
    Suppliques d'Innocent VI (1352–1362). *Analecta Vat.-Belg.*, vol. V. Bruxelles, 1911.
    Les collectories pontificales dans les anciens diocèses de Cambrai, Thérouanne et Tournai au XIVe siècle. *Analecta Vat.-Belg.*, vol. X, Rome, 1929.
Bourel de la Roncière, C., Loye, J. de, Coulon, A., Cenival, P. de: *Les Registres d'Alexandre IV* (1254–1261). 6 fasc., Paris, 1895–1931.
Bradshaw, H: *Lincoln Cathedral Statutes*. 2 vols. Cambridge, 1892–1897.
Formularium notariorum curie Romane: *cf.* Barraclough.
Göller, E: *Repertorium Germanicum*, vol. I: Clemens VII. von Avignon, 1378–1394. Berlin, 1916.
Guiraud, J: *Les Registres d'Urban IV* (1261–1264). 4 vols. Paris, 1892–1929.
Guiraud, J., Cadier, L: *Les Registres de Grégoire X et de Jean XXI* (1271–1277). 4 fasc., Paris, 1892–1906.
Hanquet, K: *Documents relatifs au Grand Schisme*, vol. I (Suppliques de Clément VII). *Analecta Vat.-Belg.*, vol. VIII, Rome, 1924.
Jaffé, Ph.: *Regesta Pontificum Romanorum*. 2 vols. Lipsiae, 1885–1888.
Jordan, E: *Les Registres de Clément IV* (1265–1268). 5 fasc., Paris, 1893–1912.
Lang, A: *Acta Salzburgo-Aquilejensia. Quellen zur Geschichte der ehemaligen Kirchenprovinzen Salzburg und Aquileja.* 2 vols. Graz, 1903–1906.
Langlois, E: *Les Registres de Nicolas IV.* 10 fasc. Paris, 1886–1893.

Ottenthal, E. von: *Die päpstlichen Kanzleiregeln von Johannes XXII bis Nicolaus V.* Innsbruck, 1888.

Perroy, E: *The Diplomatic Correspondence of Richard II.* London, 1933.

Potthast, A: *Regesta Pontificum Romanorum inde ab a.* 1198 *usque ad a.* 1304. 2 vols. Berolini, 1874–1875.

Pressutti, P: *Regesta Honorii papae III.* 2 vols. Romae, 1888.

Regestum Clementis papae V. cura et studio monachorum Ordinis S. Benedicti. 5 vols. Romae, 1885–1892.

Rieder, K: *Römische Quellen zur Konstanzer Bistumsgeschichte zur Zeit der Päpste in Avignon,* 1305–1378. Innsbruck, 1908.

Sauerland, H. V: *Vatikanische Urkunden und Regesten zur Geschichte Lothringens* (Quellen z. Lothringischen Geschichte, B. 1, 2). 2 vols. Metz, 1901–1905.

    Urkunden und Regesten zur Geschichte der Rheinlande aus dem Vatikanischen Archiv. 7 vols. Bonn, 1902 *sqq.*

Schillmann, F: *Die Formularsammlung des Marinus von Eboli* (Bibliothek des preussischen hist. Instituts in Rom, B. 16). Rom, 1929.

Schwalm, J: *Das Formelbuch des Heinrich Bucglant. An die päpstliche Kurie in Avignon gerichtete Suppliken.* Hamburg, 1910.

Tangl, M: *Die päpstlichen Kanzleiordnungen von* 1200–1500. Innsbruck, 1894.

Tellenbach, G: *Repertorium Germanicum,* II. Verzeichnis der in den Registern und Kameralakten Urbans VI, Bonifaz' IX, Innocenz' VII und Gregors XII vorkommenden Personen, Kirchen und Orte des Deutschen Reiches, seiner Diözesen und Territorien, 1378–1415. Berlin, 1933.

Wilkins, D: *Concilia Magnae Britanniae et Hiberniae.* 4 vols. London, 1737.

III

LITERARY

Baluze, E: *Vitae paparum Avinionensium,* ed. G. Mollat. 4 vols. Paris, 1916–1928.

Bernardus Claravallensis: De consideratione libri quinque, ed. Migne, *Patrologia latina* CLXXXII, 727–807.

Boncompagnus de Florentia: Rhetorica antiqua, *Cod. arch. cap. s. Petri* H. 13, *Cod. Ottob. lat.* 448, *Cod. Monacen. lat.* 23499. *Cf.* L. Rockinger, *Briefsteller u. Formelbücher,* 128–174.

Chronicon monasterii de Melsa a fundatione usque ad a. 1396, ed. Bond. 3 vols. Rolls Series, London, 1867 *sqq.*

Epistolae Cantuarienses (Chronicles and Memorials of the Reign of Richard I, vol. II) ed. W. Stubbs. Rolls Series, London, 1865.

Gilbertus Tornacensis: *Collectio de scandalis ecclesiae. Cf.* Stroick.

Giraldus Cambrensis: *Gemma ecclesiastica,* ed. J. S. Brewer. Rolls Series, London, 1862.

Grosseteste, Robertus: *Epistolae,* ed. H. R. Luard. Rolls Series, London, 1861.

Humbertus de Romanis: *Opus tripartitum,* ed. P. Crabbe, *Concilia omnia* II, 967–1003. Coloniae Agrippinae, 1551.

Matthaeus Parisiensis: *Chronica majora,* ed. H. R. Luard. 7 vols. London, 1876–1880.

Rockinger, L: *Briefsteller und Formelbücher des* 11. *bis* 14. *Jahrhunderts* (Quellen und Erörterungen zur bayerischen u. deutschen Geschichte, IX). München, 1863.

Roth, F. W. E: Eine Briefsammlung des Propstes Ulrich von Steinfeld aus dem 12. Jahrhundert, *Zeitschrift des Aachener Geschichtsvereins* XVIII (1896), 242–311.

Schmitz-Kallenberg, L: *Practica Cancellariae Apostolicae saeculi XV exeuntis.* Münster i. W., 1904.
Schoolmeesters, E: Recueil des lettres adressées pendant le XIVᵉ siècle aux papes et aux cardinaux pour les affaires de la principauté de Liège, *Analectes pour servir à l'histoire ecclésiastique de la Belgique,* XV (1878).
Stephanus Tornacensis: Epistolae, ed. Migne, *Patrologia latina* CCXI.
Stroick, A: Collectio de Scandalis Ecclesiae, nova editio, *Archivum Franciscanum Historicum* XXIV (1931), 33–62.
Ulricus Steinfeldensis: *Epistolae. Cf.* Roth.

IV

LEGAL

Bernardus Compostellanus: Commentarius in Decretales Gregorii IX, *Codd. Vat. lat.* 2548, 3980.
Bernardus Parmensis: Glossa ordinaria in Decretales Gregorii IX. *Cf.* Decretales Gregorii Noni. (The text of the gloss in *Codd. lat. Monacen.* 6904, 14011, has also been collated.)
Bonaguida de Aretio: Summa introductoria super officio advocationis in foro Ecclesiae, ed. A. Wunderlich, *Anecdota quae processum civilem spectant,* 133–345.
   Consuetudines Curiae Romanae, ed. L. Wahrmund, *Archiv für kath. Kirchenrecht* LXXIX (1899), 3–19.
Corpus Iuris Canonici. 3 vols. Parisiis, 1612. *Cf.* Friedberg; *Decretales Gregorii Noni; Liber Sextus.*
Corpus Iuris Civilis, ed. Th. Mommsen, P. Krueger, G. Kroll, R. Schoell. 3 vols. Berolini, 1872 *sqq.*
Decisiones dominorum de Rota (Decisiones antiquae et novae Rotae Romanae). Ed. Lugduni, 1515.
Decretales Gregorii Noni pont. max. cum epitomis, divisionibus et glossis ordinariis. Venetiis, 1566.
Duranti, G: *Speculum iudiciale.* Lugduni, 1556.
Egidius de Fuscarariis: Ordo iudiciarius, ed. L. Wahrmund, *Quellen z. Gesch. d. römisch-kanon. Processes im Mittelalter,* III. i (1916); *Cod. lat. Monacen.* 6905.
   Quaestiones. *Cf.* Quaestiones Bononienses; Reatz.
Friedberg, E: *Quinque Compilationes antiquæ necnon collectio canonum Lipsiensis.* Lipsiae, 1872.
   Corpus Iuris Canonici. 2 vols. Lipsiae, 1879–1881.
Goffredus de Trano: Summa super titulos decretalium, *Codd. lat. Monacen.* 741, 9549; ed. Venetiis, 1502.
Horborch, G: *cf. Decisiones dominorum de Rota.*
Hostiensis: Summa aurea super titulis decretalium, *Cod. lat. Monacen.* 24; ed. Venetiis, 1490.
Iacobi, Petrus: Libellorum Tractatus, *Cod. Palat. lat.* 798.
Innocentius papa IV: Apparatus super quinque libros decretalium, *Codd. Monacen. lat.* 3892, 6350; ed. Venetiis, 1481.
Iohannes Andreae: *Glossa in Sextum et in Clementinas. Cf.* Liber Sextus.
Liber Sextus Decretalium D. Bonifacii papae VIII., Clementis papae V. Constitutiones, Extravagantes tum viginti D. Ioannis papae XXII. tum communes. Haec omnia cum suis glossis suae integritati restituta. Venetiis, 1660.
Lux, C: *Constitutionum Apostolicarum de generali beneficiorum reservatione ab a. 1265 usque ad a. 1378 emissarum, tam intra quam extra corpus iuris exstantium, collectio et interpretatio.* Wratislaviae, 1904.
Petri Blesensis opusculum de distinctionibus in canonum interpretatione adhibendis sive, ut auctor voluit, speculum iuris canonici, ed. Th. A. Reimarus. Berolini, 1837.

Quaestiones disputatae per doctores Bononienses in iure canonico, *Cod. Monacen. lat.* 8011.
Reatz, T: *Aegidii de Fuscarariis, Garsiae Hyspani Quaestiones de iure canonico.* Gissae, 1859.
Roffredus Beneventanus: Opus libellorum super iure pontificio, *Cod. lat. Monacen.* 4111; ed. Coloniae Agrippinae, 1591.
Wahrmund, L: *Quellen zur Geschichte des römisch-kanonischen Processes im Mittelalter.* 5 vols. Innsbruck, 1905–1931.
Wunderlich, A: *Anecdota quae processum civilem spectant.* Gottingae, 1841.

LATER AUTHORITIES

V

EARLY TREATISES

Bourgeois du Chastenet: Nouvelle histoire du concile de Constance, *Preuves.* Paris, 1718.
Espen, Z. B. van: *Jus ecclesiasticum universum.* 2 vols. Coloniae Agrippinae. 1729.
Febronius, J. (*i.e.* N. de Hontheim): *De statu Ecclesiae et legitima potestate Romani pontificis liber singularis.* Bullioni, 1763.
Gomes, L: *Commentarius in iudiciales regulas Cancellariae.* Parisiis, 1546.
Marta, A: *Tractatus de clausulis.* Venetiis, 1615.
Rebuffus, P: *Praxis beneficiorum.* Romae, 1595.
Ridolphini, P: *De ordine Procedendi in Iudiciis in Romana Curia Praxis Recentior.* Romae, 1659.
Rosa, T. de: *Tractatus de executoribus litterarum apostolicarum.* Moguntiae, 1769.
Thomassinus, L: *Vetus et nova Ecclesiae disciplina circa beneficia et beneficiarios.* 10 vols. Magontiaci, 1786–1787.
Tiberius, Sallustius: *De modis procedendi in causis, quae coram Auditore Camerae aguntur, Practica Iudiciaria.* Bracciani, 1633.
Vivianus, I: *Praxis Iurispatronatus.* Venetiis, 1670.

VI

MODERN LITERATURE: LEGAL

Andt, E: *La procédure par rescrit.* Paris, 1920.
Barraclough, G: *Public Notaries and the Papal Curia. A Calendar and a Study of a Formularium Notariorum Curie from the Early Years of the fourteenth century.* London, 1934.
Bethmann-Hollweg, M. A. von: *Der Civilprozess des gemeinen Rechts in geschichtlicher Entwicklung.* 6 vols. Bonn, 1864–1874.
Briegleb, H. K: *Einleitung in die Theorie der summarischen Processe.* Leipzig, 1859.
Brunner, H: *Grundzüge der deutschen Rechtsgeschichte.* 3rd ed. Leipzig, 1908.
Brys, J: *De dispensatione in iure canonico praesertim apud Decretistas et Decretalistas usque ad medium saeculum decimum quartum.* Brugis, 1925.
Buckland, W. W: *A Textbook of Roman Law from Augustus to Justinian.* 2nd ed., Cambridge, 1932.
Collinet, P: *Procédure par libelle.* Paris, 1932.
Davis, H. W. C: The Canon Law in England, *Zeitschrift der Savigny-stiftung, kanon. Abteilung* III (1913) 344 sqq.
Delannoy, P: *La juridiction ecclésiastique en matière bénéficiale sous l'ancien régime en France.* Paris, 1910.

Digard, G: *La papauté et l'étude du droit romain au XIII° siècle* (Bibliothèque de l'École des Chartes, vol. LI). Paris, 1890.

Endemann, W: Civilprozessverfahren nach der kanonistischen Lehre, *Zeitschrift für deutschen Civilprozess* XI (1891), 177–326.

Engelmann, A: *Der Civilprozess. Geschichte und System*. B.II, Geschichte des Civilprozesses, H.3, Der romanisch-kanonische Prozess. Breslau, 1895.

Fliniaux, A: Les anciennes collections des Decisiones Rotae, *Revue hist. de droit français et étranger* (4e série), IX (1925), 61–93, 382–410.

Fournier, M: L'Église et le droit romain au XIII° siècle, *Nouvelle revue hist. de droit français et étranger* XIV (1890), 80–119.

Fournier, P: Les officialités au moyen-âge. *Étude sur l'organisation, la compétence et la procédure des tribunaux ecclésiastiques ordinaires en France de 1180 à 1328*. Paris, 1880.

    Un tournant dans l'histoire du droit (1060–1140), *Nouvelle revue hist. de droit français et étranger*, XLI (1917), 129–180.

Fournier, P. et Le Bras, G: *Histoire des Collections canoniques en Occident*. 2 vols. Paris, 1931–1932.

Friedberg, E: *Das Kanonische und das Kirchenrecht*. Leipzig, 1896.

Göller, E: Wilhelm Horborch und die Decisiones antiquae der Rota Romana, *Archiv f. kath. Kirchenrecht* XCI (1911), 662–680.

    Der Gerichtshof der päpstlichen Kammer und die Entstehung des Amtes des Procurator fiscalis im kirchlichen Prozessverfahren, *Arch. f. kath. Kirchenrecht* XCIV (1914), 605–619.

    Aus einem Hamburger Pfründeprozess unter Clemens V. im Jahre 1312, *Römische Quartalschrift* XXXVI (1928), 114–121.

Gross, C: *Das Recht an der Pfründe. Zugleich ein Beitrag zur Ermittlung des Ursprunges des Jus ad rem*. Graz, 1887.

Haring, J: Die affectio papalis, *Arch. f. kath. Kirchenrecht* CIX (1929), 127–177.

Heiner, F: *Der kirchliche Zivilprozess*. Köln, 1910.

Hinschius, P: *Das Kirchenrecht der Katholiken und Protestanten in Deutschland*. System des katholischen Kirchenrechts. 6 vols. Berlin, 1869–1897.

Keeton, G. W: *The Elementary Principles of Jurisprudence*. London, 1930.

Koeniger, A. M: *Grundriss einer Geschichte des katholischen Kirchenrechts*. Köln, 1919.

Landsberg, E: *Die Glosse des Accursius und ihre Lehre vom Eigenthum*. Leipzig, 1883.

Lega, M: *Praelectiones in textum iuris canonici de Iudiciis Ecclesiasticis*. Vol. I: De iudiciis ecclesiasticis civilibus. Ed. altera, Romae, 1905.

Maitland, F. W: *Roman Canon Law in the Church of England*. London, 1898. *Equity; also the Forms of Action*. Cambridge 1909.

Muther, D. Th.: *Zur Geschichte des Römisch-canonischen Prozesses in Deutschland während des 14. und zu Anfang des 15. Jahrhunderts*. Rostock, 1872.

Sägmüller, J. B: *Lehrbuch des katholischen Kirchenrechts*. 2 vols. 3rd ed., Freiburg i. B., 1914.

Schneider, F. E: *Die Römische Rota*. Vol. I: Die Verfassung der Rota. Paderborn, 1914.

Schulte, J. F. von: *Das katholische Kirchenrecht*. 2 vols. Giessen, 1856–1860. *Geschichte der Quellen und Literatur des canonischen Rechts von Gratian bis auf die Gegenwart*. 3 vols. Stuttgart, 1875–1880.

Steinwenter, A: Der antike kirchliche Rechtsgang und seine Quellen, *Zeitschrift d. Savigny-Stiftung, kanon. Abt.* XXIII (1934), 1–116.

Stintzing, R: *Geschichte der populären Literatur des römisch-kanonischen Rechts in Deutschland am Ende des 15. und im Anfang des 16. Jahrhunderts*. Leipzig, 1867.

Vinogradoff, P: *Common-Sense in Law*. London, 1913.
  Roman Law in Medieval Europe. 2nd ed. (ed. F. de Zulueta), Oxford, 1929.
Wenger, L: *Institutionen des römischen Zivilprozessrechts*. München, 1925.
Wohlhaupter, E: *Aequitas canonica*. Paderborn, 1931.

VII

MODERN LITERATURE: HISTORICAL

Amiet, L: *Essai sur l'organisation du chapitre cathédral de Chartres (du XIe au XVIIIe siècle)*. Chartres, 1922.
Baier, H: *Päpstliche Provisionen für niedere Pfründen bis zum Jahre* 1304. Münster i. W., 1911.
Baix, F: De la valeur historique des actes pontificaux de collation des bénéfices, *Hommage à Dom Ursmer Berlière*, 57–66. Bruxelles, 1931.
Bannister, A. J: *The Cathedral Church of Hereford*. London, 1924.
Barraclough, G: The Making of a Bishop in the Middle Ages: the Part of the Pope in Law and Fact, *Catholic Historical Review* XIX (1933), 275–319.
  Un document inédit sur la soustraction d'obédience de 1398, *Revue d'histoire ecclésiastique* XXX (1934), 101–115.
  The Constitution 'Execrabilis' of Alexander IV, *English Hist. Review* XLIX (1934), 193–218.
  Bernard of Compostella, *English Historical Review* XLIX (1934), 487–494.
  Formulare für päpstliche Suppliken aus der ersten Hälfte des 13. Jahrhunderts, *Archiv f. kath. Kirchenrecht*.
Barth, F. X: *Hildebert von Lavardin und das kirchliche Stellenbesetzungsrecht*. Stuttgart, 1906.
Bastgen, H: *Die Geschichte des Trierer Domkapitels im Mittelalter*. Paderborn, 1910.
Below, G. von: *Die Ursachen der Reformation*. München u. Berlin, 1917.
Bidagor, R: *La Iglesia propia en España* (Analecta Gregoriana, vol. IV). Roma, 1933.
Binder, B: *Das Domkapitel zu Gnesen: Seine Entwicklung bis zur Mitte des 15. Jahrhunderts*. Griefswald, 1912.
Böhmer, H: *Kirche und Staat in England und in der Normandie im 11. und 12. Jahrhundert*. Leipzig, 1899.
  Das germanische Christentum. Ein Versuch, *Theologische Studien und Kritiken* LXXXVI (1913), 165–280.
  Das Eigenkirchenwesen in England, *Texte und Forschungen zur englischer Kulturgeschichte (Festgabe für F. Liebermann)*, 301–353. Halle, 1921.
Bresslau, H: *Handbuch der Urkundenlehre für Deutschland und Italien*. 2 vols. 2nd ed. Leipzig, 1912 sqq.
Brooke, Z. N: *The English Church and the Papacy from the Conquest to the reign of John*. Cambridge, 1931.
Carlyle, R. W. and A. J: *A History of Mediaeval Political Theory in the West*. Vol. 5. London, 1928.
Churchill, I: *Canterbury Administration*. 2 vols. London, 1933.
Clergeac, A: *La curie et les bénéficiers consistoriaux. Étude sur les communs et menus services*. 1300–1600. Paris, 1911.
Deeley, A: Papal Provision and Royal Rights of Patronage in the Early fourteenth century, *English Hist. Review* XLIII (1928), 497 sqq.
Dittrich, F: Beiträge zur Geschichte der katholischen Reformation im ersten Drittel des 16. Jahrhunderts, *Historisches Jahrbuch* V (1884), 319–398.

Dufourcq, A: *Le Christianisme et l'organisation féodale*. 6th ed., Paris, 1932.
Ehrhard, A: *Das Mittelalter und seine kirchliche Entwickelung*. Mainz, 1908.
Ellis, J. T: *Anti-Papal Legislation in Medieval England* (1066–1377). Washington, 1930.
Eubel, K: Zum päpstlichen Reservations- und Provisionswesen, *Römische Quartalschrift* VIII (1894), 169–185.
Fierens, A: Ons Prebendenwezen onder de Pausen van Avignon. Een inleidend Overzicht (*Verslagen en Mededeelingen der K. Vlaamsche Academie voor Taal- en Letterkunde*, Gent, 1921, 809–848).
Fink, K. A: *Die Stellung des Konstanzer Bistums zum Päpstlichen Stuhl im Zeitalter des avignonesischen Exils*. Freiburg i. B., 1931.
Finke, H: *Die kirchenpolitischen und kirchlichen Verhältnisse zu Ende des Mittelalters nach der Darstellung K. Lamprechts*. Rom, 1896.
Fuchs, V: *Ordinationstitel von seiner Entstehung bis auf Innocenz III*. Bonn, 1930.
Gebhardt, B: *Die Gravamina der deutschen Nation gegen den römischen Hof*. Breslau, 1895.
Ghellinck, J. de: *Le mouvement théologique au XIe et au XIIe siècle*. Paris, 1914.
Gibbs, M. and Lang, J: *Bishops and Reform*, 1215–1272. Oxford, 1934.
Gnann, A: *Beiträge zur Verfassungsgeschichte der Domkapitel von Basel und Speyer bis zum Ende des 15 Jahrhunderts*. Freiburg i. B., 1906.
Göller, E: Die Gravamina auf dem Konzil von Vienne, *Festgabe Heinrich Finke*, 195–221. Münster i. W., 1904.
    Zur Geschichte des zweiten Lyoner Konzils und des Liber Sextus, *Römische Quartalschrift* XX (1906), 81–87.
    Zur Geschichte des kirchlichen Benefizialwesens und der päpstlichen Kanzleiregeln unter Benedikt XIII, *Archiv f. kath. Kirchenrecht* LXXXVII (1907), 203–208.
    Zur Geschichte der Rota Romana, *Arch. f. kath. Kirchenrecht* XCI (1911), 19–48.
Graham, R: The Taxation of Pope Nicholas IV, *English Hist. Review*, XXIII (1908), 434 *sqq*.
Gratien, P: *Histoire de la Fondation et de l'Évolution de l'Ordre des Frères Mineurs au XIIIe siècle*. Paris, 1928.
Grauert, H. von: *Magister Heinrich der Poet in Würzburg und die römische Kurie* (Abhandlungen der k. bayerischen Akademie d. Wissenschaften, phil.-hist. Klasse, XXVII). München, 1912.
Haller, J: *Papsttum und Kirchenreform: Vier Kapitel zur Geschichte des ausgehenden Mittelalters*. Berlin, 1903.
    Die Ursachen der Reformation. Tübingen, 1918.
Halphen, L: Les universités au XIIIe siècle, *Revue historique* CLXVI (1931), 217–238, CLXVII (1931), 1–15.
Hartridge, R. A. R: *A History of Vicarages in the Middle Ages*. Cambridge, 1930.
Hashagen, J: *Staat und Kirche vor der Reformation: Eine Untersuchung der vorreformatorischen Bedeutung des Laieneinflusses in der Kirche*. Essen, 1931.
Hatch, E: *The Growth of Church Institutions*. 4th ed. London, 1895.
Heckel, R. von: Das päpstliche und sicilische Registerwesen, *Archiv für Urkundenforschung* I (1908), 371–510.
    Untersuchungen zu den Registern Innocenz' III, *Hist. Jahrbuch* XL (1920), 1–43.
    Das Aufkommen der ständigen Prokuratoren an der päpstlichen Kurie, *Miscellanea Francesco Ehrle*, II, 290–321. Roma, 1924.
    Beiträge zur Kenntnis des Geschäftsgangs der päpstlichen Kanzlei im 13. Jahrhundert, *Festschrift für H. Brackmann*, 434–456. Weimar, 1931.

Hergenröther, J: *Handbuch der allgemeinen Kirchengeschichte.* Vols. 2, 3, ed. J. P. Kirsch. 6th ed., Freiburg i. B., 1925.

Hilling, N: *Die Römische Rota und das Bistum Hildesheim am Ausgange des Mittelalters* (1464–1513). Münster i. W., 1908.

Hofmann, W. von: *Forschungen zur Geschichte der kurialen Behörden vom Schisma bis zur Reformation.* 2 vols. Rom, 1914.

Imbart de la Tour, P: *Les origines de la Réforme.* 3 vols. Paris, 1905–1914.

Jackowski, L: Die päpstlichen Kanzleiregeln und ihre Bedeutung für Deutschland, *Archiv f. kath. Kirchenrecht* XC (1910), 3–37, 197–235, 432–463.

Kallen, G: *Die oberschwäbischen Pfründen des Bistums Konstanz und ihre Besetzung* (1275–1508). Stuttgart, 1907.

Kirsch, J. P: *Die päpstlichen Kollektorien in Deutschland während des 14. Jahrhunderts.* Paderborn, 1894.

　　Ein Prozess gegen Bischof und Domkapitel von Würzburg an der päpstlichen Kurie im 14. Jahrhundert, *Römische Quartalschrift* XXI (1907), 67–96.

Kisky, W: *Die Domkapitel der geistlichen Kurfürsten in ihrer persönlichen Zusammensetzung im 14. und 15. Jahrhundert.* Weimar, 1906.

　　Das freiherrliche Stift St. Gereon in Köln, *Annalen des histor. Vereins für den Niederrhein* LXXXII (1907), 1–50.

Kothe, W: *Kirchliche Zustände Strassburgs im 14. Jahrhundert.* Freiburg i. B., 1903.

Kurth, G: Liège et la cour de Rome au XIV° siècle, *Bulletin de l'institut historique belge de Rome* II (1922), 1–43.

Leineweber, L: *Die Besetzung der Seelsorgebenefizien im alten Herzogtum Westfalen bis zur Reformation.* Arnsberg i. W., 1918.

Leuze, O: *Das Augsburger Domkapitel im Mittelalter.* Augsburg, 1908.

Löhr, J: *Methodisch-kritische Beiträge zur Geschichte der Sittlichkeit des Klerus, besonders der Erzdiözese Köln, am Ausgang des Mittelalters.* Münster i. W., 1910.

Lunt, W. E: The first levy of papal annates, *American Historical Review* XVIII (1912), 48–64.

　　The Valuation of Norwich. Oxford, 1926.

Lux, C: *Die Besetzung der Benefizien in der Breslauer Diözese durch die Päpste von Avignon* (1305–1378). Breslau, 1906.

Macdonald, A. J: *Authority and Reason in the early Middle Ages.* Oxford, 1933.

Mackenzie, H: The anti-foreign movement in England, 1231–1232, *Haskins Anniversary Essays,* 182–203. New York, 1929.

Mackinnon, J: *The Constitutional History of Scotland from Early Times to the Reformation.* London, 1924.

Marti, O. A: Popular Protest and Revolt against Papal Finance in England from 1226 to 1258, *Princeton Theological Review* XXV (1927), 610–629.

Mollat, G: Jean XXII fut-il un avare? *Revue d'histoire ecclésiastique* V (1904), 522–534, VI (1905), 33–46.

　　La Collation des bénéfices ecclésiastiques sous les papes d'Avignon (1305–1378). Paris, 1921.

　　L'application du droit de régale spirituelle en France du XII° au XIV° siècle, *Revue d'histoire ecclésiastique* XXV (1929), 425–446, 645–676.

　　Les papes d'Avignon (1305–1378). 6th ed. Paris, 1930.

Nelis, H: L'application en Belgique de la règle de chancellerie apostolique de idiomate beneficiatorum, aux XIV° et XV° siècles, *Bulletin de l'institut hist. belge de Rome,* II (1922), 129–141.

Pastor, L: *Geschichte der Päpste seit dem Ausgang des Mittelalters.* Vol. 1. 4th ed., Freiburg i. B., 1901.

Paulus, C: *Welt-und Ordensklerus beim Ausgange des 13. Jahrhunderts im Kampf um die Pfarr-rechte*. Essen, 1900.

Pfaff, I: Zur Geschichte des Kanonisten Wilhelm Horborch und seiner Werke, *Zeitschrift d. Savigny-Stiftung, kanon. Abt.* XIII (1924), 513–518.

Pfaff, V: Kaiser Heinrichs VI. höchstes Angebot an die römische Kurie (1196), (*Heidelberger Abhandlungen zur mittleren u. neueren Geschichte LV*). Heidelberg, 1927.

Pottel, B: *Das Domkapitel von Ermland im Mittelalter*. Leipzig, 1911.

Priebatsch, F: Staat und Kirche in der Mark Brandenburg am Ende des Mittelalters, *Zeitschrift für Kirchengeschichte* XIX (1898), 397–430.

Puttkammer, G. von: *Papst Innocenz IV*. Münster i. W., 1910.

Rashdall, H: *The Universities of Europe in the Middle Ages*. 2 vols. Oxford, 1895.

Rauch, K: Stiftsmässigkeit und Stiftsfähigkeit in ihrer begrifflichen Abgrenzung, *Festschrift H. Brunner*, 737–760. Weimar, 1920.

Ruess, K: *Die rechtliche Stellung der päpstlichen Legaten bis Bonifaz VIII*. Paderborn, 1912.

Sägmüller, J. B: *Die Tätigkeit und Stellung der Cardinäle bis Papst Bonifaz VIII*. Freiburg i. B., 1896.

   Die Idee Gregors VII. vom Primat in der päpstlichen Kanzlei, *Theologische Quartalschrift* LXXVIII (1896), 577 sqq.

   Die Entstehung und Bedeutung der Formel 'salva Sedis apostolicae auctoritate' in den päpstlichen Privilegien, *Theologische Quartalschrift* LXXXIX (1907), 93 sqq.

Schäfer, H. K: Zur Kritik mittelalterlicher kirchlicher Zustände, *Römische Quartalschrift* XX (1906), 123–141, XXIII (1909), 35–64.

Schelenz, E: *Studien zur Geschichte des Kardinalats im 13. und 14. Jahrhundert*. Marburg, 1913.

Schneider, P: *Die bischöflichen Domkapitel, ihre Entwicklung und rechtliche Stellung*. Mainz, 1885.

Schulte, A: *Der Adel und die deutsche Kirche im Mittelalter*. Stuttgart, 1910 (Nachtrag zur 2. Auflage, 1922).

Smith, A. L: *Church and State in the Middle Ages*. Oxford, 1913.

Störmann, A: *Die städtischen Gravamina gegen den Klerus am Ausgange des Mittelalters und in der Reformationszeit*. Münster i. W., 1911.

Stroick, A: Verfasser und Quellen der Collectio de Scandalis Ecclesiae (Reformschrift des Fr. Gilbert von Tournay O. F. M. zum II. Konzil von Lyon, 1274), *Archivum Franciscanum Historicum* XXIII (1930), 3–41, 273–299, 433–466.

Stubbs, W: *The Constitutional History of England in its origin and development*. Vols. 2, 3. 5th ed., Oxford, 1903–1906.

Stutz, U: *Geschichte des kirchlichen Benefizialwesens von seinen Anfängen bis auf die Zeit Alexanders III*. Berlin, 1895.

   Die Eigenkirche als Element des mittelalterlichen germanischen Kirchenrechts. Berlin, 1895.

   Gratian und die Eigenkirchen, *Zeitschrift d. Savigny-Stiftung für Rechtsgeschichte, kanon. Abteilung* I (1911), 1 sqq.

   Das Eigenkirchenwesen in England, *Zeitschrift d. Savigny-Stiftung, kanon. Abteilung* XII (1922), 409–415.

Sznuro, J: Les origines du droit d'alternative bénéficiale, *Revue des sciences religieuses* (1925–1926), XVII, 1–13, XIX, 389–415, XXI, 1–25.

Teige, J: Beiträge zum päpstlichen Kanzleiwesen des 13. und 14. Jahrhunderts, *Mittheilungen des Instituts für österr. Geschichtsforschung* XVII (1896), 404–440.

Thaner, F: Ueber Entstehung u. Bedeutung der Formel: *Salva sedis apostolicae auctoritate* in den päpstlichen Privilegien (*Sitzungsberichte der kais. Akademie der Wissenschaften, Phil.–hist. Classe* LXXI, Wien, 1872, 807–851).

Tihon, C: Les expectatives in forma pauperum particulièrement au XIVe siècle, *Bulletin de l'institut historique belge de Rome* V (1925), 51–118.

Les expectatives in forma pauperum de Grégoire XII (1er janvier 1407), *Bulletin de l'inst. hist. belge de Rome* VI (1926), 71–101.

Valois, N: *Guillaume d'Auvergne*. Paris, 1880.

La France et le Grand Schisme d'Occident. 4 vols. Paris, 1896–1902.

Vaucelle, E. R: *La collégiale de Saint-Martin de Tours des origines à l'avènement des Valois* (397–1328). Tours, 1907.

Werminghoff, A: Neuere Arbeiten über das Verhältnis von Staat und Kirche in Deutschland während des späteren Mittelalters, *Historische Vierteljahrschrift*, Neue Folge XI (1908), 153–192.

Nationalkirchliche Bestrebungen im deutschen Mittelalter. Stuttgart, 1910.

Ständische Probleme in der Geschichte der deutschen Kirche des Mittelalters, *Zeitschrift der Savigny-Stiftung, kanon. Abteilung* I (1911), 33–67.

Verfassungsgeschichte der deutschen Kirche im Mittelalter. 2nd ed., Leipzig, 1913.

Wood-Legh, K. L: The Appropriation of Parish Churches during the Reign of Edward III, *Cambridge Historical Journal* III (1929), 15–22.

Some Aspects of the History of the Chantries during the Reign of Edward III, *Cambridge Hist. Journal*, IV (1932), 26–50.

Wunderlich, P: *Die Beurteilungen der Vorreformation in der deutschen Geschichtsschreibung seit Ranke*. Erlangen, 1930.